CITIES ON THE MOVE

LONDON going out of Town — or — The March of Bricks & Morter.

To Joseph Foynbee Esq FRS — with the best regards of GeoᵗᴴCruikshank.

May 12ᵗᴴ 1860

Designed Etched & Published by George Cruikshank.   November 15ᵗᴴ 1829

CITIES ON THE MOVE

ARNOLD TOYNBEE

HT
111
T66

1970
OXFORD UNIVERSITY PRESS
NEW YORK AND LONDON

Contents

Maps

Diagrams

(*Both taken from* CONSTANTINOS A. DOXIADIS, Ekistics—An Introduction to the Science of Human Settlements, *by permission of Hutchinson, London, and Oxford University Press Inc., New York.*)

Preface

THIS book is sponsored by the Institute of Urban Environment of the School of Architecture, Columbia University, and is part of its series of publications. I am happy that the book is appearing under these auspices. The study of urban environment and of architecture is of vital importance for mankind's future.

The aim of the book is to examine the present 'urban explosion' in the light of the previous history of cities. The 'urban explosion', like the 'population explosion' with which it is bound up, is sensational and formidable, but it, too, is not an entirely new departure in human history. Like everything in life, it is an event in time, and therefore cannot be fully understood if it is not looked at in relation to the past. The mechanized city is the heir of the traditional city. The coming World-City, which is going to spread its tentacles round the globe, will be a human settlement of the same species as tiny Jericho and Ur and Weimar. On its immensely larger scale, Ecumenopolis will still be a city, and a study of the likenesses and the differences between it and its predecessors may aid us in trying to learn how to live in it.

In retrospect it can now be seen that the history of human settlements is a unity, and that it is also a promising avenue of approach to a unified study of the history of human affairs. It is promising because 'Ekistics' is the common ground and natural meeting-place of a number of lines of study that have been pursued, till recently, more or less in isolation from each other. Architecture, town-planning, the study of communications, economics, sociology, psychology, medicine, biology are all concerned, and, whether we study them separately or in association with each other, we have to study them in the time-dimension in order to study them realistically.

I owe my initiation into 'Ekistics' to Dr. Constantine Doxiadis, the pioneer in the unified study of human settlements who coined a new name for a new subject. 'Ekistics' is new in the sense that, in bringing together a number of formerly separate 'disciplines', it has opened up new horizons.

The present little book would probably never have been written if I had not had the good fortune to meet Professor Abrams on Dr.

Doxiadis' Delos cruise of 1967. This series of conference-cruises has been giving Dr. Doxiadis' guests stimulating opportunities of meeting fellow-students of Ekistics who have been drawn into this common field of interest from many different quarters. I cannot give here a complete catalogue of all my debts, but I also cannot forbear to mention the names of three scholars from whom I have been learning by talking to them, listening to them, and reading their published works.

If Dr. Doxiadis' book, *Ekistics*, published in 1968, had been written by anyone else, I should have guessed that it was the author's definitive work. It sums up much of his previous published work; it is monumental; it is a classic; but, knowing Dr. Doxiadis, as I do, and also being informed, as I am, of some of the further work that he now has on the stocks, I am aware that he has taken the publication of *Ekistics* in his stride and is already pressing on beyond it. I have learnt much, too, from Professor Charles Abrams' *Man's Struggle for Shelter in an Urbanizing World* and *The City is the Frontier*, first published in 1964 and in 1965 respectively. Vision is not always mated with a mastery of facts and figures, nor idealism with common sense, nor compassion with a recognition of the limits of what is practicable. When these qualities do co-exist in one and the same personality, this is a fruitful combination. My third big debt is to Professor Jean Gottmann. He and I met first at Princeton, New Jersey, at the Institute for Advanced Study. One of Dr. Doxiadis' Delos cruises brought us together again; and now Professor Gottmann holds the Chair of Geography at the University of Oxford; so he and I have become fellow-islanders.

I owe much to Professor Gottmann's *Megalopolis: The Urbanised Northeastern Seaboard of the United States*. His command of a vast mass of information is made doubly instructive by the sensitiveness and acumen with which he has interpreted his data, and his points are illuminated visually by a wealth of maps, plans, charts, and tables. Professor Gottmann and the Twentieth Century Fund, which holds the copyright, have generously allowed me to quote three passages of *Megalopolis*. I am grateful, because Professor Gottmann here makes points that are of importance, for my argument, with greater authority and in a more telling form that I could have commanded if I had tried to put these points in my own words. The quotations will be found on pages 213, 217, and 234. I have given the exact references, with acknowledgments, in a footnote in each place.

I will take this opportunity of also paying tribute to a fourth student of Ekistics whom I cannot meet in the flesh and whose name I do not know, but whose work has been a constant inspiration to me ever since I first read it while I was an undergraduate at Oxford. The unknown benefactor to whom I am now giving thanks is the author of the Hippocratean treatise on *The Effects of Variety in Atmospheric Conditions, Water, and Locations* on human life.

ARNOLD TOYNBEE

December 1968

1: The Traditional City
and the Present Urban Explosion

THE title—'Cities on the Move'—that I have given to this book
would have seemed paradoxical to any reader, anywhere on the
face of this planet, at any date earlier than the closing decades of
the eighteenth century, and even then, for a time, Britain would
have been the only patch of the Earth's land-surface on which the
apparent paradox would have begun to look like an actual current
event. In the traditional language of the law, 'movable property'
has been the antithesis of 'real estate', and 'real estate' has meant land
and buildings that were styled 'real' in virtue of their being fixtures.

There were pastoral nomads who did live in moving camps
consisting of clusters of tents or huts that were repeatedly unpacked
and erected and were then repeatedly taken down and loaded on
to carts or camels, as the horde, with its flocks and herds, kept on
the move in its annual orbit between its summer and its winter
pastures. Jews and Christians were familiar with this nomadic way
of life at second hand, from the description of the lives of the
Patriarchs in the Book of Genesis; but few of them had ever set
eyes on a contemporary pastoral nomad horde either encamped
or on the march. The portrayal of nomadism in the Old Testament
had made an impression on their minds because, from the standpoint of these sedentary societies, this way of life was peculiar and
exceptional. So it was, also, in the eyes of the people of all the
other sedentary societies; and, since the beginning of the Neolithic
Age, the sedentary part of this planet's human population had
always been the great majority. The surviving vagrant food-
gatherers and hunters, and the pastoral nomads who had seceded
from the sedentary world, had been a small minority. The sedentary population had not become acquainted *en masse* with their

nomad fellow occupants of the Earth's land-surface except on those catastrophic occasions on which some nomad horde had suddenly erupted out of 'the desert' into 'the sown', bringing massacre and devastation with them and perhaps staying on to impose their yoke on their sedentary victims until the nomad tyrants were either expelled or assimilated.

These eruptions of nomads from the steppe had, however, been unusual interruptions of the normal tenour of sedentary life, and, since the seventeenth century, there had been no more of them. The pastoral nomadic way of life had been doomed when, in the seventeenth century, the Russian and Chinese Empires collided with each other in the basin of the Amur River. In meeting there they had closed the ring of sedentary populations encircling the Great Eurasian Steppe. Today the last survivors of the nomads are being debarred by force from continuing to carry on their seasonal migrations across international frontiers that, for them, have been meaningless. In Inner Mongolia, Manchuria, and Tibet the nomads are being swamped by Chinese peasant colonists; in the Soviet Union they are being herded into collective farms and factories; in Sa'udi Arabia they are being attracted into the American oil-towns by the possibility of earning wages there that, for them, are fabulously lavish.

The sedentary majority of mankind has taken this suppression of the nomadic way of life as a matter of course and has, on the whole, approved of it, in spite of the harshness with which it has been carried out by the Chinese and by the Russians. The disappearance of an exceptional, antiquated, and, for sedentary peoples, dangerous nomadic mobility has been accepted without regret. Our seventeenth-century ancestors who saw the beginning of the end of pastoral nomadism would have been astonished—and probably incredulous—if it had been foretold to them that the mobility which was being suppressed in its traditional pastoral form was now going to shift its venue to the hitherto sedentary world and to undermine the stability that had reigned there ever since agriculture had advanced to a degree of efficiency that had made it possible to cultivate the same fields, year in and year out, instead of continuing to practise the crude primitive agricultural technique of slashing and burning the bush, snatching one crop from the clearing fertilized by the wood-ash, and then drifting on, to do the same on other virgin forest land.

Our pre-nineteenth-century ancestors would have been not only surprised but perturbed if they could have seen present-day descendants of theirs who had seceded from the sedentary way of life as the pastoral nomads had seceded from it some three or four thousand years earlier. They would hardly have believed that any human being who had once lived in a fixed house would feel more at home in a travelling car. The trailer-towns in present-day Florida would have reminded our forefathers of the pastoral nomads' encampments of huts or tents. The motorist who spends more of his time in his car than out of it would have been mistaken by his sedentary forebears for a new kind of composite monster, as the peoples of Middle America mistook Cortés' six cavalrymen for centaurs. The daily orbit of the present-day commuter between his suburban dormitory and the office or factory in which he spends his working hours and earns his living would have recalled the annual orbit of the nomad shepherd or herdsman; and it would have seemed not only surprising but appalling that 'civilized' sedentary populations should have been driven by economic necessity once again to become peripatetic.

Our ancestors would have been still more amazed to see their descendants' cities, as well as these cities' inhabitants, get on the move. They would have supposed that the foundations of the cities' serried houses were as immovable as the close-set trees in the wood of Dunsinane. They would not have dreamed that one day cities would emulate the legendary behaviour of that ominous wood by breaking out of their ring-walls and flooding over the countryside, to devastate it more thoroughly and more lastingly than it had ever been devastated by any nomad horde. Nor would our ancestors have dreamed that, simultaneously, the cities would have devastated themselves, too, by turning their once sound hearts into sickly slums whose sickness would be both physical and psychological.

By 1969 some people in technologically 'advanced' countries have become aware that our cities are now on the move, and have become alive to the consequent menace to the well-being of mankind and perhaps even to its survival. We have awoken late in the day, and we cannot yet tell whether we shall have been too late to save ourselves from being overwhelmed by the onrush of our mobile cities. Present-day cities are moving at the speed of an avalanche rather than of a lava-flow, not to speak of a glacier. There was, however, at least one man, born in England before the end of the eighteenth century, who saw what was happening and depicted it as a warning to his contemporaries and to posterity. The seer whom I have in mind is the caricaturist, George Cruikshank, who was born in 1792 and lived till 1878.

One of the pictures hanging on the staircase of the tall terrace-house in London in which my sisters and I were born and brought up was a cartoon of Cruikshank's—an etching, filled in with colour-wash, bearing the title 'London going out of Town—or—The March of Bricks and Morter', with a note that it had been 'designed, etched, and published by George Cruikshank, November 1st, 1829'. This copy of the print is inscribed by the artist's own hand: 'To Joseph Toynbee Esq. F.R.S., with the best regards of Geo. Cruikshank, May 12th, 1866'. Joseph Toynbee, our grandfather (1815–66), was a younger and shorter-lived contemporary of Cruikshank's and was a friend of his. This particular cartoon was an appropriate gift; for our grandfather, who was the first ear, nose, and throat specialist in London, was also one of the pioneers in the belated struggle to provide elementary sanitation and other first-aid for public health in the new urban wilderness that the march of bricks and mortar had conjured into existence in a society that this man-made catastrophe had caught unawares and unprepared.

In this cartoon the heart of London, represented by the dome of St. Paul's and the top of the Monument, is just visible in the left background, almost crowded out by ranks of 'New Street' houses advancing implacably towards the spectator. The foremost rank, which is still under scaffolding, is already placarded with signs 'To Let'. In the left foreground a group of chimney-pots and cowls is on the march, and the leader, which is bigger than the rest, is clutching a tall notice, rammed into the ground, which announces: 'This Ground to be Lett on a Building Lease; Enquire of Mr. Goth, Brick maker, Bricklayers Arms, Brick Lane, Brixton.' Behind this notice a horse-cart is tipping refuse, authorized by a notice declaring 'Rubbish may be shot here.' The central piece in the composition is a kiln vomiting bricks which cascade towards the right of the picture in a rainbow-shaped arch. Under the arch there is a vista of belching chimneys and another host of houses swarming up Hampstead Hill. Near the hill-top is a sign-post marked 'Hampstead' and crowned with the caption: 'Our fences, I fear, will be found to be no defence against these Barbarians, who threaten to enclose and destroy us in all "manor" of ways. Detachments are on the Road already.' In the foreground immediately in front of the cascade of bricks, three animated hods have produced a line of smoke, from which there emerges the agonized figure of a willow-tree crying: 'Oh! I am morterly wounded!' Farther back, another willow, also in agony but still erect, cries: 'I must leave the field.' Between this second willow and two others far to the right, two animated haystacks are fleeing for their lives, in yokels' knee-breeches and stockings; they are trying to salvage a couple of pitchforks and a rake. The foremost of these two fugitives is exclaiming: 'Heyday! Come along, my little cocks; we must go farther afield, for we are losing ground here.' His agitated companion is crying: 'Confound these hot bricks; they'll fire all my Hay ricks.' In front of the foremost haystack, two cows, a drove of sheep, and some geese are also on the run. It is indeed high time for these terrified creatures to decamp; for, in the foreground, a wheelbarrow, wheeling another, is advancing; a self-operating saw is hacking down another willow; and fences are falling.

This picture used to catch my eye every one of the thousands of times that I passed it, going up or down stairs, during the first twenty-two years of my life. Its vigour and its ferocity were arresting, but its satire was lost on me at the time. The explosion of cities that had started in Britain at the turn of the eighteenth and nineteenth centuries had given Cruikshank's sensitive spirit and sardonic imagination a topical occasion for exposing and denouncing two major general tragedies of human life—tragedies that are the more tragic because they are inflicted on Man by Man himself and not by any inexorable fate. The first tragedy is that Man allows himself to be victimized by the artificial environment that he has created for himself by his technological prowess. The second tragedy is that he could save himself from at least the direst of the consequences of this self-victimization if he were to allow his foresight to get the better of his inertia, instead of waiting, as he does wait, frequently till the eleventh hour and sometimes till the thirteenth, before rousing himself to cope with evils of his own making—evils of which ample warning has generally been given by Cassandra's unwelcome and therefore unheeded prophetic voice.

Cruikshank's cartoon was not the only warning that I myself received in my childhood of the portentous fact that my native city, London, was on the move. Since my family was not well-off, our house, in which Cruikshank's picture hung, was 'on the wrong side of the tracks'. Drab Upper Westbourne Terrace was segregated from fashionable Westbourne Terrace by the permanent way of the Great Western Railway, at a point just before this takes its final turning into Paddington Station. As a small child in a perambulator, I used to be wheeled across the bridge over the railway four times a day *en route* to and from Kensington Gardens. I used also to be taken by my mother to visit a friend and neighbour whose house was in Westbourne Square. Her daughter who lived with her was my mother's contemporary, so old Mrs. Berry's generation must have been my grandfather's and George Cruikshank's. She used to describe how, when she was a young married woman, living in that self-same house (a tall house with a basement, like ours), she used to take her children to pick wild-flowers on the banks of a stream in the valley through which the railway now ran. This historical fact made a deep impression on me; for I found it impossible to visualize anything except the present railway-tracks occupying the hollow that was now spanned by the familiar bridge. I found it hardly credible that this hollow had still been a green valley at a date at which this living lady, in whose drawing-room I was hearing her talk, had already been a grown-up mother of my own mother's present age.

Mrs. Berry's reminiscences and Cruikshank's cartoon, between them, ought to have alerted me to what London was doing to itself. I did know that, in my childhood in the eighteen-nineties, London was the biggest city on Earth—bigger, appreciably and undeniably, than New York—but the feeling stirred in me by this knowledge was not consternation; it was pride; and I was proud of London's size, and was gratified that, in this competition for physical magnitude, my native city was maintaining its lead, because the signs of the times were not yet manifest.

In retrospect it is evident that the indicator of the malady that has overtaken London and the World's other great and growing cities is the nature and the volume of the traffic in the streets; and in my childhood the traffic in London was still archaic. At that date the only mechanized vehicles that ran, not on rails, but on the roads were steam-rollers and traction-engines. Four-wheelers and hansom cabs had not yet been pushed off the streets by taxis, and our doctor made his rounds, and our well-to-do cousin in West-bourne Terrace paid her calls, in a carriage and pair with a coach-man, not in a car driven by the owner. When the Central London Railway, the earliest of London's 'tubes', was being excavated, the clay brought up from the shafts was carried away in one-horse two-wheeled carts. The first commercially-produced automobile had not yet come out of the workshop on to the street, and, after the trickle had started, this had to swell into the post-Second-World-War deluge of mechanized vehicles before the public at large could be made to take notice of the problem of cities on the move that had already been tormenting George Cruikshank's prescient mind more than a hundred years back. The problem did not begin to cause widespread concern till the proliferation of mechanized transport in cities with horse-age streets made a mockery of the automobile's potential speed by keeping its actual crawling-pace down to the jog-trot velocity of the extinct four-wheeler.

The London of the eighteen-nineties was, of course, already far away from being the traditional city. It was no longer even the traditional capital city—and capitals had been traditional cities of an exceptional kind. All the same, the London of my childhood still retained enough of the traditional city's characteristic features for me to be able to imagine what life was like in Plutarch's Chaeronea and in Goethe's Weimar, as a palaeontologist is able to reconstruct the whole skeleton of some extinct animal from a fragment of a jaw-bone or from a single vertebra. I used to watch, after breakfast, to see Mr. Hale, the solicitor who lived in the opposite house across the street, ride off to his office on the horse that his groom had brought to the door. I used to linger by the cab-ranks to look at the horses drinking from the troughs and the sparrows scuffling with each other for the bran that had been spilled over from the horses' nosebags.

What, then, are the characteristics of the traditional city—the kind of city that was normal yesterday but is obsolete now? If we are to answer this question, we must first define what we mean by the word 'city' itself. What is there in common between the cities in which our urban ancestors lived for about five thousand years and the present-day 'conurbations'—a mushroom growth of megalopolises that are already visibly on the way towards coalescing into Ecumenopolis, the single globe-encompassing city of the not very distant future? Not very distant, considering that my great-grandchild, if not my grandchildren, will live to be immured in this coming man-made jungle of streets, highways, car parks, and high-rise buildings.

A city is a human settlement whose inhabitants cannot produce, within the city-limits, all of the food that they need for keeping them alive. This feature is common to cities of all kinds. It is common to Jericho and Megalopolis, though superficially these two cities may look as different from each other as a poodle looks from a great dane or a domestic cat from a tiger. The tiger and the cat are both felines; the great dane and the poodle are both dogs; and Megalopolis and Jericho are both cities. The proof of their common right to the title is that Jericho's inhabitants were no more able than Megalopolis's inhabitants are to feed themselves entirely from food produced within the the bounds of the area in which they lived.

The word 'entirely' is a necessary qualification because there have been cities whose area, as demarcated by a city-wall, was so much larger than the built-up and inhabited area that the citizens could stand a long siege, thanks to there being room, inside the sheltering wall, for raising some crops and for pasturing some livestock. Remains of cities with such vast perimeters, dating from the later centuries of the last millennium B.C., are still standing in North-Western Greece, in the regions that were then known as Aetolia, Acarnania, and Epirus. Equally vast perimeters, dating from the earlier centuries of the second millennium of the Christian Era, are still intact in North-Western India, in the present-day state of Rajasthan. These semi-self-feeding cities have, however, been exceptional; for city-walls are expensive to build and to keep in repair, and, even if an urban community can afford the cost of building and maintaining an unusually long city-wall, this *tour de force* is inevitably self-defeating if the purpose is to produce enough food within the walls to feed the resident population. The longer the city-wall, the larger the garrison that is needed for manning it; and consequently the enlargement of the food-producing area within the walls is likely to be offset by an increase in the number of the mouths that have to be fed.

The ability of a city to provide itself with food produced within its own bounds is therefore limited, even if the bounds are extended far beyond the edges of the built-up and inhabited part of the city's area, and even if the non-built-up part of the area includes some pasture-land and some arable. As a matter of historical fact, the inclusion of food-producing land within a city's walls, where any such land has been included, has usually been incidental. The usual reason for including un-built-up land within a city's walls has been not economic but military.

At Syracuse, for instance, the city-walls were extended by Dionysius I, between the years 403 and 398 B.C., as far afield as the strong-point Euryalus, which commands the apex of Epipolae, the plateau, shaped like an isosceles triangle, that overhangs the narrow built-up area between the foot of the plateau and the seashore. In 414–413 B.C., Syracuse, within the more closely-drawn fortifications of the day, had only just escaped being cut off from its hinterland by its Athenian assailants. These had almost succeeded in building a beleaguering wall from sea to sea across the near end of the plateau. The extension of the walled-in area of Syracuse as far inland as Euryalus made it difficult to repeat the Athenian attempt to invest Syracuse from the landward side completely. However, the expanded Syracuse, after having successfully withstood several Carthaginian attempts to take it, fell eventually, in 212 B.C., to the Romans, and the reason why it fell was because the Syracusans could not raise a big enough garrison to man effectively the whole of their city's vast Dionysian perimeter.

At Antioch the lie of the land was, in essentials, the same as at Syracuse, but here in a heightened degree. At Antioch, too, the built-up and inhabited area was a narrow low-lying strip. It was confined to the valley of the Orontes, along the south bank of the river, and it was overhung, not just by a plateau, as at Syracuse, but by a mountain. At Antioch the city-wall was carried up to the peak of Mount Casius, as at Syracuse it was carried as far as the apex of the plateau of Epipolae; but at Antioch the empty area that was included within the perimeter for strategic reasons was still less productive than Epipolae's rugged limestone surface. It was a steep bare mountain-side which could hardly provide pasture even for goats. Thus the militarily imperative inclusion of Mount Casius within Antioch's perimeter burdened the city with the disadvantage of having an inordinate length of wall to man, and this without giving it the countervailing advantage of having a food-producing area inside its straggling wall.

The Rajput stronghold at Chittor was more highly favoured by nature than either Antioch or Syracuse. Chittor is a plateau with a surface that is more fertile than Epipolae's and with an escarpment that is more precipitous than Mount Casius' southern flank. Moreover, the foot of Chittor's escarpment is protected, along about half its length, by a river that provides a natural moat. If the River Orontes had done as much for Antioch, or the sea-coast for Syracuse, these two Greek cities would have counted themselves fortunate. Yet even Chittor proved not to be impregnable.

An exception which proves the rule that the enlargement of a city's perimeter is self-defeating is the impregnability of Udaipur, the site to which the Rajput rulers of Mewar State moved after the

Mughal Emperor Akbar had stormed their previous stronghold at Chittor and had forbidden them to re-fortify it. Udaipur is so huge a fortified city that it would be less misleading to call it a miniature fortified canton. Its fortifications, like Chittor's, are natural. Udaipur is a basin of fertile land surrounded by a natural ring-wall of mountains that needs only here and there to be strengthened by human art. When Udaipur's water-supply had been assured by the construction of artificial lakes, this stronghold could not be reduced either by thirst or by starvation, and its mountain-perimeter was so extensive that a hostile army, large enough to invest it, could hardly have been mustered and, if it had been mustered, could hardly have been kept supplied with even iron rations. When Akbar's great-grandson Awrangzeb tried to take Udaipur, he failed to emulate Akbar's feat of taking Chittor. Awrangzeb's army was repulsed and it then had to retreat, discomfited.

The perimeter of Udaipur is exceptionally strong and the area enclosed by it is exceptionally fertile and exceptionally well provided with water. But there is one contingency which, in war-time, may prove too much for the best fortified and best provisioned city. Even a city that, like Udaipur, comprises an unusually large amount of food-producing land within its fortified perimeter is likely in peace-time to draw the major part of its food-supply from a rural area outside the city's defences, and, when the countryside is invaded, the rural population, with their flocks and herds, will take refuge within the fortifications of the city that, in peace-time, is their market. Thus in war-time the city's civilian population and its military garrison will be swollen by a horde of rural refugees, and these will not only add greatly to the number of the mouths that will have to be fed; camping, as they will have to camp, in a narrow space under insanitary conditions, their shanty-town is likely to become a hot-bed of infectious disease that may spread to the permanent urban community.

This is what happened at Athens in the second year of the Atheno-Peloponnesian War of 431–404 B.C. Since the Athenians could not face their Peloponnesian and Boeotian opponents in the field, they had to evacuate the Attic countryside and to concentrate the rural population of Attica inside the Long Walls that linked the City of Athens with its ports, Phaleron and the Peiraeus. The rural refugees were protected effectively against enemy action; the perimeter of Athens-Phaleron-Peiraeus, immense though it was, was somehow manned and the population inside the perimeter, including the refugees, was somehow fed. (The Long Walls made it possible to import food from overseas, across waters that the Athenian navy commanded.) The disaster that the Athenian Government had not foreseen, and could neither prevent nor overcome, was the infectious plague that broke out among the refugees and spread to the permanent inhabitants of the city. In this war, bacteria took a far greater toll of Athenian life than the Athenians' human enemies, their fellow Greeks.

Thus, in the age in which cities sought security by surrounding themselves with ring-walls, it proved impossible for a city's inhabitants to feed themselves entirely from food produced within the limits of their city's fortified perimeter. The extension of a city's perimeter for military reasons proved to be a self-defeating expedient even for military purposes, and incidentally it failed to make the city self-sufficient in terms of food-supply, even in peace-time, while in war-time it exposed the city's swollen population to the menace of being decimated by some lethal infectious disease. City-walls have now been made an obsolete form of defence by the mechanization of life that set in before the close of the eighteenth century, in Britain first of all. In the present age of increasing and accelerating mechanization the built-up areas of the World's cities have been expanding so rapidly that the streets whose names commemorate the location of a city's former walls—'Wall Street' in New York, 'London Wall' and 'Barbican' in London, the circuit of the 'boulevards' in Paris—are now embedded in the present-day city's heart. A new ring-wall, built today, would have to be pulled down tomorrow in order to be replaced by a larger ring that would then have to be pulled down and be replaced in its turn, and, since the invention of aircraft, none of these successive rings would have defended the city effectively, even if the latest and largest ring had been built with all the technological virtuosity that went, between the two world wars, into the building of the Maginot Line. Today, cities are attacked and defended no longer on the ground but from the air.

When, in 1840–4, Paris, by then already on the move, was encircled by King Louis Philippe with a gigantic girdle of Vaubanesque ramparts, this was still an effective gesture. It signified that France might be willing to go to war with a coalition of all the other European powers over 'the Eastern Question'. Louis Philippe's fortress-Paris did stand a siege in 1870–1, but in the end it had to capitulate, not to siege-guns, but to hunger. By that date it was a *tour de force* to feed the population of Paris, even for one week, with food that was to be found inside the area enclosed within the ramparts. For the next half-century the ramparts merely constricted the growth of Paris, without serving any military purpose. After the First World War, they were demolished, and, if they had been left standing, they would have been of no more avail in 1940 than the Maginot Line was for averting the fall of Paris and the fall of France.

The experience of the siege of Paris in 1870–1 demonstrated (if a demonstration was needed) that, even in that archaic phase of the age of mechanization, modern mechanized cities on the move, like the traditional static walled cities of the past, were incapable of feeding themselves with food produced within their own bounds. Modern mechanized cities cannot feed themselves, even partially, as a few of the traditional walled cities once could. The inhabitants of a mechanized city have to fight an endless battle in order to retain any open spaces at all within their city's bounds, and the first claim on un-built-up urban space is for mechanized traffic; the second claim is for parking-places for mechanized vehicles; the third claim is for recreational playgrounds and parks. It would be fantastic to file a claim for earmarking any intra-urban space for arable and pasture as a contribution to providing the city's population with its food. Even the largest of the traditional walled cities have proved, on examination, to bear out the definition of a city as being a settlement whose inhabitants cannot produce, within the city limits, all of the food that they need.

The validity of this definition is confirmed by a glance at any one of the gigantic mechanized cities of today.

If this definition is accepted, it follows that a city cannot exist without having an external source of food-supply in an agricultural hinterland that is productive enough to provide a surplus of food beyond the requirements of the local food-producing rural population. This means that no city ever has been, or ever could be, economically self-contained. Every city has to be linked, by effective means of transportation, with a food-surplus-producing agricultural area; and, in order to induce the producers to deliver their surplus food, the city's inhabitants have to offer to them, in exchange, commodities that they need—or at any rate want— and that are recognized by both parties to the transaction as being of equivalent value. Food cannot be the city's *quid pro quo*, since the rural suppliers of food do not need to import any and the urban consumers of food have none to export. The only commodities that townspeople have to offer to rural food-producers are manufactures and services (commercial, legal, religious, medical, and in some cases also administrative, though the city's administrative services are not always welcome and are sometimes forced upon their rural neighbours against their will). The city's production of goods and services has to be active and intense; for food, though it is the first necessity of life, is not the only import that an urban population has to buy. It must also buy building-materials. (Even if it can make enough bricks from clay within the city-limits, it will have to import timber.) In addition, it must buy metal for making tools. Above all, it must buy the raw materials for its manufactures, and these will include not only metals for hardware but potter's clay for crockery, fibres for textiles, and innumerable other items in an interminable shopping-list.

In the long run a city's imports and exports must balance each other in terms of value. The penalty for a chronic deficit would be the eventual cutting off of supplies and a consequent reduction of the city's population—ultimately to zero. In the past, cities that have paid their way have not imported more in value than they have exported, but they have brought in more in bulk than they have thrown out. The volume of their imports of food, building materials, and raw materials for manufactures has exceeded the volume of the sewage and other refuse that they have got rid of, and, consequently, in the course of time, their surface has risen in height.

A dramatic illustration of this tendency of cities to rise is the *tell* of Jericho—the oldest city so far known except perhaps for one other that has been unearthed at Lepenski Vir in Jugoslavia.[1] The *tell* of Jericho would be still higher than it is if the topmost strata—including the stratum whose walls are said to have collapsed at the blast of Joshua's trumpets—had not weathered away. Yet, even so, the spectacle is impressive enough when one stands on the crown of what is left of the Jericho *tell* and peers into the trench that has been cut through it by the archaeologists down to the level at which their trowels struck virgin soil. Jericho's external source of food-supply was an oasis irrigated from a spring, at a stone-throw's distance from the city-limits, and the virgin soil in which the original proto-Neolithic city was laid out was on the level at which the oasis still lies. But, in the course of the next four or five thousand years, successive destructions and reconstructions, dilapidations and renovations, transformed Jericho from a city on the plain into a city perched on the summit of a man-made miniature mountain.

At Jericho, as in most other early cities, the normal building-material was sun-dried mud-brick, and cities built of this material tend to rise in height quickly; for, when one set of buildings constructed of this material decays or is deliberately destroyed, the brick relapses into its original state of nature and, for the renovator, the least laborious procedure is, not to remove the rubble left by his predecessors, but to level it and build a fresh set of sun-dried mud-brick buildings on top of it, which his successor will then eventually level and build on likewise. Consequently, South-Western Asia stands thick with *tells*. Conspicuous counterparts of Jericho are Irbil (Arbela) in Northern 'Iraq and the two mounds at Charsadda in North-Western Pakistan. (Charsadda

---

[1] On the Serbian (that is, the right) bank of the River Danube, near the point where the river bends north-eastward into its last reach above the Iron Gates.

was the capital of Gandhara before the Kushan emperors transferred their seat of government to Peshawar in the second or third century of the Christian Era.) When archaeologists excavate the sites of ancient settlements, they usually find, as they have found at Jericho and Charsadda and Troy, a number of layers of debris deposited by successive human settlements, the layer deposited by the latest settlement lying nearest to the present surface of the ground, while the lowest layer, which will be the earliest, rests on virgin soil. A rise in the height of settlements in the course of time seems, in fact, to be the general rule.

The average height of settlements in the war-zones of the Second World War must have risen appreciably as a result of bombing and reconstruction; for, though the building-materials used in modern Europe are less easy to pulverize than sun-dried mud-bricks, mid-twentieth-century bombs and bull-dozers are more powerful instruments of destruction and of levelling for reconstruction than any that the successive destroyers and rebuilders of Jericho had at their command.

The sensational recent improvements in the means of transporting heavy loads in bulk did make it possible to remove some of the debris produced by the bombing of London and to convey it across the Atlantic to be used for building new ground along the East River rim of Manhattan Island. Of course the ships that had brought invaluable cargoes of food and munitions from the United States to Britain over Atlantic waters that were infested by enemy submarines would not have carried rubble on their equally dangerous return voyage if Britain in war-time had had any valuable commodity to export. Since, at the time, Britain's productive capacity was almost wholly given over to raising food for home consumption, and to manufacturing munitions that were to be used in Europe, the ships that brought cargoes of American supplies had to return in ballast and the wreckage of London was the ballast that was within the nearest reach. However, this uneconomic long-distance dumping of urban debris was an exceptional performance, even in an age in which Man has been devoting much of his rapidly growing technological power to the achievement of senseless prodigies. The wreckage of Hamburg was treated after the war in the traditional way. It was bulldozed to flatten out a new site for the building of a new Hamburg on a higher level than the level of the Hamburg that had just been destroyed. If, about the year A.D. 10,000, archaeologists dig a trench from top to bottom of the *tell* on which successive Hamburgs will have stood, each planted on the debris of its immediate predecessor, the spectator will see here as imposing a pile of man-made strata as he can see at Jericho today.

The bombing that ravaged Victorian London brought Roman London to light. When, after the end of the Second World War, the debris of Victorian London were being probed in order to find solid ground below them to carry the foundations for ponderous new buildings, these soundings revealed almost the whole of the tracée of the Roman city-wall, of which, previously, only a few fragments, here and there, had been located, and a Roman temple, dedicated to the god Mithras, was uncovered close to the starting-point of Watling Street, the Roman road that ran diagonally across Britain from Thames-side to Mersey-side. These excavations gave the measure of the rise in the level of the surface of the City of London within a span of eighteen centuries. It is impossible to estimate how much of this rise was due, before the Second World War, to deliberate destruction and how much to natural decay and to the excess of intake over discard which is a normal feature in the life of any city. The fate of London after the Roman evacuation and during the English invasion is unknown, and we also lack precise information about the extent of the destruction that was the price of London's defeat, in A.D. 895, of a Danish armada's attempt to force a passage, past London, up the Thames. We do not know, either, how much artificial damage Athens may have suffered when it was captured by a Catalan from a French war-band in 1311, or the exact amount of the grievous damage that it did suffer when it changed hands between the 'Osmanlis and the Venetians in 1687 and in 1688. So we cannot tell how far the rise of the present level of the city's surface above the base of the Old Metropolitan Cathedral, since the building of this little church nine centuries ago, has been due to normal causes.

The normal rise in the level of a city's surface during a period within which the city has suffered no deliberately inflicted damage is, however, illustrated at Oxford by the present difference between the levels of the surface of Broad Street and the base of the Old Ashmolean Building. Within the time-span of less than three centuries that has elapsed since this building's foundations were laid, Oxford has suffered no artificial devastation. It was never bombed during the Second World War. Yet the Old Ashmolean Building, which must have stood at street-level originally, stands at basement-level today.

In our own time, two of the many technological revolutions that we have witnessed have been the increase in the productivity of agriculture and animal husbandry and the increase in the efficiency of means of transportation. Both these technological revolutions started during the later decades of the eighteenth century, and, since then, they have gathered speed till, after the close of the Second World War, they worked up to their present impetus. Throughout the span of seven or eight millennia that elapsed between the building of the first city at Jericho and the outbreak of the Industrial Revolution in Britain, the productivity of agriculture was low and the means of communication were poor in terms of present-day standards, and consequently, by the same standards, the populations of cities were small—though no doubt they seemed formidably large to visitors from the agricultural countryside or from the steppe. Before the outbreak of the Industrial Revolution the only cities that were large even by present-day standards were the capitals of extensive and populous states, and these were rarities. The largeness of Babylon in terms of contemporary Greek standards is brought out by Herodotus[1] in his mention of the report that, when in 538 B.C. the outlying wards of Babylon were already in the Persian assailants' hands, the inhabitants of the central wards were not immediately aware that their city had fallen. In even the largest contemporary Greek city, a break through by an enemy at any point on the city's perimeter would have been visible or audible instantaneously to all the city's inhabitants. Babylon, Egyptian Thebes, Alexandria,

[1] Herodotus, Book I, chap. 191.

Rome, Constantinople, and the successive capitals of China since her political unification in 221 B.C.: this enumeration of large pre-Industrial Revolution capitals is almost complete, and the number can be counted on the fingers of one pair of hands.

All but a handful of the host of cities that rose and fell or rose and survived during those seven or eight millennia before the Industrial Revolution were market-towns serving a surrounding countryside with a radius that was short enough to allow the rural food-producer to bring his produce into the city, sell it there, and get back to his rural home again between daybreak and nightfall; and the same length of radius was also short enough to allow the urban pedlar, coming and going in the inverse direction, to tour the surrounding villages, pack on back, and to re-enter the city before its gates were closed for the night. At the outbreak of the Industrial Revolution in Britain, the typical town there was still a market-town of this traditional type. The following description of 'Casterbridge'—a fictitious name that is a thin disguise for the historic Roman city of Dorchester—would have served almost equally well to describe Jericho as it was in the sixth millennium B.C. The passage will be found in Chapter Nine of Thomas Hardy's novel *The Mayor of Casterbridge*. In the opening sentence of the book, the story is dated before 1830. It will be noted that this imaginary date coincides with the actual date at which George Cruikshank etched his cartoon called 'London going out of Town'.

Casterbridge was in most respects but the pole, focus, or nerve-knot of the surrounding country life; differing from the many manufacturing towns which are as foreign bodies set down, like boulders on a plain, in a green world with which they have nothing in common. Casterbridge lived by agriculture at one remove further from the fountain-head than the adjoining villages—no more. The townsfolk understood every fluctuation in the rustic's condition, for it affected their receipts as much as the labourer's; they entered into the troubles and joys which moved the aristocratic families ten· miles round—for the same reason. And even at the dinner-parties of the professional families the subjects of discussion were corn, cattle-disease, mowing and reaping, fencing and planting; while politics were viewed by them less from their own standpoint of burgesses with rights and privileges than from the standpoint of their country neighbours.

Like all cities that there have ever been, Casterbridge and Jericho made their living by selling manufactures and services in exchange for food, and for them, as for most other cities before the Industrial Revolution, their staple trade was with a surrounding agricultural area whose circumference was rather less than half a day's journey distant from the city's marketplace. However, even Jericho and Casterbridge needed to import other things besides the food that was produced within this short range of their walls. The forests from which a city drew its timber, the mines from which it drew its metal, and the quarries from which it drew its building-stone were rarely as close at hand as the arable and pasture from which it drew its food. For these other commodities, which come second only to food itself as necessities of city life, most cities at most times and places have had to go farther afield, and, before the application of steam-power to traction a century and a half ago, water-transport by river, canal, or sea was incomparably cheaper and quicker than overland transport by porter, wheelbarrow, pack-animal, or wagon.

Roman roads are justly famous. In Western Europe, there were no roads of equal excellence again in this backward region for fourteen centuries after the upkeep of the Roman roads had been abandoned in the fifth century of the Christian Era. Yet it was not the Roman roads that supplied the City of Rome with the necessities of life and that held the Roman Empire together. Rome as described by Strabo, who was writing in Augustus' reign, was built of timber cut in the Appennines and floated down the River Tiber. Imperial Rome, when it had become the capital of an empire embracing the whole perimeter of the Mediterranean, was fed, not on grain grown in Peninsular Italy—not even on Italian grain grown within Rome's immediate neighbourhood—but on sea-borne grain grown in Sicily and in North-Western Africa, within easy reach of their coasts, or even as far afield as Egypt. The basin of the River Po could not compete with these overseas countries for the Roman market, though it produced a large surplus of food after the Romans had conquered it and colonized it and developed it economically. Only its pigs could be driven on the trotter to Rome over the Appennines. The River Po and its tributaries, down which cereals could be floated, opened on to the head of the Adriatic, and the voyage from Adria or Spina to Rome round the 'heel' and 'toe' of Italy was too long to be profitable, so the Po basin's cereals were a drug on the local market.

Rome was the highest point on the River Tiber that could be reached by sea-going ships, and, in the pre-railway age, this was a commercially favourable location for a city. The reason why today Albany, not New York, is the capital of New York State is that Albany was the farthest point up the River Hudson that was accessible for seventeenth-century Dutch sea-going ships. However, the sea-going ships of the latest centuries B.C. found increasing difficulty in reaching Rome as the average size of cargo-ships increased and as the mouth of the Tiber silted up. In the imperial period of Rome's history the normal practice was to trans-ship sea-borne goods, destined for Rome, on to lighters that could be towed up the Tiber to the City. Originally this trans-shipment had to be carried out at sea till the Empire's financial resources could be mobilized for excavating an artificial harbour connecting the sea with the river above the river's mouth. This way of provisioning Rome was as expensive as it was elaborate; but it was less expensive and more efficient than it would have been to bring cereals to Rome overland from the fertile fields of Campania. Campania's excellent natural harbour at Puteoli, which had been used for serving Rome during the last two centuries B.C., was replaced by the artificial harbour Portus at the Tiber's mouth because the overland haulage from Puteoli to Rome had been found to be prohibitively clumsy and costly. Travellers from Rome to the Levant had to ride on horseback or in palanquin from Rome to Brindisi, in order to take ship there. They eased and speeded up this arduous first stage of their journey by spending the first night out from Rome on board a canal-barge that was towed through the Pomptine Marshes while the traveller was enjoying a night's rest.

The Mediterranean Sea was the medium of communication by means of which the City of Rome was kept supplied and the

Roman Government's officials and couriers travelled to and fro between the capital and the provinces. In terms of communications, the Roman Empire was a circummediterranean empire, and the limit of its expansion into the hinterland was the maximum distance to which it was practicable to extend the overland lines of communication of Roman armies based on Mediterranean ports. The Arab armies that conquered a more extensive empire in the seventh and eighth centuries of the Christian Era were more mobile than the Roman armies had been; but their conquests, too, were limited to the maximum distance at which they could operate from their ports. The Arab empire-builders' ports were not sea-ports; for, of all the types of terrain on the land-surface of the globe, the steppes are the most conductive, though they are neither so conductive nor so extensive as the sea. In the age of the Umayyad Caliphate the steppe-ports in which the troops drawn from Peninsular Arabia were cantoned were strung along the eastern edge of Syria and the south-western edge of 'Iraq, on the line at which 'the desert' marches with 'the sown'.

The largest land-empire that has ever been put together so far is the Mongol Empire. At its maximum extent, which it reached towards the close of the thirteenth century of the Christian Era, this empire embraced the whole of China, the whole of what are now Chinese and Soviet Central Asia, Iran, 'Iraq, and the greater part of Russia. The Mongols succeeded in conquering this vast area and in temporarily holding it together because their empire's configuration was the same as the Roman Empire's had been. The Mongol Empire, too, was a ring of territories linked with each other by a central conductive medium, in this case not a land-locked sea but a steppe encompassed by lands inhabited by sedentary agricultural and urban populations. This Eurasian steppe, which extends from the Khingan Mountains in Manchuria to the Carpathians, with an enclave of steppe-land still farther to the west in the Hungarian Alföld, is far larger than the Mediterranean, and the Mongol Empire was proportionately larger than the Roman Empire; but, since steppes are less conductive than seas are, the Mongol Empire was shorter-lived than the Roman Empire.

The First Persian Empire, which was established in the sixth century B.C., anticipated the Roman Empire, the Arab Empire, and the Mongol Empire in building roads and operating a postal service along them for the imperial government's use. The Persian Empire was not provided by nature with either a central sea or a central steppe, and its builders recognized that—with the means of overland conveyance in the pre-railway age—a network of roads, however good, was an inadequate apparatus for holding together an empire that extended westward to Egypt and Cyrenaïca and eastward to the Indus basin. The Persian Emperor Darius I surveyed a throughway for navigation from the Kābul River tributary of the Indus across the Arabian Sea to the head of the Gulf of Suez, and he linked up this water-route with the Nile and the Mediterranean by reconditioning the ship-canal, linking Suez with the Nile Delta via the lakes and the Wadi Tumīlāt, that had been dug by the Pharaoh Necho II (609–593 B.C.). Darius also sent a squadron to explore the colonial extension of the Greek World to the west of the Straits of Otranto. His son and successor, Xerxes, tried—though this unsuccessfully—to emulate another feat of Necho's: the circumnavigation of Africa by a squadron of Phoenician ships in Necho's service.

In the pre-railway age, Egypt's natural endowment made her the most convenient country in the World for providing for a city's needs. When the jungle-swamp that had originally covered the valley and the delta of the Nile from the foot of the First Cataract to the mouths of the Delta had been transformed into a kitchen garden through the draining and irrigating of its fertile alluvial soil, any city planted anywhere in Egypt was bound to have an ample source of food-supply at its gates, and it was also bound to have a navigable waterway within close reach, since it could not be far from the bank of the Nile or of one of the Nile's Deltaic arms. In using the Nile as a waterway, Man made one of his earliest moves towards supplementing, and ultimately replacing, human and animal muscle-power by harnessing the potentially far more potent physical forces latent in inanimate nature. Travelling on the Nile downstream, the human rower's muscle-power was assisted by the river's current; travelling upstream against the current, the boatman, hoisting a sail, could overpower the force of the current by enlisting the greater force of the prevalent North Wind without having to put a hand to an oar. The cliffs running parallel to the Nile valley at close range provided excellent stone of various kinds for the mason's and the sculptor's purposes, and granite quarried just below the First Cataract could be floated down-river for carving a statue or building a temple in a city in the Delta. From the Delta, a coastal voyage north-eastwards to Byblos would bring an Egyptian ship within short logging-distance of the forests on Mount Lebanon. The copper mines on the west side of the Sinai Peninsula were within a comparably short distance from the east coast of the Gulf of Suez, and the coast could be reached from Upper Egypt via the portage from the eastward bend of the Nile at Coptos to the Egyptian Red-Sea port of Qusayr (Leukos Limen). After the cutting of the canal from the delta of the Nile to Suez, the Sinai copper-mines could be reached from any part of Egypt by continuous voyage—and not only the Sinai copper-mines. Once launched on the Red Sea, Egyptian ships could reach Punt (? Somalia), and Alexandrian mariners could sail, as they learned to sail perhaps *circa* 100–80 B.C., direct across the Arabian Sea to the west coast of India and to Ceylon. Thereafter, an Alexandrian depot for the distribution of Mediterranean wares was established on the east coast of India at Arikamedu, a few miles south of Pondichéry, and, before the end of the second century of the Christian Era, at least one Alexandrian ship had reached a Chinese port.

In Sumer (present-day South-Eastern 'Iraq), nature was less generous in providing for a city's needs. When the alluvial soil of the lower basin of the Tigris and Euphrates had been turned into fields, as fertile as Egypt's, by the clearing of the jungle and the draining of the swamp, Sumerian cities, like Egyptian cities, did have a source of food-supply at their gates, but their means of communication by water did not compare with Egypt's, for, though Sumer had two great rivers to Egypt's one, these were navigable only downstream. Their currents were swifter than the Nile's, and in Sumer there was no prevailing South-East Wind to carry a sailing-boat upstream in the teeth of the rivers' resistance. This was the more awkward because there were no sources of timber, stone, and metals close at hand. The nearest forest was on Mount Amanus, in the north-western corner of Syria; the nearest mines and quarries were on the western rim of the Iranian plateau. However, necessity is the mother of enterprise as well as of invention. The Sumerians were not content with inventing tools made of clay baked to an almost metallic degree of hardness; they were enterprising enough to fetch metal and timber and even stone from their distant sources of supply and to produce and export manufactures to pay for their imports. The range of the Sumerian cities' economic activity was actually wider than the Egyptian cities' economic range was before Phoenician and Greek oceanic mariners started to operate from Egyptian ports.

These differences, however, were only relative; for all cities, from the primary market-towns onwards and upwards, necessarily live by trading with areas outside their own city limits. The city's intrinsic and perennial dependence on trade took physical form inside the city in the city's marketplace—the mother of warehouses, mercantile offices, banks, stock-exchanges, computers, and all the other sophisticated trading apparatus to which the marketplace eventually gave birth. The city's exceptionalness in the pre-industrial age, and its consequent constant danger of being obliterated by being reabsorbed into the agricultural and pastoral countryside or into the wilderness, took physical form in the city-wall and in the citadel, in which the citizens could make a last stand if the lower city were taken by assault.

Since the date, perhaps eight thousand years ago, of the foundation of the earliest city on the site of Jericho, there have been few times and places in which cities have not needed to seek security against attack, and, in the age before the advent of the bombing plane and the rocket, defences, natural or artificial, were at ground-level or water-level. At ground-level, artificial defences took the form of walls—or of the earthworks that replaced walls when the 'improvement' of artillery made previously impregnable

walls of masonry vulnerable, as the triple land-wall of Constantinople proved to be in the year 1453.

In the age of city-walls, unwalled cities were rarities. The
pre-Hellenic Cretan city of Cnossos seems to have been unwalled
throughout the millennium and a half during which it was
inhabited before it was destroyed *circa* 1400 B.C., but, towards the
end of that age, the younger cities that were founded on the
adjacent mainland of Greece—for instance, Mycenae and Tiryns—
were fortified as massively as any cities ever have been. The
reasons why pre-Hellenic Cnossos was able to do without walls
may have been (these are merely guesses) that in the Minoan Age
the island of Crete was united politically and that her navy commanded the surrounding seas. It is more remarkable that Nara,
the earliest formally-laid-out capital of the Japanese Empire, was
unwalled likewise; for, though Japan, like Crete, is surrounded by
the sea, the smallest of the four principal Japanese islands is larger
than Crete, and in the early years of the eighth century of the
Christian Era, when Nara was being built, the Imperial Government's writ may not yet have run effectively at the north-eastern
end of the main island, Honshu, at whose south-western end Nara
stands. Yet, at Nara, only the palace was walled, and this palace
was not a citadel. At Nara the palace wall's function was to provide
privacy, not security. The contrast between unwalled Nara and
the castles built in Japan in the feudal age that set in towards the
end of the twelfth century is as striking as the contrast between
unwalled Cnossos and the fortifications of Mycenae and Tiryns,
and the resemblance between these Mycenaean fortress-towns
and the feudal-age Japanese castles is no less remarkable. The
massive polygonal masonry of which the lower storeys of a
Japanese castle are built might have been the work of a Mycenaean military architect. The Japanese castles and the Mycenaean
fortresses are normal examples of urban settlements in the pre-
bombing age. Nara and Cnossos are singular exceptions to the
general rule.

In the choosing of sites for cities in the pre-bombing age,
military defensibility at ground level or water level was in almost
all cases an important requirement; and the founders of a city

sought out a natural fortress for the placement of their citadel at any rate, and, where possible, for the placement of the rest of the city as well. The two main kinds of natural fortress that are effective against attack from ground level or water level are isolated outcrops of rock and mazy swamps.

Examples of crag-citadels are the acropolises of Athens and Pergamon, the Acrocorinthus, the citadel of Ankara, and the Rajput fortress of Chittor, where the citadel and the city are coextensive. It is also possible to create an artificial equivalent of a crag-citadel on an open plain. An example of this *tour de force* of human labour is the now deserted city of Balkh (Bactra), the former capital of Bactria (now Afghan Uzbekistan), which is the plain between the north foot of the Hindu Kush Range and the south bank of the River Oxus. At Balkh the city's gigantic mud-brick walls are perched on a proportionately gigantic man-made bank; and in one corner of the huge four-square perimeter there is a gigantic man-made citadel: an artificial mound that is of the same order of magnitude as the largest of the natural crag-citadels in Turkey or Greece or Italy.

Examples of swamp-citadels are Mantua in the Po basin and Ravenna on the Adriatic coast of Italy to the south of the Venetian lagoon. When, *circa* 400 B.C., a Gallic Völkerwanderung descended on the Po basin like an avalanche, Mantua was the only one of the Etruscan cities, previously founded there, that survived—one, so it was said, out of a total of twelve. Ravenna, at that time an Umbrian city, survived the Gallic Völkerwanderung too, though the vanguard of the Gallic invaders surged past Ravenna, down the coast, almost as far south-eastward as Ancona. Ravenna, at the time of this emergency, was an island in a lagoon, as Venice has managed to continue to be by taking measures to prevent its lagoon from silting up. By the time when, eight centuries later, the Gallic Völkerwanderung was followed by a German one, Ravenna had become enveloped in marshes. The government of what was left of the western half of the Roman Empire took refuge in this natural hide-out in A.D. 404, and when, after an interlude of barbarian rule, Italy was temporarily brought back under Roman rule by the Roman Imperial Government at

Constantinople, Ravenna became and remained the capital of the Constantinopolitan Government's viceroy in the dwindling remnants of the Empire's Italian dominions. In both the Gallic and the German Völkerwanderung Rome was quickly taken by the barbarian invaders—on the first occasion *circa* 387/6 B.C. and on the second occasion in A.D. 410. By contrast, Ravenna never fell to the Gauls, and though, from A.D. 476 to A.D. 539, it was the headquarters of the successive Rugian and Ostrogothic occupations of Italy, it did not fall to the Lombards till A.D. 750, though the Lombards had broken into Italy in A.D. 568. Ravenna, not Rome, was the stronghold, in Italy, of the Constantinopolitan Roman Empire, and this historical fact is commemorated in Italy's present-day geographical nomenclature. In present-day Italy the name 'Romagna' ('the Romans' country') is borne, not by the district round Rome, but by the district round Ravenna.

The Sumerian cities, which are the oldest known to us except for Jericho and the recently discovered Neolithic city of Lepenski Vir in Jugoslavia, must originally have been swamp-fastnesses of the type represented by Ravenna and by Mantua. Each of them must have started as the urban centre of a small isolated patch of food-producing land that had been won from the swamp by draining and irrigation. The still unreclaimed swamp of the lower Tigris-Euphrates basin must have insulated these budding cities from each other, and at this stage the Sumerian cities must have been poor but secure. The completion of the process of converting the marshes into a network of canals and fields brought with it a reversal in the Sumerian city-states' fortunes. They now found themselves insecure though rich. They had been enriched by the enlargement of their respective agricultural and pastoral domains; they had lost their security through coming into contact with each other; for contact brought with it collisions over the control of canals, and over the ownership of fields in border districts. By the date at which the earliest so far recovered Sumerian records were being written, the Sumerian cities—each a sovereign state—were falling into fratricidal wars with each other, and these wars recurred with increasing violence till they brought the Sumerian society to ruin and eventually cost the Sumerian city-states their sovereignty. In the end the Sumerian World was united politically through force of arms by Semitic powers, by Agade in the first instance and by Babylon finally. This is not the only time that Man has turned a technological triumph into a social calamity. Again and again this has been the nemesis of a moral backwardness that is out of step with Man's technological prowess.

Thucydides, in his introduction to his history of the Atheno-Peloponnesian War of 431–404 B.C., has observed that, in the archaic age of Hellenic history, the Greek city-states were pulled in opposite directions by the conflicting requirements of trade and defence. Trade called for a location for the city as close as possible to good food-producing land and to good water-transport, which, in the Aegean basin, means maritime transport, since in this region there are no navigable rivers. On the other hand, defence called for a location out of reach of pirates, brigands, and invading armies, which, in this region, means a location on a mountain inland. Manifestly accessibility and security were difficult to combine, even for Greek cities that had become rich enough to be able to afford to provide themselves with artificial defences in the shape of man-made walls.

In the Mediterranean World the problem of reconciling these two desiderata has been solved by locating cities on islands or, second-best, on peninsulas that can be defended against attack from the mainland by a short stretch of land-wall running from sea to sea. Examples of insular cities are Tyre and Aradus (Arvad, Ruad) off the coast of what is now the Republic of Lebanon; Motya, a colonial Phoenician city off the west end of Sicily; Venice in her lagoon; and Tenochtitlan, the capital of the Aztec Empire, on a cluster of islands in a now dried-up lake. Syracuse, which ended as the city with the longest perimeter of land-walls anywhere in the Graeco-Roman World, had started, before it sprawled over on to the Sicilian mainland, on the off-shore island of Ortygia, a counterpart of Motya at Sicily's opposite extremity. Examples of peninsular cities are Sidon on the coast of Lebanon, Carthage on the coast of Tunisia, Miletus on the coast of Ionia, and Constantinople on the European shore of the Bosphorus. An important constituent of the British Empire has been a chain of peninsular and insular cities: Gibraltar, Valetta, Bombay, Penang, Singapore, Hong Kong. In the Second World War, British naval power in the Pacific was not strong enough to avert the fall of Hong Kong, Singapore, and Penang, but Bombay and Gibraltar were not attacked in this war, and Valetta held out. Gibraltar successfully withstood a siege from both sea and land in 1779–82.

It has been noted already that, for a brief spell in the fifth century B.C., Athens made herself, as far as practicable, into the equivalent of a peninsular city—and this on a Constantinopolitan scale—by linking herself with 'long walls' to her two ports, Phaleron and the Peiraeus. This expedient was, of course, inferior to the advantages with which true peninsular cities, such as Constantinople and Carthage, were endowed by nature. The length of wall that the Athenians had to build, to keep in repair, and to defend in order to ensure their freedom of access to maritime harbours was of the order of magnitude of the length of Syracuse's walls when these had been carried inland as far as the Euryalus.

Even in these cases the problem of combining accessibility with security was solvable only because, and so long as, the insular or peninsular city had sufficient command of the sea to be able to defend both itself and its maritime trade-routes. An island or peninsula is particularly vulnerable if it does not possess naval power or is not included politically in some larger state that is capable of defending its insular possessions. The smaller islands of the Aegean Archipelago have been raided and bullied and subjected time and again in most of the successive chapters of the Aegean basin's history. On the other hand, an insular or peninsular city that does possess adequate naval power is in an unusually favourable position. It can defend itself against attack, and it can buy its food and sell its wares as far away as the sea can carry its merchant-ships and as its navy can protect them.

Some insular and peninsular naval powers have acquired political empires. Carthage, Athens (for a short spell), Venice, and Britain are cases in point. Carthage turned her political empire to economic account by making it a commercial preserve for herself and for the other colonial Phoenician cities on or off the coasts of

Africa and Spain that were Carthage's satellites; but Carthage's trading area was wider than her political empire. She bought from the Greek city-states in Sicily and from the Etruscans the wares that she sold, at a middleman's profit, to her African and Spanish subjects. On the other hand, the British, at their zenith, threw their empire open to traders of all nations while they themselves traded with all the World; and the far greater part of the volume of Venice's trade was with the independent states of the Islamic, Eastern Orthodox Christian, and Western Christian worlds, whom she served as a commercial go-between. Her political dominions were less useful to her as markets and as sources of supply then as way-stations and as *points d'appui*.

The importation of food-supplies from distant sources by water is not open to insular cities that are located, not in the sea, but in a land-locked lake. An insular city in this situation cannot afford to dispense with a home-grown food-supply, even if it is the capital of an extensive and still expanding empire, as Tenochtitlan was at the moment when Cortés suddenly destroyed it. The population of Tenochtitlan had solved their food-problem ingeniously by inventing 'floating gardens' in which food-crops were grown on rafts composed of matted vegetation. On the other hand, an insular or peninsular city that commands the sea can do without an adjacent source of food-supply. So long as it produces manufactures and performs commercial services of sufficient value to pay for the food that it needs to import, it can fetch this food by sea from distant sources. Carthage did not extend her political empire over the adjacent parts of Tunisia till half a century or more after she had made herself mistress of points on, or off-shore from, the coasts of Sicily, Sardinia, and Spain. Venice did not start to build up an empire on the Italian mainland till more than a century after she had annexed the distant island of Crete. Hamburg never held any territory to speak of outside her city-limits, apart from a tiny enclave round Cuxhaven at the mouth of the Elbe. Yet, thanks to her location, Hamburg acquired a vast commercial hinterland. During the last generation before the outbreak of the First World War, Hamburg was the principal port of shipment for emigrants to the United States from an area in the north-western

quarter of the Old World that extended from Hamburg eastwards
as far as and including Russia.

Miletus, like Hamburg, never acquired a political empire; the
colonies that she planted, which were numerous, became independent city-states; but Miletus' trading area extended northward
to the north coast of the Black Sea, southward to Egypt, and westward into the western basin of the Mediterranean. When, in the
early decades of the sixth century B.C., the Lydians built up a land-
empire in Miletus' continental hinterland, they were foiled in
their attempts to subject Miletus, because Miletus had a merchant
marine and a navy and the Lydians had neither. The Lydians
found Miletus' landward fortifications too strong for them to take
by assault, and they failed to bring Miletus to her knees by
annually invading her agricultural territory outside her walls and
destroying the crops. They found that Miletus could dispense
with home-grown food, and probably she had long ago ceased to
count on this, for Miletus' home-territory is not fertile. Miletus
could ship her manufactures to the Ukraine and Egypt and could
buy return cargoes of food from there. The Lydians could not
interfere with this Milesian trade, and eventually they accepted
their defeat and came to terms. In the next century, Athens
played this Milesian game against her Peloponnesian and Boeotian
opponents in the War of 431–404 B.C., and she too was able to
play it successfully so long as she retained the command of the
Dardanelles and the Bosphorus and thereby retained access to the
Ukraine's cereal crops. Victorian Britain likewise ceased, at her
industrial, commercial, and naval zenith, to depend on her supply
of home-grown food. She now drew her food from North
America, Argentina, Australia, and New Zealand, and accordingly she came within sight of being starved into surrender when,
in each of the two world wars, her maritime approaches were
made perilous by enemy submarines.

Before the outbreak of the Industrial Revolution, cities were
exceptional spots on the land-surface of the planet. Even market-
towns, which were the standard type of city, were few and far
between. It was normal for a city to draw its food-supply from
an agricultural district in its immediate neighbourhood. The

maritime cities that imported their food from far away were conspicuous because they were rare. The general pattern of human settlement was a sprinkling, at wide intervals, of market-towns, each surrounded by its own narrow circle of fields and pastures, and each insulated from its nearest neighbours by the wilderness. A fraction of the wilderness was being turned to some account by Man precariously for goat-pasture on the mountains and for nomadic pasture on the steppes, but the greater part of the wilderness was still wholly unreclaimed. It is significant that in Italy in the last millennium B.C. Silvanus, the god of the woods, was also the tutelary god of the frontiers between states. At the time at which Silvanus acquired this second function, states in Italy must have been isolated clearings in the peninsula's coverage of forest. There were a few areas—for instance, Sumer, Egypt, and the North Indian and North Chinese plains—in which the arable and pasture lands surrounding each of the local cities had eliminated the intervening wilderness and had coalesced with each other; but such patches of continuous cultivation and pasturage were exceptional, and, since the outbreak of the Industrial Revolution has launched the World's cities on the move, it has become clear that the World's fields and pastures will never now coalesce into a continuum with a world-wide range. The example set by London of 'going out of town' is being followed by all the other cities in the World, and the fields and pastures are being overtaken and being overwhelmed by a lava-flow of new houses and streets. What has happened in Japan in my lifetime has given a preview of what, within my grandchildren's lifetime, will have happened over many other parts of the land-surface of the globe. In 1956 I could not recognize the shores of the Shimonoseki Straits which I had seen in 1929, and in 1967 I could not recognize the city of Nara which I had seen in 1929 and in 1956. A once lovely rural landscape and a once even more lovely holy city had been obliterated by 'the march of bricks and mortar'.

The chequer-board pattern of fields is not now going to spread till the separate patches of it coalesce; it is going to be broken up into isolated remnants by the spread of the world-encompassing city—Ecumenopolis—which is being brought into existence today under our eyes. Within the ambit of Ecumenopolis, though not all over the rest of the land-surface of the globe, the general pattern of human settlement is going to be the same as it was before. It is still going to be a pattern of dots sprinkled, at rare intervals, over a surface that, in the main, will be of a different colour. It will, however, be the same pattern with a difference, for the components of it will have been changed. The sprinkled dots will now be the surviving remnants of greenery; the space of a different colour in which these rare isolated dots of green will be set will no longer be the virgin wilderness; it will be a continuum of streets and buildings—and this threatens to become a wilderness of a more fearful kind than the worst that nature has begotten if Man fails to plan the shape and structure of the coming World-City before this has set hard in the intolerable form of a world-wide shanty-town.

The ecological revolution through which mankind is putting itself in our time is symbolized in the inversion of the function of walls. Their traditional function was to save cities—an exceptional and rare form of human settlement—from being overwhelmed by the aggression of fields, pasture, and wilderness. The function of walls today is to save parks and 'green belts' from being overwhelmed by the aggression of bricks and mortar. As for agriculture and animal husbandry, they are going to be pushed off the land into the sea, first on to the continental shelf and eventually, perhaps, into the depths. Fortunately the deep sea covers a far greater part of the planet's surface than is covered by dry land and shallow seas together. The sea is going to be mankind's future source of food, and the sea-bed our future source of minerals. With the world-wide city now fast bearing down upon us, we can no longer afford to exploit the resources latent in the sea by following the feckless methods of our Palaeolithic ancestors.

In the age of Ecumenopolis the fishing industry—a persisting relic of the antiquated Palaeolithic food-gathering economy—has fallen out of date. The Japanese have carried this form of food-gathering to the highest attainable pitch of efficiency, and it is no accident that the Japanese are also the pioneers in the new enterprise of farming the sea. Visit Wakayama and you will see seaweed being cultivated as a food-stuff. Visit Shirahama and you will see yellow-tail fish-spawn being artificially fertilized and the surviving brood being shepherded like Proteus' legendary flock of seals on Pharos Island. In the state of nature—i.e. the state of the maritime fauna in which the fisherman takes his toll of this— three yellow-tail eggs out of one million survive to grow into adult fish that will live long enough to keep the species in existence by producing spawn and sperm in their turn. In the novel state of domestication, the number of survivors is no longer just three out of one million; it is one hundred thousand. Here are the loaves and fishes on which the fifty thousand million future inhabitants of Ecumenopolis are going to be fed.

In cities of the traditional kind the population was congested. Since city-walls were expensive to build and keep in repair, the public authorities sought to confine the circuit to the minimum length that would contain the population when this was as closely packed as it could be. If a city could afford a length of wall that would embrace more than this minimum area, the authorities were deterred by the prospect of having to find the additional men for manning this extended perimeter. If an extension, beyond the bounds of the built-up and inhabited area, was required for imperative military reasons, such as the inclusion of a ridge or a peak, commanding the site of the city, which could not safely be left outside to be occupied by an assailant, the additional intramural space thus reluctantly acquired was likely to be too steep and rocky for use as a building-site. The geometrical lay-out of the Ionian Greek city Priene on a steeply sloping shelf half way up a mountainside was an exceptional *tour de force*. Consequently, in most cities of the traditional kind, the density of settlement was high. It was at its maximum in the Phoenician insular and peninsular cities, whose areas were tiny. At Motya the buildings were six storeys high; the city possessed no food-producing land of its own; and there was not even room on the island for a cemetery; a site for this had to be rented on the Sicilian mainland from the natives.

In the age before the Industrial Revolution the close-packed inhabitants of the planet's rare cities constituted only a very small fraction of the planet's human population. The surviving food-gatherers were probably fewer still. The vast majority of people, during the eight or possibly ten thousand years that elapsed between the invention of agriculture and animal husbandry and the outbreak of the Industrial Revolution were food-producers who lived and worked in the open country. In 1969 it is estimated that forty-five per cent of the World's population has already become urban, and, since the explosion of urbanization has occurred, so far, mainly among a 'developed' minority, the percentage that has already been reached here is already far above the world average. It is said, for instance, that in the United States today, the percentage of the population that is still engaged in producing food is smaller than the percentage that is on the campuses of the universities. This overwhelming preponderance of the numbers of the urban population, which is an accomplished fact in the United States today, will have become a world-wide phenomenon by the day after tomorrow. Yet the average present density of urban settlement in the United States, Western Europe, and Japan (which, in Tokyo, contains the World's present largest city), is estimated to be lower, on the average, than the density was in the cities of the traditional type. Among present-day cities, Hong Kong is possibly the only one in which there are as many inhabitants per square kilometre as there once were in Motya, Carthage, Tyre, Sidon, and Aradus.

On first thoughts this estimate may seem incredible. The high-rise buildings of Tokyo, New York, and Chicago dwarf the six-storeys-high buildings at Motya at the turn of the fifth and fourth centuries B.C. At the same time, however, the area of the whole of Sicily is being far exceeded by the areas of each of the megalopolises—future components of Ecumenopolis—that are now coagulating round the Great Lakes of North America, from Milwaukee, through Chicago and Detroit, to Cleveland, and along the east coast of North America from Boston, through New York and Philadelphia, to Washington, D.C., and along the south coast of the Main Island of Japan from Tokyo, through Nagoya, to Ōsaka. It is therefore probably true that the increase in the area covered by urban buildings and streets has expanded out of proportion to the increase in the absolute numbers of the urban population. There has been a vast increase in these numbers, but there has been a still vaster simultaneous increase in the areas that the urban population occupies, and this means that the density of settlement will have lessened as the cities have grown in both population and size.

This, on first thoughts, paradoxical result of 'the march of bricks and mortar' has been made possible by the concomitant improvement, through mechanization, of the means of communication. In a city of the traditional kind, most of the inhabitants had to circulate on foot; only a well-to-do minority could afford to ride through the narrow streets on donkeyback or on horseback. Consequently, most urban workers lived either in the buildings in which they worked or within a few minutes' walk of them, and this meant that they lived and worked tight-packed. Even in the London of the eighteen-nineties, which had been expanding at an accelerating pace for at least a century past, my family's neighbour, the solicitor, rode to his office on horseback; my father, who was a social worker, travelled to and fro by horse-drawn bus between our house in Paddington and the local branch offices of the Charity Organization Society on the south bank of the Thames; and the persistence of these primitive means of conveyance limited the expansion of London to some extent. The practice of 'commuting' had already begun by the eighteen-nineties, but it was still in its infancy, and it was still confined to travel by train. There was not yet any public or private mechanized road-transport for passengers.

By this year, 1969, 'commuting' between a suburban dormitory and an urban factory or office has become the rule. In the dormitory suburbs the average height of buildings is relatively low compared to the average in the business quarter—the 'City' in London, 'down town' in New York, 'the Loop' in Chicago—and one of the amenities of suburban life is that in a suburb there is room, at an economic price, for a house to have a garden. It is true that the poorer part of the urban population, which is still, as it always has been, the majority, continues to live fairly near to the inner sectors of the city, but the re-housing of the poor in high-rise blocks of flats has not increased the density of habitation in the areas in which they live. The new blocks are widely spaced to leave room for playgrounds for children and for parking places for the owners of cars, whereas the single-storey or two-storey houses which the high-rise blocks have replaced stood much thicker on the ground. Moreover, now that it is no longer usual for an urban worker to sleep at night on the upper floor of the building on whose ground-floor he works in the daytime, most workers occupy two units of urban or suburban space—one in which the worker spends his nights and his week-ends and a second in which he spends his working hours on working days. It has been said (and this is not an excessive exaggeration) that the only people who spend their nights nowadays within the precincts of the 'City' of London are the Dean and Canons of Saint Paul's Cathedral and the members of their households.

This means that the replacement of the traditional tiny walled city by the boundless city of the present and the future has changed the character of the crux of urban life. In a traditional city the crux was the congestion of a stationary population. Life was squalid and insanitary, and the intra-mural urban death-rate from disease was probably higher than the extra-mural death-rate from battle and murder. In a present-day megalopolis the crux is the congestion of the traffic now that the population has become mobile. It has taken to migrating *en masse* between its dormitories and its working-places twice in every twenty-four hours. In 1967 I was told in Tokyo that seventeen million people worked within the city limits by day, but only twelve million slept within the same area by night. Five million people were 'commuting' in and out of Tokyo; the number was increasing; and the public authorities were already at their wits' end in seeking to cope with the consequently growing traffic-problem. The zone of danger to life and limb has now shifted from the countryside to the city. In the cities of the United States, murder and battle, amounting almost to civil war, are threatening to become chronic, but the chief physical risk is that of accidents when high-powered mechanized vehicles collide with each other and with pedestrians. The toll of life taken by accidents is not, however, so grievous an affliction for these urban populations on the move as the physical fatigue, the psychological strain, and the loss of hours of working time and recuperating time which are a 'commuter's' occupational trials. These novel problems of urban life are the subject of the two concluding chapters of this book.

2: City-States

In the preceding chapter, cities have been looked at mainly in their material aspect. In this aspect, we can see that they are human settlements of a particular kind that is distinguished from other kinds by the nature of the man-made environment in which urban populations live. Cities are not villages whose inhabitants are occupied in producing crops from fields or on breeding livestock on pastures; nor are cities encampments of miners, foresters, or charcoal-burners, and, *a fortiori*, they are not moving camps like those of the nomadic pastoralists. Cities, like villages, are fixed settlements whose inhabitants are sedentary, but urban settlements are conglomerations of streets and buildings, and it is not possible to produce, within a city's bounds, all the food—or, indeed, in most cases, any of the food—that its inhabitants require. This definition of the nature of cities in material terms is correct, and is also illuminating, as far as it goes; but it is, of course, incomplete. Man is one of the social animals; any kind of human settlement therefore has a social aspect as well as a physical one; and an urban settlement is no exception to this universal rule. A city's population is either a self-contained—that is to say, sovereign—community or else it is a part of some sovereign community that includes other members besides this particular city's inhabitants; and, where an urban population is part of a larger community, there is a wide gamut of possible relations between the part and the whole.

The larger community of which the city is a part may delegate to the city a degree of autonomy that is almost tantamount to local sovereignty in practice, though not juridically. Short of that, there are many gradations of municipal self-government that a non-sovereign city may be granted, and it may also have even the minimum degree of self-government withheld from it and may be administered directly by officials of the government of the state in which it is incorporated. This has been the fate of some capital cities, for instance Alexandria, when it was the capital of the Ptolemaic Empire, and Washington, D.C., the capital of the United States. However, it is unusual even for capital cities to be denied even the most elementary degree of self-government; for, though the existence of an active, and potentially self-assertive, municipal authority in the city which is the seat of government of a larger political unit may be a nuisance, and even occasionally a menace, to the sovereign government which is installed in the same built-up area of streets and houses, it may be a still greater burden for the sovereign government to have to undertake the task of municipal administration, even in a single big city, in addition to its own inescapable primary duties.

Usually, therefore, it has been found to be more convenient, on balance, to allow even a capital city to enjoy a certain amount of municipal autonomy. A city is not only a particular kind of settlement; it is also a particularly complicated kind, and each city has its own individual configuration, character, and problems. A city is therefore likely to be administered most successfully by representatives of its own citizens who are familiar with all sides of its life and who are free to give first priority, in their working time, to their duties as municipal administrators.

The aspect of urban life that we are now considering is the political one, and the subject of the present chapter is the political category of cities that have been at the same time sovereign states. The Graeco-Roman World has been one of the societies in which city-states have been the standard kind of states, and the English words 'political', 'politics', 'polity', 'policy', and 'police' are all adaptations of derivatives of the Greek word 'polis', which originally meant a physical citadel, then came to mean the city into which a citadel had expanded, and, concomitantly, also came to mean the state which was a Greek city's political aspect. The equivalents of these English words of Greek origin are to be found in the vocabularies of most of the languages spoken in the present-day Western World. The adoption and adaptation of these Greek terms of political art is one of the many evidences of

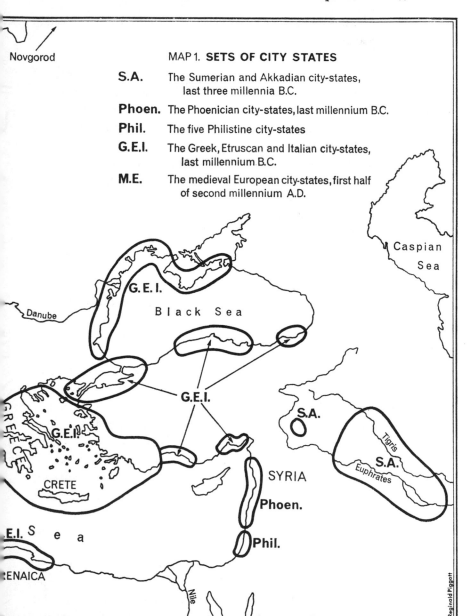

MAP 1. **SETS OF CITY STATES**

S.A. The Sumerian and Akkadian city-states, last three millennia B.C.

Phoen. The Phoenician city-states, last millennium B.C.

Phil. The five Philistine city-states

G.E.I. The Greek, Etruscan and Italian city-states, last millennium B.C.

M.E. The medieval European city-states, first half of second millennium A.D.

Novgorod

Caspian Sea

Danube

Black Sea

G.E.I.

G.E.I.

S.A.

Tigris

S.A.

Euphrates

GREECE

G.E.I.

CRETE

SYRIA

Phoen.

Phil.

E.I. S e a

ENAICA

Nile

Reginald Piggott

the Western Civilization's cultural debt to its Graeco-Roman predecessor.

A city-state may be defined as a state in which there is only a single city or in which a single city is so superior in terms of population and power to any minor cities that may be included in its territory that this one city's paramountcy in the state is indisputable. The fully enfranchised citizens of the city and of the state will be identical with each other, whether the city-state's constitution is oligarchical or is democratic. (The difference between an oligarchical and a democratic regime is one, not of kind, but of degree; these two types of regime blend with each other through a series of intermediate gradations.) In the preceding chapter it has been noticed that, in the age before the outbreak of the Industrial Revolution, most cities were market-towns that bought their food-supply, and sold their wares, in a food-producing district in their immediate neighbourhood. City-states that have lived mainly or wholly by dealing with larger and more distant markets and sources of supply have been in a minority, though this minority includes some of the most famous representatives of the species, the Phoenician cities, Miletus, Corinth, Athens, Venice, Genoa, Pisa, Hamburg, Bremen, Frankfurt. Most of the cities that have at the same time been states have been market-towns of the common kind, and these sovereign market-towns have normally included within their political frontiers the immediately surrounding rural area from which their food-supply has been drawn. In city-states of this type, in which the population has been partly rural and not exclusively urban, the respective political statuses of the urban and the rural section of the population have been very diverse in different cases.

In the Roman city-state the voters registered in the urban voting-districts were deliberately placed at a disadvantage; for, though they possessed full citizen-rights individually, their voting-districts were outnumbered overwhelmingly by the rural voting-districts, and this insured that the rural voters should have the decisive voice, since the voting-units were not the individual citizens but the voting-districts, and each of these delivered a block vote conforming to the decisions taken by a majority of its members. By contrast, in the Spartan city-state, the only fully enfranchised citizens of the state were a relatively small body of 'peers' who were full-time professional soldiers permanently cantoned in the city of Sparta itself. The agricultural land in the immediate neighbourhood of the city was perhaps cultivated by 'inferiors' who were Spartan citizens but were not enfranchised. The greater part of the territory of the Spartan city-state (as distinguished from the territories of Sparta's satellite city-states and of her sovereign allies) was inhabited by serfs, who cultivated the fields and tended the livestock and paid to the Spartiate 'peers' a tribute in kind which provided these with the economic means of devoting their whole time to military duties and spending the whole of it in Sparta city when they were not on campaign beyond the frontiers of the Spartan city-state's dominions. Two other Greek city-states besides Sparta, namely Syracuse and Heraclea Pontica, also had relatively extensive rural territories inhabited and cultivated by serfs, though, in these two colonial Greek city-states, the serfs were non-Greek 'natives', whereas in the Spartan city-state the serfs were Greeks, like the Spartiate 'peers' themselves. In the Athenian city-state the constitutional relation between the urban and the rural section of the population was different again. Here the members of both sections alike were fully enfranchised citizens (with the considerable exception of the slaves, the freedmen, and the resident aliens).

Athens, Sparta, Heraclea, Syracuse, and Rome were normal city-states in the sense that they contained within their frontiers a rural as well as an urban area and population—in contrast to the Phoenician cities, Venice, Hamburg, Bremen, and Lübeck, whose territories, at least originally, were practically conterminous with the area enclosed within the city limits. Rome, Syracuse, Heraclea, Sparta, and Athens, were, however, exceptional among the city-states of the Graeco-Roman World in the size of their territories. In the great majority of the Greek and Italian city-states in the age of the Graeco-Roman Civilization the city was a market-town and the state's territory also included a surrounding rural district, but this district was small enough to allow the inhabitants of the villages that were farthest away from the city to come into the city to do their marketing and then to get back to their village between daybreak and nightfall. Since, before the mechanization of the means of traction, overland communications were inefficient and expensive and maritime communications were precarious, city-states consisting of a single market-town and its immediate rural surroundings have been a very common form of state in the past. Indeed, in the pre-mechanization age, states on a larger scale than this have been exceptional, though the few states that did succeed in attaining this larger scale played immensely important parts during the five thousand years of human history that elapsed between the dawn of civilization and the invention of steamships and steam-driven locomotives running on rails—an invention that made it technologically possible, for the first time, to establish and operate a state of literally world-wide physical dimensions.

By the year A.D. 1969, the spurt of technological progress that began about two hundred years ago has greatly reduced the role of Man's natural environment in controlling and limiting human activities. Today aeroplanes can be flown, and rockets can be catapulted, with accuracy from any point on the planet's surface to any other point, regardless of whether the surface above which the aerial conveyance or missile is travelling happens to be land or water, and, if it is land, whether it is plain or mountain, 'sown' or 'desert', steppe or swamp. In the past, on the other hand, the configuration and the make-up of the planet's surface have exercised a potent—though perhaps never an omnipotent—influence on the course of human affairs and, among other things, on the scale and the political structure of states.

The kinds of terrain—crag and marsh—that have been sought for as sites for citadels have also been propitious for the formation of states of the city-state type. The earliest city-states of which we have a record are the Sumerian states that were reclaimed—in isolation from each other in the first phase of their history—from the swamps in the lower Tigris-Euphrates basin. The city-states that were the standard type of state in the Graeco-Roman World arose in the last millennium B.C. round the shores of the Aegean Sea and in Peninsular Italy in mountainous country in which the rare patches of plain that were good for agriculture and for pasture were insulated from each other by mountain ranges, as the Sumerian city-states had once been by still unreclaimed swamps. In Egypt, on the other hand, the numerous and populous cities which the fertile alluvium of the lower Nile valley and the Delta was able to support economically did not develop politically into so many separate sovereign states because in Egypt, as has been noted in the preceding chapter, the means of communication provided by nature were exceptionally good by the standards of the pre-mechanization age. The current of the River Nile and the prevailing North Wind worked together in Egypt to facilitate the political unification of the country from the foot of the First Cataract to the mouths of the Delta. Egypt was united politically at least half a millennium earlier than South-Eastern 'Iraq was.

However, the correspondence between terrain and political structure has been far from exact. The physiography of the North European plain is almost as propitious for political unification as the physiography of Egypt is. Yet, in the Middle Ages of Western history, Flanders and the Northern Netherlands and Northern Germany were a seed-bed of city-states which were no more than nominally subject to the French Crown and to the Roman Empire of the German People. Northern Germany was not united politically till the establishment of the Norddeutscher Bund in 1867, and neither this nor its successor the Second German Reich nor the Weimar Republic nor the present Federal Republic of Germany (Western Germany)—nor, indeed, even Hitler's Germany—has been a unitary state. Each of them has been a federation, and, in these successive German federal states, two North German city-states—Hamburg and Bremen—have retained their identities, as separate components (Länder) of the federal union, down to this day, while a third, Lübeck, retained its identity down to 1937. Conversely Japan, which, like Peninsular Italy and Greece, is a land of rare plains insulated from each other by mountains, produced only one solitary city-state, Sakai. At the beginning of her authentically recorded history, Japan was a unitary empire, and in 1868 she became a unitary empire again. During the seven centuries ending in 1868 the political map of Japan was a mosaic of local states which had been held together during the latest two and a half of those centuries under the hegemony of the most powerful of them, but, except for Sakai, these Japanese states had not been city-states. They had been feudal states, each of them ruled from a castle by a baron commanding a war-band of retainers.

The political structure of pre-Meiji Japan had, in fact, been like the structure of Mycenaean-Age Greece, as far as this can be reconstructed by piecing together Homeric reminiscences, dumb masonry and potsherds, and a handful of vocal contemporary documents inscribed on clay tablets in the 'Linear-B' script. This is a reminder that the period during which the Greek World, in its political structure, was a world of city-states was limited to the millennium ending in the third century of the Christian Era; and this is only one quarter of the four thousand years of Greek history of which we have a surviving record, if we count, as we should count, as part of the record the archaeological evidence that antedates the earliest written testimony that has yet been recovered in Greece.

We have no written records to tell us what was the political status of the two Neolithic-Age cities that have been unearthed so far, namely Jericho and its recently discovered counterpart at Lepenski Vir in Jugoslavia. The building of these two cities antedates the invention of the earliest system of writing in use anywhere in the World. The earliest known to us, and probably also the earliest in fact, is the cuneiform script which was developed to convey the Sumerian language and was afterwards adapted to convey a Semitic language, Akkadian-Babylonian-Assyrian. The date of writing of the oldest decipherable Sumerian records that have been disinterred by modern archaeologists is not much later than the beginning of the third millennium B.C., and at this date the area occupied by the Sumerian cities and their respective rural domains—an area now known as South-Eastern 'Iraq—was not yet united under a single unitary government. Each of the Sumerian cities was a sovereign state, and they were already exercising the sovereign right to go to war with each other.

In the course of the last fifteen hundred years B.C., city-states made their appearance at three points on the shores of the Mediterranean basin. The earliest of these were the Phoenician city-states along the coasts of the present-day Lebanese and Syrian republics. The Philistine city-states were planted, before the close of the second millennium B.C., along the coast of Palestine by invaders from the Aegean basin or possibly from some point still farther away in South-Eastern Europe. After the beginning of the last millennium B.C., Greek city-states arose on both sides of the Aegean Sea, and Etruscan city-states were planted, by invaders from some region in the Levant that has not yet been identified, along the northwestern section of the west coast of Peninsular Italy between the right bank of the River Tiber and the southern foot of the north-western Appennines.

The citizens of all these three Levantine groups of city-states competed with each other in colonizing other shores of the Mediterranean and its backwaters—for instance, the Sea of Marmara and the Black Sea—where the natives were more backward both politically and technologically and were therefore weaker than their Levantine dispossessors were. In the division of the spoils the Greeks won the lion's share. Their geographical position, astride the Aegean Sea, enabled them to monopolize the exploitation of the Sea of Marmara and the Black Sea, and their superiority over the Phoenicians and the Etruscans in numbers enabled them at the same time to compete with these for the exploitation of the western basin of the Mediterranean.

Not all the native peoples of this region succumbed. Some of the natives of the interior of Sicily and of Peninsular Italy managed to hold their own against the Levantine invaders by adopting the institution of city-states from them; and eventually Rome—a Peninsular Italian city-state that was neither Etruscan nor Greek-nor Phoenician—succeeded in imposing political unity, under Roman rule, on the whole perimeter of the Mediterranean Sea. Throughout this vast area that the Romans brought under their political dominion, they deliberately patronized and promoted the city-state form of political organization, preserving it where it already existed and introducing it where the natives had not previously adopted it, on their own initiative, as the Romans themselves had. At the turn of the second and third centuries of the

Christian Era, the Roman Imperial Government completed this process by giving city-state constitutions to the Egyptian cities that were the seats of the administration of the departments into which Egypt had been articulated for administrative purposes since before the dawn of the Egyptian civilization. Thereafter, for a short spell of time, the Roman Empire was a body politic constituted almost entirely of cells that were city-states in their political structure. They were not, of course, sovereign city-states; but it was a cardinal point in the Imperial Government's policy to give the Empire's constituent city-states as large a measure of local self-government as they showed themselves capable of exercising efficiently.

The East Roman Empire survived in the medieval Greek World, and its government had become so highly centralized that city-states maintained themselves here only in small numbers, and this only on the Empire's fringes: for instance, Kherson in the Crimea (on the site on which, long afterwards, the Russians founded Sébastopol); Ragusa and Venice in the Adriatic; Amalfi, Naples, and Gaeta on the west coast of South-Eastern Italy. Of these, all except Venice and Ragusa were nipped in the bud; these two alone achieved sovereign independence, and both of them retained it till 1797.

Venice and Ragusa gravitated towards the West when the East Roman Empire's superiority over them became a dead letter, and city-states played a prominent role in the life of the Western World in the medieval chapter of its history. In medieval Western Christendom there were two regions in particular in which city-states arose and flourished. The more important of the two was Northern and Central Italy; the other was the North European plain, from Flanders and the Northern Netherlands across Northern Germany as far to the east as medieval Western Christendom's eastwards-expanding borders. These two main clusters of medieval Western city-states were linked by a third group in Southern Germany, where city-states—for instance, Augsburg in Swabia and Frankfurt-am-Main and Nürnberg in Franconia—were strung along the overland routes of the trade between the Italian group and the northern one. The Italian group of city-states had outlying members beyond the bounds of Italy—for example, Marseilles, Barcelona, and Ragusa, which were Italianate in their economic and political way of life, though their citizens were not Italians in nationality.

A foreign observer—let us say an East Roman acquainted with Graeco-Roman history—who studied Western Christendom at any date between the opening of the twelfth century and the close of the fourteenth might have forecast that the political structure of Western Christendom was going to be a reproduction of the structure of the Graeco-Roman World. Western Christendom was going, our imaginary observer might have prophesied, to become a society in which, on the political plane, city-states would have driven all competing forms of polity off the field. He might have concluded that the nascent Western nation-states, as represented, for instance, by France and England, had no future; they were being dominated by the Western city-states economically, and eventually their native inhabitants would be led, for the sake of self-preservation, to transform their antiquated kingdoms into clusters of city-states on the standard Western pattern.

By the year 1100 the East Roman Empire—a centralized empire of the Pharaonic Egyptian and the post-221-B.C. Chinese kind—was already feeling the pressure of the rapidly growing economic and naval power of the maritime Italian city-states—Venice first and foremost, but also Amalfi, Pisa, and Genoa. The medieval Western city-states took, from the beginning, a leading part in the aggressive expansion of medieval Western Christendom at the expense of Eastern Orthodox Christendom and the Islamic World, and, as time went on, they pocketed a larger and larger share of both the economic and the territorial profits of the joint colonizing enterprises on which they had embarked in partnership with their feudal Western Christian neighbours and coreligionists. The city-states had the whip hand, because the expansion of medieval Western Christendom, in the Baltic as well as in the Mediterranean, was largely dependent on maritime transport in this age of inefficient overland means of communication, and in the Middle Ages the greater part of Western Christendom's shipping was built, owned, and operated by the maritime Western city-states.

Though the feudal main body of the Westerners who went on the First Crusade reached Syria and Palestine overland, those who stayed to found and hold Western principalities in this distant *terre d'outre-mer* found themselves dependent on the maritime Italian city-states for maintaining their life-line with their West European base, and the Italian men of business—quick to see and to seize their advantage—extorted extensive commercial and political privileges in the Crusader states from the hard-pressed Frankish knights. The Fourth Crusade was manipulated by the Venetians to serve their own ends, for Venice had the ships that the French participants in this Crusade needed to carry them to the Levant, and the French arrived at Venice without the money to pay for their passage. The Venetians bargained with their French fellow Crusaders that, in lieu of the money-payment that the French could not make, the French should perform for Venice some military services at the Venetian Government's dictation. The French Crusaders had first to capture for Venice the Dalmatian city Zara; next they had to replace a dispossessed emperor on the East Roman imperial throne at Constantinople; and eventually they had to take the City of Constantinople by storm; to pay their debt to the Venetians out of their share of the loot; to partition the East Roman Empire; and to concede to Venice three-eighths of the territorial spoils. When the East Romans (i.e. the medieval Greeks) eventually regained possession of Constantinople, they found that their only way of shaking off the Venetian yoke was to put their necks under the equally oppressive yoke of the Venetians' rivals, the Genoese.

In the Baltic and the North Sea, events took a parallel course. The Hansa—an association of the German city-states that had arisen on the North-European plain—wrested the command of these seas from the Scandinavians. They colonized the south and east coasts of the Baltic, all the way from Mecklenburg to the south coast of the Gulf of Finland, with daughter city-states— for instance, Danzig, Riga, and Reval—and they dominated the Christian descendants of the Vikings in their home countries. In the course of the thirteenth and fourteenth centuries, the Hansa states succeeded in imposing on the Scandinavian states a commercial and naval servitude that almost amounted to a colonial regime. Our imaginary East Roman observer would, no doubt, have reported that Denmark, Norway, Sweden, and Finland were heading for the same doom as France and England.

In the early years of the fourteenth century, it would have been reasonable, in the light of the course of events during the past three hundred years, to predict that, in Western Christendom, the future lay with the city-states and that this was going to become the standard form of Western polity, as, once upon a time, it had become the standard form in the Graeco-Roman World. Yet, if the non-Western observer of Western affairs had lived on into the later decades of the fourteenth century, an unexpected turn of events would have led him to revise his forecast. In Western Christendom in the course of the fourteenth century, the fortunes of the city-states began to wane and the fortunes of the nation-states to wax; and the subsequent passage of six more centuries of Western history has seen the nation-state, not the city-state, become the standard form of Western polity. The hundreds of city-states that once occupied commanding positions in the political landscape of Western Europe have been reduced progressively in numbers, and the survivors, all but one, have forfeited their former sovereign, or virtually sovereign, status. On the political map of the Western World in 1969 there is only one solitary fully sovereign city-state, namely San Marino; and twentieth-century San Marino is as strange a curiosity as sixteenth-century Sakai—with which, however, San Marino cannot be compared, since Sakai, unique though it was, played an important role in the economic life of Japan in its day.

Since the outbreak of the Industrial Revolution, a city that is both a major focus of modern economic activity and a sovereign city-state with a territory of minimal size has become an anachronism, and it has become a misfit even when the city-state in question has ceased to be sovereign and has become one of the states-members of a federation, since every city of this kind has been bursting its bounds under the Industrial Revolution's impact.

San Marino, of course, has not been confronted with Hamburg's and Bremen's problems; for San Marino is a tiny hill-town perched on a spur of the Appennines far away from any main route. San Marino never has been a focus of economic activity, and, in an age in which the World's large and populous cities have been becoming still larger and more populous, the populations of little rustic cities like San Marino have been dwindling as a result of the emigration of their citizens to places in the main stream of the World's affairs, where they have a better prospect of finding remunerative work. The impression made by San Marino nowadays is that it earns its living mainly from the tourist trade. It can hardly earn it from agriculture or animal husbandry, for its tiny territory is as rugged as that of Miletus.

Since only two of all the former city-states in Germany have preserved their political identities as Länder of the present Federal Republic, the last refuge of city-states in the present-day Western World is Switzerland. Like the Second Reich and its forerunner the Norddeutscher Bund, Switzerland is a federation some of whose states-members are city-states, while others are states of a different political structure. The balance of forces, however, is not the same. In the Second German Reich the three Hansa city-states were rare relics of the structure of the First Reich, and they were overshadowed by Prussia and other states of a far larger calibre than theirs. By contrast, in Switzerland the principal city-state cantons—Zürich, Berne, Basel, Geneva—overshadow the tiny San-Marino-like 'forest cantons', which are the historical nucleus of the Swiss Confederation. These Swiss city-states survive because they have been wise enough to pool their former separate sovereignties. The city-state of Geneva, which was a sovereign independent ally of the Swiss Confederation until after the Napoleonic Wars, had the foresight to read the signs of the nineteenth-century times. She negotiated her admission to membership of the Confederation in 1814. If Geneva had then chosen still to try to stand alone, it seems improbable that she could have survived politically as a city-state in isolation.

In the World of 1969 the most important sovereign independent city-state is Singapore, which launched out adventurously into independence on 9 August 1965, in preference to remaining associated with her neighbour the federal union of Malaysia. The parting was by mutual consent. An overwhelming majority of the citizens of Singapore are Chinese, and they did not wish to be incorporated in a federal union in which the Malays might claim to have the last word, while the Malays, on their side, were relieved to be able to avoid the reinforcement of the Chinese component in the population of Malaysia by the addition of Singapore's relatively large contingent of Chinese citizens. In contrast to the Singaporians, the Gibraltarians are determined not to have independence imposed upon them, since they think, not without reason, that, for Gibraltar, it would be a short step from independence to forcible re-annexation by Spain. It is hard to guess what choice the people of the Chinese city-state of Hong Kong will make, if one day they are given the option between Hong Kong's continuing to be a British colony and its becoming independent like Singapore. An independent Hong Kong would be at Continental China's mercy, as an independent Gibraltar would be at Spain's. However, Hong Kong could already be taken by Continental China at any moment if China deemed this to be in her own interest; so, for Hong Kong, the juridical change from colonial status to independence might not appreciably aggravate the precariousness of her political position. It seems certain that Hong Kong will be re-annexed by China some day, and it also seems not improbable that eventually the sovereign independent city-state of Singapore will also go the same way.

In a world in which the scale of all institutions and all activities has been rapidly increasing in magnitude, a sovereign independent city-state, standing alone politically, has become too small a political unit to be practicable any longer. It is significant that the date at which, in the Western World, the nation-state form of polity began to get the better of the city-state form was more than four hundred years earlier than the revolutionary improvement of the means of transportation through the application of steam-power to traction. In the Western World, city-states had failed to prevail even in an age in which the inefficiency of overland communications favoured the survival of states of pedestrian and pack-horse dimensions. *A fortiori*, states of this miniature size were doomed after the invention of steamships and steam-powered locomotives for overland haulage on rails. In the light of the trend in Western life towards an increase in scale, Geneva's decision in 1814 to enter the Swiss Confederation seems more prescient than Singapore's decision in 1965 to launch out on a career of sovereign independence. Possibly the Singaporians might have hesitated to take this hazardous plunge if the Malayan citizens of the Malaysian federation had not worked together with the Singaporian Chinese aspirants to independence to force the Singapore Government's hand.

In the Western World, as has been noted, city-states have now become a virtually obsolete form of polity, and this turn of events in Western history, which might have been surprising to a non-Western observer in the fourteenth century, can be seen, on a synoptic view, to have been a common political development in societies that, on the political plane, have started life as clusters of city-states. In the histories of some of these societies the originally sovereign independent city-states have been eliminated, as they have now been in the Western World, by the triumph of some competing form of local state with a different political structure. In other societies the city-states have preserved their separate existence at the cost of renouncing their separate sovereignty, as, in the Western World, they have in the exceptional case of the city-state cantons of Switzerland. In other cases again, groups of city-states have been pieced together, not by voluntary federation on a footing of equality, but by the imposition of some preeminently powerful city-state's hegemony on weaker city-states in its neighbourhood, which it has deprived forcibly of their sovereignty without annexing their territories to its own and without depriving them of their city-state constitutions. This has produced empires, ruled by an imperial city-state, that have been more extensive than even the largest city-state could have been in isolation. Most of these empires that have been established by dominant city-states over their weaker neighbours have failed to grow into anything bigger than a local state of supra-city-state size; but, at the western end of the Old World, one city-state,

Rome, did once succeed in founding an empire that embraced the entire domains of the Graeco-Roman and Phoenician societies and also large additional territories inhabited by populations of many different kinds and different degrees of culture.

In the history of the Graeco-Roman society there was a spell, lasting for about a century and a half, during which the course of political events took the turn that it has taken in the history of the Western society since the closing decades of the fourteenth century of the Christian Era. In the latter part of the fourth century B.C. the contending states of Continental European Greece were overshadowed and dominated—though this only temporarily as it turned out—by culturally more backward kingdom-states— Macedon and Epirus—that were of the same type as the medieval Western kingdom-states in Western Europe and in Scandinavia which got the better of their city-state neighbours and rivals. In the Greek World to the east of the Straits of Otranto, it might have looked in the third century B.C. as if the only city-states that were going to survive, as such, were those that had been voluntarily pooling their separate sovereignties by entering into the Aetolian and Achaean Confederations (polities that were Greek counterparts of Switzerland). However, the rulers of the Greek monarchical successor-states of the First Persian Empire that were established by Macedonian war-lords found that they could maintain their hold over the masses of their non-Greek subjects only by founding Greek colonial city-states at key points in their dominions and by giving these new Greek city-states a large measure of autonomy. Nor did the post-Alexandrine Greek monarchies, which had extended their domain southwards to Egypt and eastwards to the Jaxartes, ever succeed in dominating the city-states in the Mediterranean basin to the west of the Straits of Otranto.

In the third decade of the third century B.C. King Pyrrhus of Epirus tried and failed to break the Carthaginian Empire and to prevent the completion of the establishment of Rome's hegemony over the Greek and non-Greek states in South-Eastern Italy. By the year 217 B.C. an Aetolian statesman was warning Aetolia's adversaries in Greece, the King of Macedon and his allies, that, if the Greek states to the east of the Straits of Otranto did not now renounce their family quarrels and make common cause with each other, they would all fall under the domination of the victor, whichever this might be, in the great war that was being waged, to the west of the Straits, between two imperial city-states, Carthage and Rome. The warning was not heeded and the prophecy was fulfilled. In 201 B.C. Rome brought Carthage to her knees, and within the next thirty-three years she established her ascendancy over all the Greek states in the Levant, city-states and kingdoms alike. This further turn in the course of Graeco-Roman history put the local kingdom-state form of polity out of the running and made the city-state form 'the wave of the future' after all.

It has been noted already that the Roman Empire was a body politic composed of city-state cells. These city-states, that were subject to the imperial city-state Rome, were placed by Rome's fiat in different categories that were distinguished from each other by differences in their juridical relation to Rome and in the degree of their autonomy, but two features were common to them all: they had all been deprived of their sovereignty *de facto* but, at this price, they had all preserved their local territories and their self-government in the management of their own domestic affairs. In A.D. 416 a Gallic Roman post, Rutilius Namatianus, sought to sum up Rome's political achievement in the epigrammatic line of verse '*Urbem fecisti quod prius orbis erat*'—'You had made into a city what was previously a world'. This formula had been juridically correct since A.D. 212, when Roman citizenship had been granted to, or—it might be more accurate to say—had been imposed on, all but a small residue of those inhabitants of the Roman Empire who were not already Roman citizens by that date. It would, however, have been nearer to the reality if Rutilius had said that Rome had turned what had previously been a world of sovereign city-states into a world in which the same city-states had been united politically, without being *gleichgeschaltet*, under the sovereignty of one of their number, Rome.

The only city-state in the medieval Western World that might conceivably have emulated Rome's empire-building achievement was Milan, the largest, most populous, most centrally located, and most powerful of the medieval Italian city-states in the basin of the River Po. In the fourteenth century, Milan momentarily came near to bringing under her hegemony all the other contemporary city-states between the Alps and the Appennines. In the event, Milan was thwarted by the combined opposition of Venice and Florence, and the greater part of her budding empire was wrested from her. We can, however, imagine Milan overcoming Venice's and Florence's resistance, as Rome had overcome Tarentum's and Samnium's, and uniting Italy under her own supremacy as Rome had done sixteen or seventeen centuries earlier. With the wealth and power of the whole of fourteenth-century Italy at her command, Milan then might have succeeded in extending her hegemony over Transalpine Western Europe after waging a victorious war with the northern group of western city-states that were associated with each other in the Hansa.

Rome is the only city-state in either the Graeco-Roman or the Western World that has succeeded in building a world-empire—that is to say, an empire that has embraced almost the whole of that part of the World that has been within the empire-builders' ken. Rome's achievement was extraordinary; for she started as a city-state of the normal minute size. Her original frontiers were not more than from six to ten miles distant from the Forum and the Capitol. However, in the Sumero-Akkadian World, empires proportionately equivalent to the Roman Empire had previously been built successively by the Akkadian city-state Agade, the Sumerian city-state Ur, and the Amorite city-state Babylon, and in both medieval Western Christendom and the Mediterranean basin during the last millennium B.C. there are a number of examples of local empires built by city-states.

The Carthaginian empire over the major part of the western basin of the Mediterranean and its African and Spanish shores and hinterlands has been mentioned already. The other Phoenician colonial city-states in the western basin of the Mediterranean submitted to Carthage's hegemony as a lesser evil than the alternative of being overwhelmed by the influx of the Greeks into this region. The Carthaginian empire had a lesser counterpart and rival in the empire acquired by the Greek colonial city-state Massilia (Marseilles) along the north shore of the western Mediterranean from the Italian Riviera to the Catalan Costa Brava inclusive. The Siceliot Greek colonial city-states Syracuse and Akragas each built up a miniature hegemony over the weaker Greek colonial city-states on the coasts of the island and over the natives in the interior. To the east of the Straits of Otranto Athens, Sparta, and Thebes successively imposed their hegemony on the whole of Continental Greece and the Aegean basin, but in each case the achievement was ephemeral.

Thebes never succeeded in permanently reducing even her sister Boeotian city-states to the status of satellites of Thebes. In Boeotia, Orchomenos and Thespiae succeeded in thwarting Thebes as, in medieval Italy, Venice and Florence succeeded in thwarting Milan. Sparta, however, did succeed, within the limits of Laconia, in doing what Thebes failed to do within the limits of Boeotia. For rather more than five centuries ending in the year 195 B.C., the other Laconian city-states were Sparta's satellites. Each of them retained its local autonomy within its own territory, and from first to last they all continued to be normal Greek city-states of the market-town order of magnitude. Their Spartan overlords did not constrain these satellites of Sparta's to adopt the peculiar institutions that the Spartans imposed on themselves at some date in the seventh century B.C. Sparta's satellites did, however, have to furnish contingents to Lacedaemonian expeditionary forces on call from the Spartan Government, and, unlike Sparta's allies outside Laconia, Sparta's Laconian satellites inside Laconia had no say in the political decisions, taken at Sparta, that might involve the satellites in fighting in Spartan-made wars.

Venice acquired an overseas colonial empire in the Levant more than a century before she began to build up a land-empire over the Italian city-states that were her neighbours on the terra firma— Treviso, Padua, Vicenza, Verona—in order to thwart Milan. In the Levant, Venice had a commercial and naval rival in Genoa—a more formidable rival than Massilia had been for Carthage. The Genoese overseas empire came to include Pera, the suburb of Constantinople beyond the Golden Horn, and the ports of Caffa

and Tana on the distant Crimean Riviera. The Hansa confederation's virtual colonial empire in Scandinavia was a counterpart
of the Venetian and Genoese domination over the declining East
Roman Empire.

These city-states that acquired political empires of various kinds
were exceptional, and so too were city-states that, without acquiring political empires, did acquire substantial sources of supply and
markets for their wares beyond the range of their own territories.
The overwhelming majority of city-states have been market-
towns whose territories were limited to the immediately adjoining
countryside and whose principal business relations were with the
rural population that came into town on market-days to sell food
and to buy wares and services. The smallness of the size and the
simplicity of the economy of a city-state of this normal type had
an effect on the character of the state's political life. Public affairs
in a standard petty city-state were conducted much like family
affairs. All enfranchised citizens participated directly in the city-
state's government; and this direct participation was also the rule
in city-states which, like Athens, had an exceptionally large territory and population and an exceptionally wide franchise.

A city-state with the population and the area of Attica was,
however, the largest in which the direct participation of the whole
of the enfranchised citizen-body could be a reality. When Rome,
which had started with a territory only a fraction of the size of
Attica, created additional voting-districts inhabited by enfranchised Roman citizens as far south-eastwards in the Roman state's
expanding territory as the right bank of the River Volturno and
as far northwards as the shore of the Adriatic Sea, Roman citizens
domiciled in these outlying districts could not exercise their
voting-rights, and, *a fortiori*, could not stand as candidates for
public office, unless they had the money and the leisure to undertake frequent journeys to the City of Rome and to make pro-
tracted stays there. In a city-state it was normally the rule—a rule
deriving from the identification of the state with the city—that
public business could not be transacted anywhere in the state's
territory except within the official limits of the city itself. This
normal rule held good in Rome and was not relaxed when more

and more of the districts inhabited by enfranchised Roman citizens came to lie much farther away from Rome than half a day's walking-distance. Thus the inordinate expansion of the Roman city-state's territory, and the consequent relegation of a larger and larger proportion of the enfranchised section of the Roman citizen-body to domiciles more and more distant from the City of Rome itself, led to the virtual disfranchisement of all but a minority of the juridically enfranchised citizens who were now domiciled at a distance.

This was a paradoxical result of the unparalleled increase in the Roman city-state's size and power, and a second paradoxical result was that, while the political value of the Roman citizenship was diminishing, its personal value was increasing. As Rome's power grew, the arrogance and high-handedness of her public officers grew proportionately, and Roman citizenship was the only status that gave anyone under a Roman public officer's jurisdiction any guarantee of being properly treated or, if he were improperly treated, any hope of obtaining redress. Citizens of communities that were allied to Rome or were subject to her were defenceless. Saint Paul was a Roman citizen by birth, though he was a Jew whose home-town was the Greek city of Tarsus in the south-east corner of Anatolia, and, at several critical moments in his hazardous career, his Roman citizenship stood him in good stead in his encounter with public authorities. By Saint Paul's day it was utterly impossible for the vast majority of the Roman citizen-body to take a direct part in the transaction of public business in the Forum at Rome. The domiciles of Roman citizens were scattered, by now, from Tarsus in Cilicia to Seville in Spain; the number of Roman citizens now ran to several millions, and even the small minority of them that still lived in Rome or in its environs had no opportunity of voting or of standing for election, since the public assemblies were no longer being convened and the Senate had become the electoral body. The city-state that had grown into a world-empire was now governed by an autocrat assisted by a professional civil service.

The wideness of the extent of the geographical distribution of the enfranchised Roman citizen-body since the closing decades of the fourth century B.C. was, of course, unusual. The wideness of the extension of the Athenian franchise and the plenitude of the powers of the Athenian public assembly during two centuries ending at about the same date were unusual too. Most city-states—Graeco-Roman, Phoenician, medieval Western, Sumerian—have had far smaller territories and citizen-bodies not only than imperial Rome but than Athens, and in most cases only a minority of the relatively small citizen-body has had effective political power. In fact, the effective governing body in a city-state—the *politeuma* as it was called in Greek constitutional terminology—was in many city-states on a scale on which, as in a family, all the members could be, and actually were, personally acquainted with each other. I have been told that it used to be customary for any member of the Genoese aristocracy to address any other member in the second person singular. This form of address signified that all Genoese aristocrats felt themselves to be virtually each other's kinsmen. In the days when Genoa was a sovereign city-state—and these days lasted till the temporary annexation of Genoa and her territory to Napoleonic France—the Genoese city-state was in the Genoese aristocracy's hands. In such small-scale circumstances, politics were almost literally a family affair, and so they were in the Roman city-state, after the Roman nobility had virtually monopolized the holding of public office and before it had been virtually deposed from power by an autocratic regime that was arbitrarily inaugurated by a series of war-lords before being regularized, under a perfunctory disguise, by Augustus.

Family life is intimate, but intimacy is no guarantee of harmony or of mutual forbearance, and family quarrels, when they break out, are sometimes bitter. In city-states, the conduct and spirit of politics have had the drawback, as well as the advantage, of not being impersonal, as they are apt to be in a bureaucratically-governed state with an extensive territory and a large population. In city-states, politics have been, on the whole, more violent than they have been in most other forms of polity, and perhaps it is no accident that, in the French Revolution, a conspicuously violent role was played by citizens of two cities, both by that date incorporated in France, which had once been sovereign city-states.

A battalion, raised in Marseilles, made a famous march on Paris to take a hand in the overthrow of the monarchy; Robespierre was a citizen of Arras. Marseilles had been an outlying member of the Mediterranean group of the medieval Western city-states that was thickest on the ground in Northern and Central Italy; Arras had been a member of the group on the North European plain. Since the triumph of absolute monarchy in the Western world at the transition from the Middle Ages to the modern age of Western history, the people of Arras and Marseilles had been inhibited from indulging in the violence that has been characteristic of the political life of city-states. The collapse of the *ancien régime* gave the battalion from Marseilles and the man from Arras the opportunity of reverting to the political behaviour of their forefathers, and they seized this chance to revive the turbulence of the piazza, the forum, and the agora in the bigger theatre of a nation-state. The city-state turbulence that had thus been injected into the political life of France after the outbreak of the First French Revolution in 1789 broke out again in 1830, 1848, and 1871, and the name 'commune', that was assumed in 1871 by the abortive revolutionary regimes in Paris and in Lyon, is evidence that this fourth bout of turbulence in modern France was intended by its fomenters to be a revival of the political tradition of city-state life in the Western World in the medieval chapter of western history. The surprising upheaval in Paris and in other French cities in May 1968 showed that the spirit of medieval Marseilles and Arras, which by that date had been dormant in France for nearly a century, was not yet extinct.

It is to be hoped that the legacy of violence, which the modern Western society has inherited from the medieval Western city-states, will not continue to make itself felt in an age in which the accelerating progress of technology, applied to the invention of new and ever more deadly weapons, has made street-fighting as fearful as warfare in the jungle and on the rice-paddy. There is, however, another feature of city-state life that would be a blessing if it could be introduced into the life of the present-day megalopolises that are now on the move towards coalescing into the coming World-City. Familiarity may breed contempt, mutual hostility, and violence, but it may also be a cure for the spiritual maladies of loneliness and of alienation from society that are the characteristic ecological diseases of populations that live and work in an urban environment in which they do not feel at home. The discovery of a cure is imperative; for social isolation is not only painful in itself; it too is a potential generator of violence.

In a megalopolis the great majority of the inhabitants are aliens in the sense that they or their parents or, at the farthest remove, their grandparents have been transported from a rural setting in which their ancestors have lived for thousands of years on end into an urban nightmare to which no earlier generation has ever been exposed. These present-day ex-rural *déracinés* have been dumped in a warren of streets and houses in which they are physically at close quarters but are spiritually still far apart from each other. Their crying need is to be given a chance to strike fresh roots in their new, unfamiliar, and excruciating environment and to become each other's neighbours there in the social as well as in the physical sense. The most promising social strategy for meeting this need is to try to articulate each of the megalopolises of today and the whole of the Ecumenopolis of tomorrow into cells on the city-state scale and with the city-state standard of sociality. The coming world-city will be endurable only if it is organized—and this in good time—as a settlement and a society composed of cells of the size and character of 'Casterbridge' in 1829, the year in which Cruikshank was etching his cartoon of London going out of town, or of Weimar in 1832, the year in which Goethe died there.

Such city-state-like cells of Ecumenopolis cannot be provided with that intimate relation with a surrounding agricultural countryside that was one of the amenities of life in a market-town. There will be no room in Ecumenopolis for that. Fields and pastures on terra firma will have been transformed into food-factories, and agriculture and animal husbandry of the traditional kind will have been pushed off the land into the sea. Weimar and 'Casterbridge' did, however, also enjoy a second amenity. Their inhabitants were in personal relations with each other, and these relations were intimate, whether they were friendly or hostile. An inhabitant of a city on this human-size scale might experience there, within his lifetime, successive alternating vicissitudes of social harmony and social strife, but, even in the most unpleasant or actually dangerous circumstances, he could be sure that he would not ever be lonely. He could count on always finding himself in company, whether for weal or for woe, whatever might be the political atmosphere in his city at the moment.

Can this city-state standard of sociality be attained in Ecumenopolis by physical and social planning with this end in view? This question—a vital one for mankind's future—is discussed in the closing chapter of the present book.

3: Capital Cities:
Their Distinctive Features

In a city-state the city and the state are identical. A capital city, like a city that is a city-state, is a seat of government, but, unlike a city-state, a capital city is a seat of government merely; it is not a state as well. A state that is big enough to have a capital is governed *from* the capital, not *by* it.

It has been noted already that, so far from being a sovereign urban community, a capital may be destitute of even a bare minimum of municipal self-government—and this by the will of the sovereign government that has chosen this city to serve as its base of operations for administering a territory that extends beyond the limits of the capital and the immediately surrounding countryside. Washington, D.C., the capital of the United States, is governed, together with the rest of the Federal District of Columbia in which it lies, by a commission consisting of members of the United States Congress, not by elected representatives of those United States citizens who are domiciled in the District. Alexandria, when it was the capital of the Ptolemaic Empire, was not allowed to have the city-council (boule) that the citizens of a Greek city considered to be one of the essential institutions of any city, even of one that was not a sovereign state. The City of Rome had ceased to be a self-governing city-state by the time when it had become the capital of a circummediterranean body politic composed of city-state cells. By Augustus' time, Rome's own territory, outside Rome's city limits, as well as the territories of Rome's allies and subjects, had been articulated into a mosaic of non-sovereign but self-governing municipalities. Rome herself was now the only city in the Ager Romanus that had no municipal self-government. She was the seat of government of the Roman

Empire, but she herself was administered by a bureaucrat, the *prafectus urbi*, who was the Emperor's appointee. The City of London succeeded in acquiring and preserving an ample measure of municipal self-government just because the seat of the government of the Kingdom of England was not the City of London but was the adjoining City of Westminster. In the seventeenth-century trial of strength, at Westminster, between two organs of the government of the Kingdom, the Crown and the Parliament, the City of London's support of the Parliament drove the Crown to evacuate Westminster and to retreat, up the Thames valley, to Oxford.

A capital city may not only have to pay for the role that has been assigned to it by being denied self-government; its retention of the role itself is always precarious. Since a capital city is, by definition, the seat of government of a state with which the capital is not coextensive, the state's territory is likely to include other cities besides the capital, and it is open to the government of the state, at its sovereign pleasure, to transfer its seat to some other city if, for one reason or another, some other city suits it better than the capital of the day. A city that is a city-state is bound to be its state's seat of government so long as the state itself exists as a distinct political entity. A city that is a capital has had this role conferred on it by choice, and the choice is revocable.

A capital is likely to lose its role, sooner or later, to some other city within the sovereign government's dominions if the capital is the seat of government for the historical reason that it has previously been the seat of a smaller state which has been the nucleus out of which the present state has grown. This fate eventually overtook the Egyptian city Thebes, which had been the capital of the Thebaid before it became the capital of the New Empire of Egypt, and the same fate also eventually overtook Rome, which had first been a solitary city-state and had then become the paramount city-state in Peninsular Italy before it became the capital of an empire embracing the whole perimeter of the Mediterranean basin. As for Turin, which had been the capital of the Kingdom of Sardinia (that is to say, actually the capital of Piedmont plus Savoy), it forfeited its role immediately when the Kingdom of Sardinia grew into the Kingdom of Italy in 1859–61. The capital was moved from Turin to Florence in 1865, and was then moved on to Rome after the remnant round Rome of the Papal State had been annexed to the Kingdom of Italy in 1870.

Even if a city that has hitherto been a capital is not disqualified by the territorial expansion of the state whose government has had its seat there, there are possible changes of other kinds that may make it expedient to remove the seat of government from the capital of the day. Even if the area of the state does not either expand or contract, the state's demographic, economic, military, or cultural centre of gravity may shift its locus within frontiers that remain the same, and a change in the internal structure of the state on any of these several planes of social activity may call for a change in the location of the state's seat of government. The capital of the day is, *ex officio*, the most important city in the state politically, but it is not necessarily the most important city in any other respect. For instance, it is not necessarily the biggest city or the most important city economically or militarily or culturally.

Indeed, a capital is unlikely to be pre-eminent on any of these counts, at any rate at the start, if it is a new city that has been built expressly in order to serve as a capital. The Hague, Washington, D.C., Ottawa, New Delhi, Canberra, Islamabad, and Brasilia are cases in point. The Hague is smaller and is less important on all counts except politically than Rotterdam and Amsterdam, Washington than New York and Chicago and Detroit; Ottawa than Montreal and Winnipeg; New Delhi than Calcutta and Bombay, Canberra than Sydney and Melbourne; Islamabad than its predecessor Karachi and than Lahore; Brasilia than its predecessor Rio de Janeiro and than São Paulo and Recife. A city that has not been artificially created in order to serve as a capital but that has become a capital for historical reasons may find itself at the same disadvantage. By the time when Rome had united the whole perimeter of the Mediterranean under her rule, she may have outstripped all the other cities in her empire in point of size of population; but she was less important economically than Alexandria, and less important culturally than Alexandria, Athens,

Pergamon, and Rhodes. Moreover, now that the Roman armed forces had ceased to be militias raised *ad hoc* and had become professional formations stationed permanently at strategic points, Rome had become a less important *place d'armes* for the Roman army than Köln or Antioch, while her home-port Ostia at the mouth of the Tiber had been superseded for naval purposes by Misenum and Ravenna, which were now the respective bases of the two Roman imperial fleets.

The capital cities that have been created expressly to play this role in the course of the last two centuries cannot compare, in point of size of population, with the commercial and industrial cities that have shot up simultaneously and have grown to inordinate sizes with the aid of mechanization. On the other hand, in the age before the outbreak of the Industrial Revolution, in which the standard type and scale of city was the market-town, the capitals of the rare giant states were, in relative terms, the biggest concentrations of population. Even a capital city that was not a hive of industry or a focus of commerce would be relatively populous. It would be inhabited, not only by the sovereign and his court and the staff of his central administration, but also by a corps of imperial guards, with possibly a mobile central reserve army as well, and these state-employed inhabitants of the capital would themselves employ a host of servants and another host of artisans and shopkeepers to make and sell the luxury goods for which the personnel of the central administration would provide a lucrative market. (The surplus product of the whole empire would have found its way into official pockets in the capital in the form of salaries paid out of receipts.) A capital city would therefore require a large, constant, and assured supply of food and of raw materials for luxury industries, and, as the pre-mechanization age was an age in which overland transport was inefficient and expensive, while maritime transport was precarious, one of the distinctive features of a capital city in the pre-mechanization age was the limiting factor of supply. A capital city's population would be too large, and the standard of living of the official section of this population would be too high, for the capital to be able to depend on local supplies, even if the immediate neighbourhood happened to be rich in sources of food, fibres, timber, and metals. A capital city could neither become nor remain a capital if it could not import large supplies from distant sources by water.

Rome was able to satisfy this condition without difficulty so long as she was the capital of a commonwealth whose area was limited to Peninsular Italy. Standing, as she did, on the bank of the Tiber, which is the biggest and longest river in the Peninsula—a river that was navigable for barges far up its course—Rome, in this first phase of her history as a capital, was able to supply herself with grain from higher up the Tiber valley, as well as with timber from the Appennine forests overhanging the Tiber's source. When, however, in the course of half a century ending in the year 168 B.C., the Romans expanded the area under their political control from Peninsular Italy to the whole perimeter of the Mediterranean basin, the population of the City of Rome consequently grew to a size at which it could no longer live solely on the river-borne supplies that it could draw from Central Italy. The City now had to draw the major part of its food-supplies from overseas; the military and political ascendency that Rome had established by this date over Sicily enabled her to requisition food-supplies from there; the granaries of Sicily were subsequently supplemented by those of North-West Africa and Egypt, and the export of grain from Sicily and from Egypt presented no problems, since no cornfield in Sicily was far from the coast, while every cornfield in Egypt was close to the waterway of the River Nile or one of its arms. The City of Rome's problem at this stage of its history was the conveyance of these sea-borne supplies on the last stage of their journey.

As has been noted already, the costly work of excavating an artificial maritime harbour, Portus, connected by a water-link with the Tiber above the river's mouth, could not eliminate the clumsy and still costly operation of trans-shipping the sea-borne cargoes into river-barges that could reach the City's riverside quays. This handicap, under which imperial Rome laboured, did not afflict Constantinople, the New Rome by which the Old Rome was eventually superseded in the role of serving as the capital of the Roman Empire. Constantinople possesses a first-rate natural maritime harbour in the Golden Horn, a sheltered deep-water inlet of the Bosphorus that runs inland for the whole length of Constantinople's northern waterfront, and an obliging current automatically diverts into the Golden Horn a ship drifting down the Bosphorus laden with a cargo of grain grown in the Ukraine and carried from there, down any one of half-a-dozen navigable rivers, to sea-ports on the shores of the Black Sea and the Sea of Azov. Rome's inferiority to Constantinople in point of accessibility for the delivery of sea-borne supplies was one consideration, though not the only one, that led to the eventual transfer of the capital to Constantinople from Rome, in spite of the enormous prestige that had enabled Rome to hold her position as the capital of the Mediterranean World for the five centuries that had elapsed between the Roman state's crowning victory at Pydna in 168 B.C. and the laying-out of Constantinople in A.D. 324.

The same problem of supplying the capital of an empire beset the imperial government of China after the political unification of the Chinese World in 221 B.C. In the course of the twenty-two centuries that have now elapsed since that epoch-making event in the history of mankind, China has temporarily relapsed into political disunity on four occasions; but on each occasion the normal unity has been re-established sooner or later; the aggregate length of the bouts of disunity adds up, all told, to only about six-hundred years out of nearly two thousand two hundred; and the tendency has been for these exceptional spells of disunity to become shorter. The earliest of them, which ran from the fall of the Posterior Han dynasty to the re-unification of China by the founder of the Sui dynasty, lasted for about four centuries; the most recent bout of disunity in China lasted only for the eighteen years A.D. 1911–1929; and China is politically united today, except for the survival of a counter-government in the island of Taiwan.

During almost the whole of the aggregate period of sixteen centuries of political unity so far, the capital of a politically united China has been some city in the North. In 1969 the capital is Peking ('Northern Capital'), at the northern extremity of the North China plain, which was also the capital from 1421 till the brief political break-up of China after the fall of the Ch'ing

(Manchu) dynasty in 1911. From 221 B.C. to A.D. 23, and again from A.D. 589 to A.D. 904, the capital was in the 'Land within the Passes', i.e. the present-day province Shensi, which lies to the west of the wall of mountains that overhangs the western edge of the North China plain. Access from this plain or from any other part of either Northern or Southern China to 'the Land within the Passes' is particularly difficult, as this region's traditional descriptive name indicates. The least difficult access is up the course of the Yellow River along the gorges in which the river cuts its way through the mountain-wall just below the point where it makes its right-angle turn from a southerly to an easterly direction and starts on its last lap, which carries it across the North China plain towards the sea. From A.D. 25 to A.D. 221, the capital was at Loyang, near the south-western corner of the North China plain, in the lower valley of the River Lo, which is the first right-bank (here south-bank) tributary of the Yellow River below the point where this issues from its gorges. From A.D. 960 to A.D. 1124, the capital was at Kaifêng, on the south bank of the Yellow River about half-way across the North China plain and also about half-way between the Yellow River's point of exit from the gorges and its mouth. Thus the capital of a politically united China has usually been located in North China, though, within this region, its location has oscillated between three different localities: Shensi, Honan, and Hopei. There have been only two short spells during which a united China has been governed from Nanking ('Southern Capital') on the south bank of the lower Yangtse River. The first of these spells lasted from 1368 to 1421; the second from 1929 to 1937.

The original unification of China, which was completed in 221 B.C., was the work of one of the previous local states, Ch'in, whose home territory lay 'within the passes'. Its capital, the city of Hsien Yang, stood a short distance to the north of the north bank of the Wei River, a right-bank tributary of the Yellow River. (Their confluence is just above the point where the Yellow River plunges into the gorges through which it breaks out into the North China plain.) Ch'in State expanded progressively, eastwards and southwards, and this expansion reached its climax

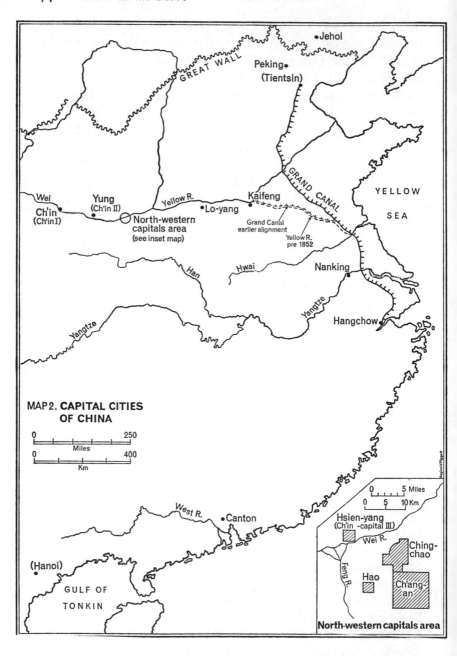

MAP 2. **CAPITAL CITIES OF CHINA**

when, within the ten years 230–221 B.C., Ch'in conquered and annexed all the six other local Chinese states that had maintained their independence till then. As Ch'in expanded, the size of the population of its capital increased, and, when the state finally incorporated the whole of the rest of the Chinese World, its government was confronted with the problem that faced the Roman government when the City of Rome became the capital of an empire embracing the whole basin of the Mediterranean.

Indeed, the problem of supplying the capital's swollen population was more difficult for Ch'in to solve than it was for Rome, and this for two reasons. Ch'in's expansion, in its climactic final bout, was more sudden that Rome's expansion was, and the conveyance of food to Hsien Yang by inland waterways was more arduous than the carriage of it to the Tiber-mouth by sea. In enlarging her once modest dominions into a vast empire, Ch'in, like Rome, had acquired the command over sources of supply that could meet the demands of a city that was now the capital of an empire, and no longer just of a local state, but, in both empires, these adequate sources of supply were distant from the imperial capital. Rome's sources were the cornfields of North-West Africa and Egypt; Ch'in's sources were the rice paddies of the Yangtse basin. The Ch'in dynasty was relieved of the task of solving this transport problem by being overthrown in 209 B.C., only a dozen years after it had completed the unification of China under its own rule, and in the ensuing anarchy Ch'in's capital, Hsien Yang, was destroyed in 207 B.C. The problem was taken over by Liu P'ang, the founder of the Prior Han dynasty, who re-united China in 202 B.C., and whose work proved more durable than Ch'in Shih Hwangti's had been. Liu P'ang planted his own imperial capital for a united China at Ching-chao, on the opposite side of the Wei River to the site of Hsien Yang. Ch'ang-an, the capital of the Sui dynasty, by whose founder China was re-united for the third time in A.D. 589, was laid out on the same side of the Wei River as the site of Ching-chao, on an immediately adjoining site; and Ch'ang-an was taken over by the Sui's successors the T'ang.

The four dynasties that ruled over a united China from an

imperial capital 'within the passes' had located their capital in a region that was more difficult than any other within the confines of the Empire to keep supplied with food from the Yangtse-basin rice-bowl. Peking is more distant from the rice-bowl than the cluster of successive imperial capitals in the Wei valley, but it is easier to reach from the South by water; Loyang is nearer than either Peking or Ch'ang-an, and Kaifêng is both the nearest and the most accessible of all the northern capitals. The Yellow River, which offers the only water-route to the 'Land within the Passes', is awkward for navigation. Its current is swift; its course through the North China plain is obstructed by shoals; and the haul upstream through the gorges is laborious. The problem of transporting South-China rice to Peking or Loyang or Kaifêng was, however, hardly more easy to solve, for Nature has not done for the Chinese Empire what she did for the Roman Empire.

Nature provided the Roman Empire with a central waterway, the Mediterranean Sea and its backwaters; she has not provided China with any corresponding facilities for water-transport from south to north. In China, Nature has given Man two great navigable waterways, the Rivers Yangtse and Hwai; but both these rivers run from west to east, not from south to north. In China, Nature has left it to Man to create artificial south-to-north inland waterways by digging canals. China's network of canals was created bit by bit over the course of about fifteen centuries, beginning with the original unification of China in 221 B.C. The greatest single advance was made in the reign of the second Sui emperor Yangti (A.D. 605–618). The network was not completed till after A.D. 1272, the year in which the Mongol Emperor Qubilāy moved his capital to Peking from Qāraqōrum in Mongolia. For a century after that, Peking was the capital of an empire that included, at least nominally, not only the whole of China, but the whole perimeter of the Eurasian Steppe. In order to supply Peking, the Grand Canal, which had previously linked the Yangtse and the Hwai with the Yellow River at Kaifêng, was carried northwards to the Pei-ho. After that, it was possible to convey freight and passengers from Hangchow to the Pei-ho by continuous inland voyage.

The Chinese Empire's man-made inland waterways have proved to be a more effective means of holding an empire together than the Roman Empire's central sea; for a sea links together the countries round its shores only so long as it and they are under the command of a single naval power. When, in the fifth century of the Christian Era, the Vandals launched a rival navy on this sea that the Romans had legitimately called *mare nostrum* since it had been cleared of pirates by Pompey in 67 B.C., and when, two hundred years later, the Arabs, in their turn, launched a maritime offensive against the Roman Empire, the Mediterranean became an 'estranging sea'. As soon as the command of the Mediterranean was disputed with the Romans by hostile powers, 'the Roman Sea' cleft the Roman Empire asunder, whereas the Grand Canal has held China together.

The City of Rome and the successive northern capitals of the Chinese Empire have not been the only capital cities that have availed themselves of waterways to lay vast areas under contribution to meet their proportionately vast demands. On first thoughts, capital cities might seem to be distinguished invidiously from cities of other kinds. The smallest and poorest market-town produces wares to pay for the food that it buys. A capital city apparently reaps where it has not sown. On second thoughts, however, it will be recognized that capital cities do make a return for the supplies that they import, though this is not a return in kind and is not an economic service either. Capitals justify the toll that they levy on the production of distant provinces by performing for the provinces political and military services that are valuable though they may not in all cases be welcome. In exchange for the food that it imports, a capital city sends out civil servants and soldiers who conduct the administration, keep the peace within the frontiers, and defend the frontiers against attack from outside. The officials who operate from a capital city, together with their direct and indirect dependents who are domiciled with them there, are subject, like everyone else, to one of the universal laws of social life—the law that services will cease to be rendered if they cease to be rewarded with an adequate *quid pro quo*. If the government installed in a capital city fails to provide the provinces with an efficient public administration, an effective police, and a successful defence of the frontiers, the revenues in kind or in money that have been flowing from the provinces into the capital will fall off, and then both the prosperity and the numbers of the population of the capital will decrease. This was the fate of the City of Rome when the Roman Empire went into decline, and it has been the fate of the capitals of all other large states that have declined and fallen.

Accessibility for the importation of supplies by water has manifestly been a major consideration in the choice of a city for serving as a capital. In the age before the mechanization of transport, Egypt was perhaps the only country in the World whose rulers were free to leave this consideration out of account. In Egypt, any city was as eligible as any other on this count, since in Egypt all cities have the River Nile or one of its arms at their gates. Everywhere else, the accessibility of a city had to be taken into account, but this is not the only consideration that has determined the location of capitals. Some cities have been capitals in virtue of their prestige, others in virtue of their convenience for serving as centres of a network of administration, and others again in virtue of their strategic position. Choices of capitals for each of these several different reasons are surveyed in the next three chapters.

4: The Choice of Capitals for Prestige

A CITY's prestige has in some cases moved a government to retain it, or positively to select it, for serving as a capital, even if this city has nothing to recommend it on any other count and indeed if, on one or more counts, it is actually unsuitable for performing a capital's functions. To give weight to prestige is not irrational; for prestige is an important factor in the psychological relations between a government and its subjects. A government that rules from a seat in a city that possesses prestige in its own right will stand to benefit by this. The capital's prestige will communicate itself to the government that is located there, and this may at least keep the people in awe of the government and may perhaps win for it their goodwill and possibly their affection. This psychological advantage may be worth the price of drawbacks in the matters of supply, administrative convenience, and strategy.

The most direct sources of prestige for the capital of a state are historical. If the state has been brought into existence through the conquest of a number of smaller local states by one of their number, the previous capital of the empire-building state will automatically become the capital of the new empire unless and until the once local but now imperial government decides to shift its seat to some other city that suits it better in the new circumstances. In this situation, inertia and pride will work together with awe to keep the capital where it is. Pride and inertia will make the imperial government and people disinclined to shift their capital to some city which, however eligible in itself, lies outside the bounds of their own homeland; and the awe in which the imperial government's and people's country and capital will be held by their subjects will be recognized by the rulers as being a valuable political asset.

A striking example of the efficacy of these considerations is the City of Rome's retention of its role of serving as a capital city for nearly five hundred years after the Roman Commonwealth in Peninsular Italy had expanded into an empire embracing the whole basin of the Mediterranean. This expansion, which was achieved during the half-century ending in 168 B.C., made the City of Rome unsuitable for continuing to be the capital of the vastly enlarged area that had now come under Roman rule or control or ascendancy. The difficulty of supplying the City's increased population by sea has already been noticed, and this was not the only handicap with which the City had to contend in its new role of serving as the capital, no longer just of Peninsular Italy, but of the entire Mediterranean World. Rome lay, as has already been noted, inconveniently far to the west of the demographic, commercial, industrial, and cultural centres of gravity of the Mediterranean in the last millennium B.C. and the first millennium of the Christian Era, and the City's location also lost its strategic importance when the Empire's frontiers had been carried as far afield as the banks of the Euphrates, the Danube, and the Rhine. Yet it was not till A.D. 324 that the Emperor Constantine I started to build a New Rome on the superbly and manifestly felicitous site of the Greek colonial city Byzantium—a site which, according to Herodotus in his widely-read work written in the fifth century B.C., had caught a passing Persian statesman's eye already before the close of the sixth century B.C.

When, *circa* 1570 B.C., Egypt was re-united politically for the second time by a local Egyptian state whose capital was Thebes, this city became, for the first time, the capital of all Egypt, in spite of its lying, as it did, far to the south of the Egyptian World's centre of gravity; and Thebes retained this role for nearly two centuries till the revolutionary emperer Akhenaton deliberately deposed Thebes by building a new capital for the Egyptian Empire at Tall-al-'Amarnah, about half way down-river between Thebes and the natural site for a capital of a united Egypt, namely a site at the head of the Delta. Thebes' achievement is impressive, but it was not so great a *tour de force* as Rome's, for Thebes held her position for less than half the length of time for which Rome held hers, in spite of an advantage that Thebes enjoyed in common with every other city in Egypt. Thanks to the River Nile, Thebes, unlike Rome and unlike the successive capitals of China in the 'Land within the Passes', had no difficulty in importing supplies in the volume required by an imperial capital.

Calcutta was the capital of the whole subcontinent of India for more than half a century (1849–1912) after the completion of the political unification of the subcontinent under British rule. Calcutta inherited this privilege from her previous role of having served, for nearly a century before that, as the capital of the British Raj's principal nucleus and growing-point, which had been Bengal. Calcutta was an unsuitable capital for all India. Bengal lies in a corner of the subcontinent, and it is isolated by a barrier of hills from the great plain of Hindustan, which contains a number of eligible sites for capitals—for instance Patna, Allahabad, Agra, Delhi, and Lahore. Calcutta was not even well-placed for serving as the principal Indian terminus of the maritime line of communications that linked the British Government of India with Britain, the country which was the ultimate base and source of the British Raj's power. Calcutta is on the far side of India from Britain. The island of Bombay, off-shore from the west coast of India, is considerably nearer to Britain via both the Cape of Good Hope and the Suez Canal, and Bombay is also easily accessible from the sea, whereas sea-going ships have to be piloted to Calcutta up the Hoogly branch of the Ganges-Brahmaputra delta. Calcutta's feat of holding its position in these adverse circumstances is remarkable.

Equally remarkable is Cuzco's feat of holding its position as the capital of the Inca state after this state, which had started as a small local one, had expanded into an empire embracing the entire domain of the Andean civilization. The Andean World's demographic and economic centre of gravity lay in the series of exquisitely irrigated and cultivated lower valleys of rivers that cross the coastal plain of Peru on their way from the Andean highlands to the sea. These lowland valleys were the Andean World's principal centres of population, and they contained its biggest cities—for example, the gigantic city of Chan-chan, a New-World counterpart of Babylon. By contrast, Cuzco was a highland city on the extreme eastern verge of the Andean civilization's domain. Cuzco is perched on the Atlantic slope of the Pacific-Atlantic watershed. In present-day Peruvian geographical terminology, its location is on the far side of the Andes and of the Altiplano, in the Montaña. In spite of this geographical handicap, Cuzco's prestige, as the historical capital of the Inca imperial people, was so great throughout the subjugated remainder of the Andean World that Cuzco held its position till the Inca Empire was suddenly and unexpectedly overthrown by Spanish invaders.

Babylon was more successful than Cuzco, Calcutta, Thebes, or Rome. It was originally the local capital of a parvenu dynasty, and its location in the alluvial plain of the lower Tigris-Euphrates basin was not central; Babylon was not far from the alluvium's north-western limit. But the third political unification of the lands of Sumer and Akkad was the work of a Babylonian empire-builder, Hammurabi, and, as a result, Babylon not only became the capital of the whole country; it managed to retain this role for fourteen centuries before being replaced by Seleucia-on-Tigris.

The most striking testimony to the psychological value of the prestige of an empire-building people's homeland is presented by two cases in which the imperial dynasty actually laid out an artificial imperial capital in its native country to play this role in default of the existence there of any already established city that could serve this purpose.

When the Mongols had conquered the domains of the sedentary civilizations surrounding the Eurasian Steppe, they laid out a capital for themselves, Qāraqōrum, in the heart of the high half of the Steppe, the present-day Mongolia—to the east of the Zungarian Gap, between the Altai Mountains and the Tien Shan, which is the corridor linking the eastern and the western halves of the Steppe with each other. The site of Qāraqōrum did have the natural advantage of being a convenient centre of communications for an imperial people who were pastoral nomads, and, during the half-century for which it was the capital of the most extensive land-empire that has ever been put together so far, Qāraqōrum drew to itself prisoners of war, merchant adventurers, missionaries, and ambassadors from the four corners of the Old World. Friar William of Rubruck, who travelled to Qāraqōrum and back in the years 1253–5 as Ambassador for King Louis IX of France to the Mongol Khaqan Mangū, found a friend in need, on the night of his arrival at Qāraqōrum, in a woman whose home-town was Metz in Lorraine. She had been captured by the Mongols in Hungary and was now married to a Russian carpenter whose craftsmanship the Mongols appreciated. This Lotharingian lady Paquette introduced Friar William to a namesake of his, Master William Buchier, a goldsmith working in Qāraqōrum, who had a brother living in Paris on the Grand Pont. Master William's wife had been born in Hungary, but one of her parents had apparently been a West European by origin, and she spoke French as well as Cuman Turkish. The same two languages were spoken by an Englishman, likewise born in Hungary, whom Friar William met at Master William's house in Qāraqōrum on Palm Sunday, A.D. 1254.

The building of artificial capitals for the First Persian Empire in the Persian imperial people's home country Parsa (Fars) was a still greater *tour de force* than the building of Qāraqōrum. Fars is a rugged highland country on the south-western rim of the Iranian plateau, remote from all the main routes in South-Western Asia, and, after the Persians had conquered an empire extending westwards to Cyrenaïca and the Aegean basin and eastwards to what is now Soviet Central Asia and to the Panjab, the Persian Emperors had little time for visiting their out-of-the-way homeland. They had sufficient time only for being buried there. Yet the founder of the Persian Empire, Cyrus II, built an imperial capital in Fars at Pasargadae, and the second founder, Darius I, built a more magnificent one there, Persepolis. The emperors made up for the infrequency of their visits to Pasargadae by giving a gold piece to every woman in the city when they did go there.

An existing city that has not previously been even a local capital may be made into one in virtue of its having acquired prestige through having played an heroic part at some crisis in a people's history. It was partly in virtue of this that Paris was able in 987 to supplant Laon as the capital of France, London gradually to supplant Winchester as the capital of England, and Ankara in 1923 to supplant Istanbul as the capital of Turkey. Paris and London had won their laurels by successfully blocking the Vikings' passage up the River Seine and the River Thames; and Ankara had won hers by serving, in the Graeco-Turkish war after the First World War, as the rallying-point for the Turkish national movement led by Mustafā Kemāl Atatürk. On the other hand Turin failed to become the capital of a united modern Italy, though it had been the capital of the Kingdom of Sardinia, the local Italian state that had played the leading part, and this an heroic one, in bringing about the unification of Italy in the teeth of the mighty Habsburg Monarchy's resistance.

Unlike most empire-builders—for instance, the Romans, the British in India, the Incas in the Andean World, the Mongols in the hinterlands of the Eurasian Steppe, and the Persians in South-West Asia—the Piedmontese had united Italy not as conquerors but as liberators. Their role in Italy had, in fact, been the same as the role, in Egypt, of the Theban founders of the Egyptian New Empire who had liberated and re-united Egypt by expelling the Hyksos, and the Italian people recognized the services that the Kingdom of Sardinia had performed for them by conferring the crown of the new Kingdom of Italy on the House of Savoy. This house's ancestral capital Turin did not, however, succeed in the nineteenth century of the Christian Era, as Thebes had succeeded in the sixteenth century B.C., in becoming the capital of the larger state that had been brought into existence by the local state of which Turin in the one instance, and Thebes in the other, had been the capital previously. In Turin's case, the handicap of its outlying location was not compensated for, as it was in Thebes' case, by the presence of a natural means of communication to link it with the whole of Italy, as Thebes was linked with the whole of Egypt by the Nile; and, in the second-place, Turin's recently won prestige could not rival the far longer established prestige of Italy's galaxy of famous cities.

It would have been difficult for the Italians to make a choice among this host of possible claimants to serve as the capital of a united Italy if one of them had not possessed a prestige that incontestably outshone the prestige of all the rest. The choice was bound to fall on Rome; yet, on every count except prestige, Rome was a still less suitable choice for the capital of modern Italy than Turin would have been. Rome had been a convenient capital for Peninsular Italy during the century and a half ending in 168 B.C., but she is not a convenient capital for modern Italy, any more than she was for the Roman Empire between the years 168 B.C. and A.D. 324. Modern Italy includes not only the Peninsula to the south-east of the Appennines but the continental territory between the Appennines and the Alps, and in modern Italy this region is the social centre of gravity. The 'developed' half of modern Italy extends no farther south-eastward than Siena and Perugia, and Rome lies within the 'developing' (i.e. backward) Mezzogiorno. If considerations of prestige had not tipped the balance in Rome's favour, the most suitable site for the capital of a united modern Italy would have been, on every other count, either Bologna at the northern foot of the Appennines or Florence at their southern foot, where the capital did alight for a short spell in the course of its transit from Turin to Rome.

The location of the capital of modern Greece at Athens in 1834 was as inevitable as the location of the capital of modern Italy at Rome in 1870. In the fifth century B.C., the attempt made by the city-state of Athens to impose her political supremacy on the rest of the Hellenic World had been foiled, but, in the course of the subsequent chapters of Graeco-Roman history, Athens had succeeded in establishing her cultural supremacy, and the enduring monuments of her architectural, artistic, and literary achievements had given her a prestige which was potent in 1834 and is still potent in 1969. Moreover, in the nineteenth century, Athens, unlike Rome, was eligible for serving as a capital on other counts besides the prestige inherited from a glorious but by that time remote past. Athens possesses a first-rate natural harbour in the Peiraeus, and this is a valuable, and indeed indispensable, asset for a capital of a country whose territory includes a host of islands, and whose mainland is broken up by mountains into insulated compartments that are difficult to link up with each other overland by rail and road.

In 1832, when the independence of Greece was recognized by the Ottoman Imperial Government and when the original land-frontier between the Kingdom of Greece and the Ottoman Empire was agreed, Athens might have been considered to lie inconveniently, and perhaps even perilously, close to this frontier, which ran from the head of the Gulf of Preveza to the western shore of the Gulf of Volo. However, the Greek people looked forward—confidently and also legitimately—to eventually incorporating in independent Greece the continental territories, extending northward from the original Graeco-Turkish frontier, in which the Greeks were in a majority in the local population. These Greek expectations were more than fulfilled by the successive northward and north-eastward extensions of Greece's continental territory in 1881, 1912-13, and 1919. The plains of Thessaly and Greek Macedonia are more fertile, better watered, and hence more productive than the Peloponnesos and the islands; and the city of Thessaloniki, which has always been an important node of maritime and overland communications, has become an important manufacturing town too since its transfer from Turkish to Greek rule. Thus the economic as well as the geographical centre of gravity of Greece has shifted northwards between 1834 and 1969, and, in consequence, Athens today, so far from being too close to Greece's continental frontier, is, if anything, too distant from it. Indeed, if the prestige of Athens had not, by now, been reinforced by a prescriptive right dating from 1834, Athens' tenure of the privilege of serving as the capital of modern Greece might have been disputed, by this time, by Thessaloniki.

A curious case of the operation of prestige is the fate of Hsien Yang, the city 'within the passes', near the left bank of the Wei River, which had been the local capital of the State of Ch'in before Ch'in united the whole of the Chinese World under its rule. In contrast to the unification of Italy by the Piedmontese and to the re-unification of Egypt by the Thebans, the unification of China had not been a welcome act of liberation; it had been an invidious act of subjugation. The Romans in the Mediterranean, the British in India, and the Incas in Peru were not loved by their subjects; the people of Ch'in, like the Mongols, were positively hated by theirs. The Ch'in regime was harsh, dictatorial, and revolutionary; it sought to confirm the unity that it had imposed by force of arms by then imposing sweeping measures of standard-ization, in many departments of social life, that were as vexatious for the Chinese as the Nazis' policy of *Gleichschaltung* was for the Germans. Consequently, after the death of the masterful and ruth-less Ch'in ruler who was the first emperor of all China, Ch'in Shih Hwangti, the Ch'in imperial regime was swiftly overthrown by a general revolt; its capital, Hsien Yang, was sacked and razed; and China was deliberately broken up again into a number of local states.

For a moment it looked as if all the unifying work of the Ch'in empire-builders, which had culminated in Ch'in Shih Hwangti's crowning achievement, had now been undone; but these momen-tary appearances were deceptive. Ch'in Shih Hwangti had given the Chinese World peace and order, and, high though the price of this boon had been, its value had been inestimable for a society that had been afflicting itself, for at least four centuries ending in the year 221 B.C., with wars of ever increasing violence between contending local states. This anarchy had become intolerable for the Chinese people, and the prospect of a permanent relapse into it was grim. Thus the Chinese people's historical experience told powerfully in favour of Ch'in Shih Hwangti's high-handed action, and it gave the dead unifier of China a posthumous victory that was still more remarkable than his victories during his lifetime. The united China that had been broken up in 209 B.C. was once more united by 202 B.C., and the second and more tactful unifier, Han Liu P'ang, laid out his new imperial capital, Ching-chao, in his Ch'in predecessor's ancestral domain, 'the Land beyond the Passes'. He planted it, in fact, close to the River Wei, almost opposite the now devastated and deserted site of Hsien Yang.

Han Liu P'ang's choice of his site for his own imperial capital indicates that the prestige that Ch'in had won through its feat of unifying China was a more potent force than the hatred that it had aroused by the brutality with which it had done its work. Han Liu P'ang himself was not a native of Ch'in; he came from a coastal district, to the north of the mouth of the River Yangtse, in what is now the province of Kiangsu. Local patriotism might have prompted Han Liu P'ang to locate his imperial capital in his native district, and practical considerations of convenience for water-borne supply would have reinforced personal sentiment; for this is the region where the plains traversed by the lower courses of the Yangtse, the Hwai, and the Yellow River coalesce with each other, and consequently it is the region through which the Grand Canal was subsequently carried. It would have been as easy to supply an imperial capital located in Kiangsu as it was difficult to supply one that was located 'within the passes'. Han Liu P'ang's decision to lay out his imperial capital, nevertheless, on a site in the neighbourhood of the abandoned site of Hsien Yang is presumptive evidence that Han Liu P'ang felt—or at any rate perceived that the Chinese people felt—that the region which had been the geographical nucleus of Ch'in, the local state that had united China politically for the first time, was on this account the proper location for the capital of a re-united China too.

The prestige inherited from Hsien Yang kept the capital of the Chinese Empire at Ching-chao for over two centuries (202 B.C.–A.D. 23) dating from the foundation of Ching-chao by Han Liu P'ang. The combined prestige of Ching-chao and Hsien Yang was strong enough to attract the imperial capital back again to a site, Ch'ang-an, immediately adjoining Ching-chao, on the same side of the Wei River, after an interval of 566 years (A.D. 23–A.D. 589). When at last, in A.D. 589, China was re-united for the third time by the founder of the Sui dynasty after having been divided, with only one ephemeral spell of re-unification, since the fall of the Posterior Han dynasty in A.D. 221, Ch'ang-an was the site for the new imperial capital that the Sui re-unifier of China chose. Even after that long lapse of time the prestige of this location weighed more heavily in the balance than the inconvenience of 'the Land within the Passes' for two practical purposes: the importation of supplies from the rest of China upstream through the Yellow River's gorges and the administration of the rest of China from this secluded corner of the subcontinent. The Sui dynasty was as short-lived as the Ch'in dynasty had been, and this for the same reason. Its behaviour was harsh and exigent, and consequently it was hated and was quickly overthrown. Ch'ang-an, however, did not suffer Hsien Yang's fate. Ch'ang-an was not destroyed and then replaced by a new capital in the same neighbourhood. It was taken over by the Sui's successors the T'ang.

Prestige also played a part in the Posterior Han's decision to place their capital at Loyang when they became the masters of a united China in A.D. 25. Loyang had been the capital of the Chou dynasty from the year 770 B.C. till 256–249 B.C., when the Chou had been extinguished by the then reigning King of Ch'in, Ch'in Shih Hwangti's grandfather. During the span of more than 500 years for which the Chou had survived at Loyang, they had been *rois fainéants* whose suzerainty over the local states of the Chinese World had been merely nominal; yet they had bequeathed to Loyang an aura of legitimacy, and no doubt this imponderable psychological asset, as well as Loyang's comparative accessibility, counted for something with the Posterior Han when they decided to locate their imperial capital here instead of reverting to the Prior Han's capital 'within the passes'. If, in choosing Loyang, the Posterior Han did in truth have in mind the later Chou's long residence there, it is conceivable that the Ch'in may previously have been influenced, when they located their capital at Hsien Yang, by the location, in that neighbourhood 'within the passes', of the earlier Chou's capital. Before 770 B.C., the Chou's capital had been Hao (Chung Chou), and this city, like the Prior Han's Ching-chao and the Sui's and the T'ang's Ch'ang-an, was located within a short distance of Hsien Yang, on the opposite side of the Wei River from Hsien Yang's location.

Prestige, again, was one of the considerations that led the British rulers of India to transfer their capital from Calcutta to Delhi. The prestige acquired by Calcutta through its having been the capital of the principal nucleus of the British Indian Empire could not vie with the older prestige that had been accumulated by Delhi in the course of the five centuries—the thirteenth century of the Christian Era to the seventeenth inclusive—during which Delhi had been the principal capital of a series of Muslim rulers over the major part of India.

The prestige accumulated by Constantinople during the eleven centuries (A.D. 324–1453) for which it had been the capital of the Roman Empire was one of the considerations that led the 'Osmanlis at last to take this pawn off the board nearly a century after the date at which Constantinople had been encircled by the expanding Ottoman Empire. By the date of Constantinople's fall, this empire that had once included the whole perimeter of the Mediterranean had dwindled to a tiny enclave of territory round its final capital, Constantinople. After its disasters in A.D. 1071 and A.D. 1204, the East Roman Empire had led as miserable an existence as the Chou Empire after its disasters in 840 B.C. and 771 B.C.; yet in A.D. 1453 the prestige of Constantinople was still appreciable, as the prestige of Loyang still was in A.D. 25, when the Posterior Han dynasty installed itself there.

In Middle America at the time of the Spanish conquest, the Aztecs' capital, Tenochtitlan, enjoyed a prestige which drew the Spaniards to found on its ruins the capital of their New Spain, the present-day Mexico City, instead of choosing to rule Middle America from their maritime base at Vera Cruz, as the British ruled India at first from Calcutta. The promptness of the Spaniards in setting up their Middle American seat of government in the interior stands out in contrast to the comparative slowness of the British in India in transferring their capital from Calcutta to Delhi. The strength of the prestige of the site of Tenochtitlan is remarkable, considering that, by the date of the Spanish conquest, the Aztec empire-builders who had been operating from Tenochtitlan had already had time enough to incur the hatred of their Middle American victims but had not yet had time enough to carry their empire-building enterprise to completion.

5: The Choice of Capitals for Convenience

THE word 'convenience' can have two meanings when it is used apropos of the location of a capital. It can mean convenience for the importation of supplies and also convenience for the conduct of administration and the maintenance of security. The importance, for a capital, of being accessible for the importation of supplies has been discussed in the first chapter of this book; and in the third chapter it has been suggested that capital cities, like cities of other kinds, can survive only so long as they manage to pay for their imports by exports of equivalent value. A capital city's exports are not manufactures or commercial services, but a capital city is not parasitic, though its exports are not of an economic kind. The services with which an imperial capital provides the provinces in return for their tribute of food and raw materials are administrative and military. A Chinese imperial capital, for instance, would import rice and would export civil and military mandarins. A capital needs to have access to the provinces as well as to be accessible from them, and a site that is convenient for either of these purposes will presumably be convenient for the other purpose too. The incoming rice and the outgoing mandarins can be conveyed, in opposite directions, along the same canals in the same barges.

The chapter immediately preceding the present one has been concerned with the part played in the choice of capitals by a city's prestige. This psychological asset has sometimes availed to retain the capital of an expanding state in a city that the state's expansion has made inconvenient for serving as this state's capital any longer. Considerations of prestige have even led to the choice of an inconvenient site in cases in which the question at issue was not whether to retain a capital on its existing site, but was to decide between alternative possible new sites. These victories of prestige over

convenience have been illustrated from the history of the City of
Rome. Prestige retained the capital of the Roman Empire at
Rome for nearly five hundred years after Rome had become
inconvenient for this purpose; and, more then 2,000 years after
Rome had made herself the unchallengeable permanent power in
the Mediterranean basin by her victory at Pydna in 168 B.C., the
same prestige was still potent enough to make Rome the inevitable
choice for serving as the capital of modern Italy, though, for this
purpose, too, Rome was inconvenient from the start and continues to be inconvenient after having been Italy's capital for a
century. If, however, whether by design or by chance, a capital
has once been located on a convenient site, it has seldom or never
been moved from there to a less convenient site for the sake of
this other site's prestige. By contrast, there are a number of cases
in which a capital has been transferred, sooner or later, from an
inconvenient site hallowed by prestige to a site that cannot compete with this previous one in prestige but does surpass it in point
of convenience.

A classical example of such a transfer is the eventual removal of
the capital of the Roman Empire by Constantine the Great from
Rome to a 'New Rome' on the site that had been partially occupied by the Greek colonial city Byzantium. The Roman Empire
was a circummediterranean empire, and, in a competition for
serving as the capital of an empire with this geographical structure, it might look as if Byzantium were subject to one of Rome's
handicaps. While Rome's location is too far to the west,
Constantinople's might appear to be about equally too far to the
east.

The power-basis of a circummediterranean empire is necessarily
the possession of naval supremacy in Mediterranean waters. Rome
did, in fact, wrest this supremacy from Carthage in the First
Romano-Carthaginian War, and it was this Roman naval achievement that enabled Rome to establish her political ascendancy over
the whole perimeter of the Mediterranean within less than a
century after she had made herself the sovereign naval power in
this landlocked sea. Yet, in naval terms, neither Rome nor Constantinople was the best-placed site for the capital of a circum-

mediterranean maritime empire. If a naval officer had been asked to choose a site for this, he would undoubtedly have chosen one that commanded one or other or, better still, both of the sea-passages connecting the Mediterranean's eastern and western basins. The narrower of these two passages, which insinuates itself between Sicily and Italy, can be commanded either from Messina or from Reggio di Calabria; the wider passage that sunders Sicily from North-West Africa can be commanded either from Lily-baeum or from Carthage. Both passages at once can be commanded at rather longer range from Syracuse on Sicily's east coast or from Palermo on the island's north coast or, perhaps best of all, from Valetta on the Island of Malta. Of these seven cities that were all potential capitals for a circummediterranean maritime empire, two, Syracuse and Carthage, were actually competitors for this political prize, and, of these two, Carthage might have beaten Rome, though, when once Carthage had lost to Rome the command of the sea, it was a foregone conclusion that even Hannibal's genius and daring would not be able to reverse—not even by the most brilliant operations on land—the decision that had already been reached on the water. Carthage had commanded the south-western half of the western basin of the Mediterranean for about 350 years ending in her defeat in the First Romano-Carthaginian War; Syracuse had momentarily commanded the Adriatic, and had successfully harried some of the Etruscan city-states along the north-west coast of Peninsular Italy, in the second decade of the fourth century B.C.; but Rome was the eventual victor in this naval contest, though, for naval purposes, she was less favourably located than either Carthage or Syracuse.

If the site for the eventual capital of the Roman Empire had been determined solely, or even mainly, by naval considerations, either Carthage or Syracuse, not Byzantium, would have been the city by which Rome was replaced. However, sea-power is unlikely to have been in Constantine's mind when he was selecting the site for a new imperial capital. Constantine will have taken Rome's naval command of the Mediterranean for granted, since this had remained unchallenged, by his time, for nearly four hundred years running from the year 67 B.C., in which Pompey had put down the audacious Cilician pirates. The decisive considerations in Constantine's mind will have been demographic, economic, and cultural, and on these three counts the two halves of the Mediterranean Sea were not of equal weight in the scales, as they would have been if Constantine had been thinking in naval terms.

On these other counts the Levant had a decisive preponderance over the Ponent (as the western basin of the Mediterranean was called in medieval Western geographical nomenclature) from the dawn of civilization until after the opening of the second millennium of the Christian Era. Consequently it was inevitable that, when the seat of government of the Roman Empire was at last removed from Rome, it should be transferred to some site in the Levant, not in North-West Africa or Sicily; and, when once the range of choice had been narrowed down to the limits of the Levant, the inevitable location was somewhere on the shores of the narrow seas that thread their way between South-West Asia and the Eurasian Continent's European peninsula and that link the Mediterranean with its principal backwater, the Black Sea, by a continuous waterway.

Julius Caesar had been credited by his Greek, and debited by his Roman, contemporaries with the intention of transferring the Roman Empire's capital from Rome to Alexandria Troas, or to Troy itself, a pair of sites that commanded the passage of the Hellespont (the Dardanelles) from the Anatolian side; and Horace, in a passage in one of his odes,[1] hints that Augustus may have played with the same idea. On the European side of the Dardanelles, on the neck of the Gallipoli Peninsula (the Thracian Chersonesus), one of Alexander the Great's successors, Lysimachus, had laid out an imperial capital, called Lysimachea after the founder's name, for a short-lived empire that, from 301 B.C. to 281 B.C., united Anatolia with the eastern half of the Balkan Peninsula. Three centuries after Augustus had rounded off the Roman Empire's south-east European dominions by extending them up to the south bank of the Danube, the Bosphorus had replaced the Dardanelles as the most convenient reach of the

[1] *Odes* III, 3, lines 57–72.

narrow seas for crossing these en route between Asia and Europe. Constantine's predecessor Diocletian had governed the Empire from Nicomedia (Ismid) at the head of the backwater of the Sea of Marmara that bears this city's name. In opting for Byzantium, Constantine was choosing a site that lay, not just close to the Bosphorus, as Nicomedia lay, but right on the shore of this maritime thoroughfare.

The excellence of Byzantium's harbour, and the facility with which it could be supplied by sea with grain from the Ukraine and from Egypt, have been noticed already. Constantinople's strategic advantages over Nicomedia, the Troad, and Rome alike will be considered in the next chapter. In the present context it need only be noted that the site of Constantinople was also convenient as a centre for the administration of an empire embracing some or all of the regions surrounding the Mediterranean. Couriers and officials could come and go between the provinces and Constantinople more expeditiously than they could between the provinces and Rome; for Constantinople was a seaport on the edge of two land-masses, South-Eastern Europe and Anatolia, whereas Rome was inaccessible for seagoing vessels and was located on a peninsula which was insulated from the land-mass of continental Europe by the successive mountain-barriers of the Appennines and the Alps. Moreover, the important provinces of the Roman Empire were those in the Levant, and Constantinople lay far closer to these than Rome lay.

Constantinople's convenience, as well as the prestige that it had accumulated in the course of eleven centuries, made it a coveted Naboth's vineyard for the 'Osmanlis from the date, 1353, at which they established their first lodgment on European soil on the Thracian side of the Dardanelles. The Ottoman state had started as one of more than forty petty Turkish principalities that had sprung up in Anatolia on the former territories of the East Roman Empire and the Saljuq Turkish Sultanate of Rum. Within eleven years of the 'Osmanlis' crossing of the Dardanelles, they had conquered such a considerable extent of European territory that the centre of gravity of their expanding dominions had moved over from Asia to Europe, and they had consequently transferred their capital from Bursa (Prusias), the first important city that they had captured, to Adrianople. Here they were astride Constantinople's line of communications with the rest of Europe, but, so long as Constantinople itself remained unconquered, this residual enclave of East Roman territory that was now enveloped by the Ottoman Empire debarred the 'Osmanlis from travelling between the European and the Asiatic portion of their dominions by the shorter route across the Bosphorus, and permitted them to use only the more circuitous route across the Dardanelles. When the Ottoman Padishah Mehmet II took Constantinople in 1453, he was acquiring for the Ottoman Empire the capital from which the Roman Empire had been administered conveniently by the Emperor Justinian I in an age in which the Roman Empire's area had been approximately the same as the area that the Ottoman Empire came to embrace when its territorial extension was at its maximum.

For any empire that unites South-Eastern Europe with the Asiatic and African segments of the Levant, Constantinople is the almost obligatory capital; and, in virtue of his having acquired this prize, Mehmet II has been distinguished from all earlier and later Ottoman padishahs by being styled 'the Conqueror' *par excellence*. In terms of square mileage, Mehmet II's total conquests, including the Peloponnesos and the Empire of Trebizond and the Principality of Qaraman, add up to a much smaller figure than his fourteenth-century predecessor Murat I's conquests in Europe and his sixteenth-century successor Selim I's conquests in Asia and Africa. Yet, in Ottoman Turkish eyes, 'the Conqueror's' acquisition of Constantinople surpassed all previous and all subsequent Ottoman conquests in terms of value. For the 'Osmanlis, Constantinople was '*the* City', as it had been for the East Romans. Indeed, the present Turkish name for Constantinople, 'Istanbul', is a compound of three Doric Greek words that mean 'to the City'. No further specification was required, since Constantinople ranked as *the* City without a peer.

Mehmet the Conqueror would have been astonished if, on 29 May 1453, he had been told that, within 470 years, the city that for him and for all 'Osmanlis of his generation was the supreme prize, would be felt by their descendants to be a liability and an incubus, and that the capital of the Ottoman Turkish state, which the Conqueror was transferring on that day to Constantinople from Adrianople, would be transferred, by a later 'Osmanli ghazi who was not a scion of the House of 'Osman, from Constantinople to a site in Anatolia that did not even lie within the bounds of the original nucleus of the Ottoman state, but was situated still farther to the east. Today Ankara, not Istanbul, is the capital of a Turkish Republic that is the youngest of the Ottoman Empire's numerous successor-states. It has already been noted that the choice of Ankara for this new Turkish state's capital was partly determined by the prestige that Ankara had acquired as the front-line headquarters of the heroic Turkish resistance movement in 1919–22. The choice of Ankara was, however, also partly determined by considerations of convenience and of psychology.

The Ottoman Empire, like the Roman Empire before it, had grown to greatness by making itself mistress of a European peninsula, but had ended, as the Roman Empire had, as an Anatolian state with a narrowly circumscribed bridge-head on the European side of the straits connecting the Mediterranean with the Black Sea. Ghazi Mustafa Kemāl Atatürk deliberately planted the capital of the Ottoman Empire's Anatolian Turkish successor-state in the heart of the Anatolian territory that it still retained and that was the region in which its future lay. He planted the new capital outside the limits of the Ottoman Empire's original North-West Anatolian nucleus in order to signify that the new Turkey was the common national patrimony of the whole of its now predominantly Turkish population; and there was an historical consideration that prompted him to make this clear by a striking symbolic act. The great majority of the present Turkish population of Anatolia are not 'Osmanlis by origin. They are descendants of the Turkish populations of the other Anatolian Turkish principalities that the Ottoman Turks conquered in the fourteenth and fifteenth centuries with their left hand while with their right hand they were conquering the non-Turkish peoples of South-Eastern Europe. For little less than five centuries the non-'Osmanli Anatolian Turks had been, like the Greeks and Bulgars and Serbs, the 'Osmanli Turks' subjects. It is true that the Anatolian Turks had been less severely penalized than their Christian fellow subjects, since the Anatolian Turks are Sunni Muslims, and in the Ottoman Empire the Sunnah had been the established religion. Yet, under the Ottoman imperial regime, Turkish Sunnis had not been any more highly privileged than their Arab, Kurd, Laz, and Albanian co-religionists. The transfer of the capital from Istanbul to Ankara was a signal to the Anatolian Turks that they had ceased to be Ottoman subjects and had become citizens of a Turkish national state.

Thus, after Constantinople had been an imperial capital for nearly sixteen centuries, it reverted, in the twentieth century of the Christian Era, to playing the role—a relatively minor one— that was played by Byzantium before the fourth century. A city that occupies this site cannot, of course, ever be deprived of the topographical advantages with which it has been endowed by Nature. It will always be a port, with a magnificent natural harbour, at the exit from the Bosphorus into the Sea of Marmara, and it will also always be the European terminal of the most convenient ferry between Europe and Asia. Thanks to this, the population and the built-up area of Istanbul are larger in 1969 than ever before. But, like the pre-Constantinopolitan Greek Byzantium, the present-day Istanbul is merely an important ferry-terminal and port and business centre; it is not the capital of an empire—not even of an empire of the diminutive size to which the East Roman Empire had shrunk by 1453.

The transfer of the capital of Turkey from Istanbul to Ankara has counterparts, in some respects, in the transfers of the capital of British India from Calcutta to Delhi and of the capital of Brazil from Rio de Janeiro to Brasilia, and in the planting of the capital of New Spain on the site of the razed capital of the Aztec Empire, Tenochtitlan. All these transfers alike were to a site in the interior of a country in preference to a site on the country's edge; and the British Government of India, like the nationalist Government of Turkey, intended to signify by its transfer of its capital that the state was the patrimony of its native inhabitants. In this case the difference was that the capital of Turkey was being transferred from a city that had acquired its prestige in the long pre-Turkish chapter of its history to a city whose prestige was recent and was the fruit of an heroic Turkish achievement, whereas the capital of India was being transferred from a city whose prestige was bound up with the British regime to a city whose prestige had been acquired in the pre-British chapter of its history.

In Mexico the newly-founded Spanish coastal city, Vera Cruz, never competed with the site of Tenochtitlan for becoming the seat of the viceroy of New Spain. In immediately planting the capital of New Spain in the interior, the Spanish conquerors may have been influenced by the convenience of the site's location, as well as by the prestige which was the legacy of its previous role of being the capital of the Aztec Empire; but in this case the conquerors were certainly not intending to intimate to the subjugated natives that the country was theirs. Mexico City did become the crucible of a new Mexican nation in which the conquered and the conquerors were fused together by a community of religion that opened the way for inter-marriage, but this happy reconciliation was the work, not of the Spanish colonial regime in Mexico, but of a native convert to Christianity who convinced the ecclesiastical authorities of the genuineness of his series of visions on the hill, on the outskirts of Mexico City, that is now crowned by the shrine of the Virgin of Guadalupe.

As for the transfer of the capital of Brazil in 1960 to Brasilia from Rio de Janeiro, the new capital had no prestige to tell in its favour. It could not have had any, for it was planted on a never previously inhabited site. It was placed in the interior of the country as deliberately as the new capitals of Turkey and of British India were, but the purpose was not to make the population feel that the country was theirs by locating the new capital in their midst. In 1955, the date of the decision to build Brasilia, the vast interior of Brazil was still virtually uninhabited. Brasilia was sited well beyond the inland edge of the area that had been settled by that time, and the purpose of planting the new capital of the country in the wilderness was to draw the population after it. In Brazil, some such stimulus was required; for in Brazil, in contrast to the United States, the settlers from the Old World had hitherto come to a halt within a short distance of the Atlantic coast, instead of trekking adventurously farther inland to win the West. The most important organs of the city of Brasilia are its tentacles—in particular the long roads that link this new political capital of Brazil with the country's industrial and commercial capital, São Paulo, and with Belem, the port at the mouth of the southernmost branch of the delta of the Amazon River. The volume of the traffic along these roads gives the measure of the success or failure of the controversial policy of planting a new capital, at a high cost, in no-man's-land. In 1969 this traffic is on a scale that justifies the founder, President Kubitscheck's, bold and imaginative venture in 'ckistics': the art of planning human settlements.

In the transfers of the capital of France to Paris from Laon and of the capital of England to London from Winchester, the prestige that the new capital had acquired, like Ankara, by recent heroism was reinforced, in the choice of the new location, by considerations of convenience in these two cases as well. Neither Paris nor London stands so near to the geographical centre of the country of which they have respectively become the capitals as Ankara, Delhi, or Mexico City stand. Paris and London do, however, each occupy a key position in its country's network of natural communications.

Paris spans the River Seine just below the River Marne's and just above the River Oise's confluence with it. Three navigable waterways thus converge on Paris, or, for travellers upstream, fan out from Paris. Moreover, Paris, like Rome, has been attracted to the particular site that it occupies by the presence, at this point in the city's river, of an island in mid stream that makes the river easy here to bridge. Paris's key position in the communication-network of Gaul was discerned by the Caesar Julian when he was sent to Gaul to rid Gaul of her invaders from beyond the Rhine. Julian made Paris his headquarters for the conduct of his operations, and a building that may have been his residence is still standing in the Paris of 1969.

London's location on the Thames, like Paris's on the Seine, has a feature in common with Rome's location on the Tiber. London, like Rome, stands at the lowest point on its river at which the bridging of the river is possible. Moreover, any passenger or freight travelling, in either direction, by the shortest sea-route—i.e. across the straits of Dover—between the Eurasian continent and any part of the island of Britain to the north of the Thames is bound to cross the Thames by London Bridge—or, nowadays, by one or other of the many bridges by which the two banks of the Thames are linked with each other in the London that has made itself into a megalopolis by 'going out of town' (Cruikshank's telling phrase). London's location is not in the Midlands of England; yet it is a more convenient location for the capital of England than Tamworth, the relatively small and obscure city that was once the capital of Mercia, and London's location is also a far more convenient location than Winchester's—the city that was the capital of Wessex. Mercia and Wessex were the two local English successor-states of the Roman Empire in Britain that were in the running for the prize of becoming the nucleus of a new state in which the former Roman territory in Britain would be re-united. One reason why Tamworth is not the capital of England today is that Mercia lost this race; but the reason why Winchester is not the capital today is that the race was eventually won by Wessex. When England was united politically as a result of the expansion of Wessex in her victorious counter-offensive against the Danish invaders of the island, the capital of this outlying local state that had now grown into the Kingdom of England was ill-placed for serving as a united England's capital. Alfred's Winchester and Victor Emmanuel (I of Italy)'s Turin had the same ironical yet inevitable fate. The success of a local state in uniting a whole country put the local state's historic capital out of business.

On Asia's grander scale, the location of Patna (Pataliputra) in the Ganges-basin is a counterpart of Paris's location in the Seine-basin. Patna stands, like Paris, at a confluence of rivers which are natural waterways for traffic. The rivers that converge at Patna are the Jumna, the Ganges, the Gogra, and the Son. Patna is the natural site for the capital of a united Northern India, as Paris is for the capital of a united Northern France, and, in both France and the Indian sub-continent, the political unification of the North is apt to lead on to the unification of the whole country. Patna has, in fact, been the capital of the greater part of India during two periods of Indian history. Chandragupta, the founder of the Maurya dynasty, may have got his start by seizing Alexander the Great's lightly-held conquests in the Indus basin after Alexander's death, but the stroke by which Chandragupta made himself master of the whole of Northern India was his subsequent seizure, in 322 B.C., of Magadha (Bihar), the local North-Indian state of which Patna was the capital. When, about six and a half centuries later than this, the Gupta dynasty repeated the Mauryas' feat of uniting Northern India politically, they did not have to start by seizing Magadha because they were already installed there as the local rulers, with their capital at Patna. Thus Patna has been the imperial capital of the greater part of the Indian sub-continent on two occasions on which the unification has been carried out by Indian hands.

Patna is, indeed, the only natural alternative site to Delhi for the location of a capital for the whole of India, and, when the British rulers of India decided to move their capital from Calcutta to some site in the interior, they might have chosen Patna if Delhi had not played Patna's historic role more recently. By the year A.D. 1912, Delhi had become the stronger candidate of the two; for Delhi had not only accumulated prestige by having served, off and on, as the capital of India since A.D. 993/4, that is to say since Delhi had passed out of Hindu into Muslim hands. Delhi could also vie with Patna on the score of the convenience of its location. Delhi stands on the right bank of the Jumna affluent of the Ganges at the point where the Ganges basin and the Indus basin are at their closest to each other. It is significant that, within the three centuries ending in the year 993/4, in which Delhi became an imperial capital for the first time, two other cities in the same region—first Sthanesvara and then Kanauj—had already played this role.

It has been mentioned that, when Pharaonic Egypt was re-united politically for the second time *circa* 1570 B.C., Thebes, the capital of the upper Egyptian canton that had done the work, was rewarded by being retained for nearly two centuries to serve as the capital of all Egypt. This, however, was an exception to the general rule of Egyptian institutional history. The local canton that had become the nucleus of a united Egypt had, on each occasion, been a southern one, and, on the two previous occasions, the unification of the country had been followed by a transfer of the capital to a more central position in the Egyptian World. The first re-unification, which was accomplished *circa* 2052 B.C., had been carried out, like the second re-unification, by a Theban local prince, but on this former occasion the capital had been moved from Thebes to a new city, built expressly for this purpose, which was located downstream on the Nile a few miles above Memphis. The location of Memphis, and of this successor of Memphis, Iz-Taui ('The Conqueror of the Two Lands') was just above the point at which the River Nile splits into a number of branches that fan out to make the Delta.

This is the natural centre of Egypt's system of communications, and, for this reason, the capital of Egypt had been placed at Memphis when, at an early date in the third millennium B.C., Egypt had been united politically for the first time. On that first occasion the southern canton that had done the work had not been the Thebaid; its twin capitals, Necheb and Nechen, had faced each other across the Nile at a point in the extreme south, between Thebes and the foot of the First Cataract; and, after the local princes of Necheb-Nechen had united all Egypt under their rule, they had moved their capital downstream, first to Thinis and then to Memphis. Thinis was a convenient site. While it was less remote than Necheb and Nechen were from the half-way point of the lower Nile Valley, it was no more distant than they were from the point where an eastward bend in the river's course brings it closer than it comes anywhere in Upper Egypt to the western shore of the Red Sea; and from Coptos, on the east bank of the Nile, on this bend, there is a route leading from the Nile valley to a Red Sea port[1] from which the masters of Thinis could reach by sea the copper-mines on the western side of the Sinai Peninsula. However, Thinis's topographical advantages were

---

[1] See p. 24.

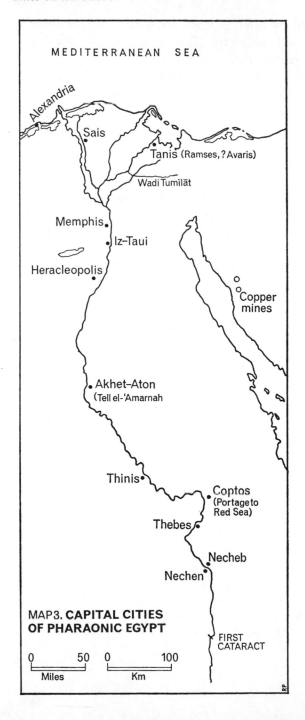

MEDITERRANEAN SEA

Alexandria

Sais

Tanis (Ramses, ? Avaris)

Wadi Tumilāt

Memphis

Iz–Taui

Heracleopolis

Copper mines

Akhet–Aton
(Tell el-'Amarnah

Thinis

Coptos
(Portage to
Red Sea)

Thebes

Necheb

Nechen

MAP 3. **CAPITAL CITIES
OF PHARAONIC EGYPT**

0   50   0   100

Miles   Km

FIRST
CATARACT

outweighed by Memphis's; for a capital of Egypt that is located at the head of the Delta is not only better placed in itself than Thinis; it also has a better line of communications, along the Wadi Tumīlāt, with the Red-Sea port of Suez. Accordingly, the Pharaohs who had established the Old Kingdom did not keep their capital at Thinis after they had moved it from Necheb-Nechen to there; they moved their capital on again to a second location at Memphis, and the capital of the United Kingdom of Egypt remained at Memphis thereafter till the Old Kingdom of Egypt declined and fell and broke up.

The sensitiveness of the Pharaonic Egyptian empire-builders to considerations of topographical convenience is remarkable; for, as has been noted already more than once, Egypt was the only country in the World before the invention of steam-traction in which Nature had made the whole country accessible from any city located anywhere in it by providing both a prevailing North Wind and a northward-flowing river. By contrast with the ease with which Nature had made it possible for Upper and Lower Egypt to communicate with each other, Nature has not provided any comparable means of communication between Northern and Southern China. In China, as has been noted already, the principal rivers all flow from west to east, and 'the Land within the Passes' is insulated from all the rest of China by a mountain-range that is pierced by the Yellow River's gorges. It might have been expected, therefore, that the Chinese would have been readier than the Egyptians to accommodate the institutional structure of a united China to the unaccommodating natural features of the subcontinent in which their lot had been cast. The pertinent feature was that the source of supply for the capital of a united China was the South, after the South had been incorporated in the Chinese Empire politically and had been developed economically by Chinese settlers and by natives who had adopted the Chinese way of life. When Southern China was opened up, it became all China's rice-bowl, and it might have been expected that the Chinese empire-builders would have located their imperial capital in the South, at the source of China's rice-supply, since China, unlike Egypt, had not been provided by Nature with ready-made means of communication between all parts of the country. The problem of communications was in any case more formidable for a united China than it was for a united Egypt, because China is vastly larger than Egypt is. Yet the Chinese have never made any voluntary concessions to the intractability of Nature in their subcontinent.

It has been mentioned already that the city of Nanking ('Southern Capital') in the Yangtse-basin rice-belt has been the capital of a united China only twice in the course of the twenty-two centuries during which China has been united politically more often than not, and it has also been noted that, on each of these occasions, Nanking's tenure of the seat of government was brief. At all other times than these two short spells, the capital of a united China has been located somewhere in the North, and for long periods in the secluded 'Land within the Passes'. Instead of accommodating themselves to Nature, the Chinese have overcome Nature by creating a gigantic system of inland waterways for transporting rice to northern capitals: Ch'ang-an, Loyang, Kaifêng, Peking. Chinese capitals located conveniently in the rice-belt have all been cities of refuge harbouring a government that had originally ruled the whole of China from a capital which had been obstinately located in the North. Ex-imperial Chinese governments have migrated to the south only when Northern China has been conquered by barbarian invaders from the Eurasian Steppe or from the Manchurian forests. These refugee governments in Southern China have felt themselves to be exiles. They have pined for the lost North, and they have longed for the day—a day which never came—on which they would liberate the North and would move back to their original capital there. They have treated their new southern capital as a temporary camp; and, if they have noticed that their migration under *force majeure* has carried them into a land of plenty, whose rice-paddies are at their provisional capital's gates, they have found no consolation in this prosaic compensatory economic convenience.

When a number of local states have been united into a single state, the method by which this unification has been brought about has usually been military conquest. One of the local states has conquered and subjugated the rest. In this situation the location of the capital of the new unified state has, of course, been decided by the government of the local state that has imposed the unification by force. This government has had the power, if it has so wished, to retain its own local capital as the capital of the larger state that it has brought into existence, and equally it has had the power to transfer the capital to a site, of its own choosing, which has seemed to it to be likely to be a more convenient base of operations for administering its enlarged dominions. In Pharaonic Egypt, as has been observed, the founders of the Old Kingdom and of the Middle Kingdom chose to move their seat of government downstream; the founders of the New Empire chose to keep it at Thebes, which had been the capital of the local state which they had expanded into an empire, though, in addition to Upper Egypt, this empire had come to include Lower Egypt and eventually Syria and Nubia too. In this situation, which has been the usual one, the choice made by the empire-builders may prove to have been ill-advised, and in any case it will have been arbitrary; but it will have been easy to make inasmuch as it will have been made by the fiat of a single power that has been capable of imposing its decision on its subjects.

The choosing of the location for the capital of a union of local states will be more difficult when the choice has to be made by common consent, and this has been the situation in cases in which the unification has been not compulsory but voluntary. One case of this kind has been considered already, namely the voluntary unification, between 1859 and 1870, of the local states among which Italy had previously been divided. Italy was fortunate, as has been noted, in containing, among its numerous famous cities, one unquestionably pre-eminent city, Rome; and Rome became the capital of the recently created Kingdom of Italy as a matter of course when, in 1870, the withdrawal of the Papal Government's French covering force made it politically possible at last to complete the political unification of Italy by incorporating in the Kingdom the remnant of the Papal State. The unquestionableness of Rome's title to become the capital of a united modern Italy made up, to some extent, for Rome's unsuitability for performing this function; and, in possessing, in Rome, an inevitable national capital, modern Italy has, on balance, perhaps been fortunate.

However, if this has been a piece of good fortune, Italy owes it to the irrelevant accident that she happens to be a country that has had a long and glorious history. Not every state that has been created by a voluntary act of union has had a counterpart of Rome at its disposal. Spain had no ready-made capital awaiting her when she was united politically by the marriage of the King of Aragon with the Queen of Castile in 1469; and it goes without saying that the new states called into existence by the federation of groups of colonies planted overseas by West-European peoples since the seventeenth century have not contained any cities invested with the prestige that is conferred by antiquity. Consequently the United States of America, Canada, and Australia have each had to do what modern Spain has done. They have had to lay out a new city to provide the capital for a state that has been brought into existence by a voluntary union, because, in each of these cases, the alternative would have been to make the capital of one of the local constituent states into the capital of the union, and there was no local capital, as there was in Italy, to which all the other local capitals would have been willing to subordinate themselves. This is why the Spaniards had to create Madrid, the Americans to create Washington, D.C., the Canadians to create Ottawa, and the Australians to create Canberra.

The creation of a new city to serve as the capital of a new state that has been brought into existence by a voluntary act of union may be the only practicable way of circumventing the impasse produced by local jealousies; but this solution of one psychological problem generates another. A new city that has been laid out, all of a piece, on a comprehensive plan is likely to be more commodious than an ancient city that has grown gradually, haphazard; and, if the new city is being designed to serve as a capital, it is also likely to be equipped with public buildings that will be either impressive or functional or will perhaps even combine these two qualities. The assets that an artificially created new city will lack in the critical first chapter of its history are the social and cultural amenities that are the gifts of age. If the new city survives this first critical period, it may gradually acquire these amenities, as the example of Constantinople demonstrates. In the fourth century of the Christian Era, Constantinople was a parvenu city by comparison with Rome; yet by the year 1923, when it ceased to be an imperial capital after having played this role, by then, for nearly sixteen centuries, Constantinople was at least as mellow as Rome had been when, in the fourth century, the sceptre had passed from Rome to this 'New Rome' which the Emperor Constantine had called into existence. Mellowing, however, is a process that takes time, and the rawness of even the best-planned brand-new capital is apt to prove uncongenial to civil servants and politicians who have been compelled, without having had any say in the decision, to migrate to this new capital from an old one in which they have felt at home.

We have already taken note of the homesickness felt by Chinese civil servants for some lost capital in the mellow northern birthplace of the Chinese civilization when they have had to take refuge in some southern city that has been rich in rice but has not been rich in ancient buildings or in traditional manners and customs. There must originally have been federal officials, marooned in newly-built Washington, D.C., who were homesick for Philadelphia or Charleston or Boston, and in Canberra today there are certainly Australian commonwealth officials who pine for Melbourne and resent having been deported from this older city. There are also certainly Brazilian officials, now parked in Brasilia, who pine for Rio and who feel like exiles in the new capital of their own country.

The choosing of a capital city is, at best, a difficult task, and attempts have been made to elude this difficulty, or at least to attenuate it, by providing a state with more capitals than one.

A pair of capitals has indeed been a necessity of life in states that straddle a mountain-range and that have their *raison d'être* in their command of the passes. One state with this peculiar geographical structure was Piedmont-Savoy, styled misleadingly the Kingdom of Sardinia. (This outlying insular possession of the House of Savoy was the only piece of their dominions that could legitimately be styled a kingdom, because it was the only piece that lay outside the bounds of the Roman Empire of the German people, and, within those bounds, the title 'Kingdom' was banned.) Piedmont-Savoy was important militarily and politically, out of proportion to the smallness of its area and population, because it controlled the passes over the western Alps between the Po basin and the Rhône basin. This state therefore needed to have a capital at the foot of the passes on both the Cisalpine and the Transalpine side. Its Cisalpine capital was Turin, and its Transalpine capital was Chambéry.

This mountain-straddling state in Western Europe was dismembered when, after the Franco-Sardinian victory over Austria in 1859, Savoy and Nice were incorporated in France, and Piedmont and Sardinia in the new Kingdom of Italy. In Asia, however, Afghanistan still straddles the Hindu Kush, and this not by a miracle, but thanks to the valour of the Afghan soldiers and the astuteness of the Afghan statesmen who, between them, saved their country from being partitioned in the nineteenth century between the British and the Russian Empires. Afghanistan is the latest representative of a series of states that have, like her, straddled the Hindu Kush from time to time. The first of these was the Greek successor-state of the Seleucid Empire in Bactria (present-day Afghan Uzbekistan, between the Hindu Kush and the River Oxus). The Bactrian Greek prince Demetrius crossed the Hindu Kush in the second decade of the second century B.C. and annexed an area of unknown extent in North-Western India; and in the first century of the Christian Era (if this dating is correct) Demetrius's achievement was repeated by the Kushans, a branch of the Eurasian nomad horde known by the Chinese as the Yuechi. The Bactrian Greek Empire's two capitals were Bactra (Balkh), on the north side of the Hindu Kush, and Taxila on the south side; the Kushan Empire's two were Balkh and Peshawar; Afghanistan's two are Balkh's successor, Mazar-i-Sharīf, and Kābul.

A pair of capitals has also been maintained in some states that have not been forced to resort to this institutional expedient, as Afghanistan and Piedmont-Savoy have been, by being situated astride of a mountain-range that divides their territory into two sections insulated from each other by this physical barrier. The

Mughal Empire in India had a capital not only at Delhi but at Agra on the same bank of the River Jumna, farther down its course. The Seleucid Empire had a capital at Seleucia-on-Tigris as well as at Antioch-on-Orontes. The Chinese Empire, when it has been united, as it has been for the greater part of the time since 221 B.C., has had a southern capital (Nanking) as well as a northern capital (Peking), though the Nankings and the Pekings of the past have not always been the cities that bear these titles today. Japan's south-western capital at Nara and then at Kyoto has been supplanted by a north-eastern capital, farther along the south-east coast of the main island, Honshu, first at Kamakura and then at Yedo (the present-day Tokyo).

This institution of a pair of capital cities has in most cases been a failure—and this even where it has been imposed by a state's physiographical structure or has been prompted by the size of a state's area. In almost every case, one of the two capitals has either been, or become, so predominant over the other that it has served virtually as the sole capital, overshadowing its partner as overwhelmingly as the presidency overshadows the vice-presidency in the practical working of the constitution of the United States. Chambéry was eclipsed by Turin in the Kingdom of Sardinia; Taxila by Balkh in the Kingdom of Bactria after its expansion to the south of the Hindu Kush; and Balkh by Peshawar in the Kushan Empire. As for Balkh's successor Mazar-i-Sharīf in present-day Afghanistan, it hardly ranks even as a secondary capital; it owes what importance it has to its prestige as a holy city. Similarly, in the Seleucid Empire, Seleucia-on-Tigris was eclipsed by Antioch-on-Orontes, though Seleucia had been the Seleucids' earliest capital and possessed two advantages—the economic advantage of being located in the lower Tigris–Euphrates basin, whose rich alluvial soil produced an abundant food-supply at Seleucia's gates, and the geographical advantage of being located at the central node of the Seleucid Empire's lines of communication. From Seleucia, one road ran north-westwards to Antioch and another north-eastwards, via Hamadan, to Balkh and to Samarkand. Yet Seleucia had only just begun life when the building of a second capital for the Seleucid Empire at Antioch virtually put Seleucia out of business as a seat of the imperial government.

In failing to make the most of Seleucia, the Seleucid Government was making a big mistake, and for this it paid a proportionately heavy penalty. The Seleucid Empire's sources of strength had lain, not in its provinces that opened on to the Mediterranean, but in these western provinces' hinterland in 'Iraq and Iran. By the year 140 B.C. the whole of this hinterland, right up to the westward elbow of the Euphrates where the river comes closest to the Mediterranean, had been lost to an Iranian power, the Parthian Empire, which had been founded by the Parni nomads from what is now Türkmenistan.

This sweeping change in the political map of South-West Asia, which spelled disaster for the Seleucid Empire, made the fortune, not of Seleucia itself, but of its suburb Ctesiphon on the opposite (i.e. the eastern) bank of the Tigris. Ctesiphon now won the position that Seleucia had so quickly lost. Ctesiphon became the sole capital of an empire that embraced the whole of 'Iraq and Iran, and it played this role for nearly eight centuries—first under the Parthian regime and then under the regime of the Parthians' Persian supplanters. Ctesiphon flourished, of course, at the expense of other cities. It was now Antioch's turn to be depressed. This former capital of the Seleucid Empire—a state whose territories had once extended from the Pamirs to the Mediterranean and the Aegean—was now reduced to becoming the seat of administration of a single Roman province.

The former capital of the Parthian Empire and the ceremonial capital of its eventual supplanter, the Second Persian Empire, were still greater losers than Antioch. The Parthian government abandoned its previous capital Hecatompylos in Parthia (the present-day Khurasan) and moved its seat to Ctesiphon as soon as it had annexed 'Iraq, and, when the founder of the Second Persian Empire, the Emperor Ardeshir of the House of Sasan, overthrew the Parthian regime, of which he had been a minor feudatory, and took over the Parthian Empire's dominions lock, stock, and barrel, he kept the capital of the empire that he had acquired in the city in which his Parthian predecessors had placed it. Ardeshir moved his seat of government to Ctesiphon from his out-of-the-way homeland, Fars. Like the second founder of the First Persian Empire, Darius I, Ardeshir gave his homeland a consolation-prize in the shape of a ceremonial capital city. Ardeshir's circular-shaped low-lying city Ardeshir-Kvarreh (near present-day Firuzabad) bore no resemblance in its layout to Darius's lofty Persepolis; but these two cities, each grand in its own way, had two features in common. Their magnificence, whose relics present so strange a contrast to the poverty of the province in which they were planted, was paid for out of contributions that had been levied from a great empire; and their founders, who commanded this great empire's resources and drew upon them for financing this extravagance, found it easier to raise the money to build their ceremonial capitals in Fars than to find the time to visit them.

In Japan the two capitals were differentiated from each other by being given different functions. Kamakura, and subsequently Yedo, became the seat of power, from which the Empire was governed *de facto* by a shogun who was in theory the Emperor's deputy, while Kyoto retained its prestige in virtue of its continuing to be the residence of this emperor who was nominally sovereign and was even officially divine, but who was actually a *roi fainéant*. Political power was bound to shift from the neighbourhood of Nara and Kyoto to the neighbourhood of Kamakura and Yedo when Japan's economic and social centre of gravity shifted north-eastwards on the main island, Honshu. In its physical configuration, Honshu resembles Peninsular Italy. It is an elongated country, compressed between two parallel coasts; it is also a mountainous country in which fertile plains are rare; and the largest and most productive of these rare plains adjoins one of the coasts at about the mid point of its length. On the south-west coast of Peninsular Italy this midway plain is Latium, the topographical setting of the city of Rome; on the south-east coast of Japan the midway plain is the Kwanto, which is commanded by the cities of Kamakura and Yedo (Tokyo). A city in this commanding location was bound to become the capital of Japan.

However, Kyoto did not surrender tamely to the inevitable future capital on the Kwanto. After Japan had been ruled from

Kamakura by the Minamoto shoguns and their Hojo regents for 148 years (1185–1333), the Ashikaga shoguns (1336–1597) found it necessary to quarter themselves in Kyoto in order to keep the Imperial Court under surveillance, and a determined, though ultimately unsuccessful, effort to govern and not merely to reign was made by the Emperor Go Daigo (1318–39). The Japanese Empire's *de facto* capital did not finally come to rest in the Kwanto till the Tokugawa shoguns (1603–1867) planted their seat of government at Yedo. This victory of the Kwanto over Yamato in their competition for being Japan's metropolitan area has not been reversed and is not likely ever to be. When, in 1868, the Tokugawa shogunate was liquidated and the Emperor's authority, which had never been abrogated juridically, was theoretically rejuvenated after it had languished for nine or ten centuries, the capital of Japan did not revert from Yedo to Kyoto; instead of that, the Emperor migrated from Kyoto to Yedo to reign, still without governing, in the Tokugawa shoguns' vacated seat and indeed actually to reside in Tokugawa Ieyasu's massive fortress-palace. Under the new name Tokyo, Yedo became, in 1868, the capital of Japan *de jure* as well as *de facto*, as Kyoto had been under the Ashikaga regime. In the course of the century that has elapsed since then, Tokyo has become the most populous city on the face of the planet. The population of Kyoto has grown concurrently, and in 1969 South Kyoto, the ancient capital's new industrial annex, is on the point of coalescing with Ōsaka and Kobe and New Sakai and Nara into a single continuous 'conurbation'. Yet, in the fearsome gestation of the world-encompassing city Ecumenopolis, Tokyo seems likely to maintain its present lead over all rival megalopolises in Japan or elsewhere.

Thus, when a state has equipped itself with two capitals, the usual outcome has been that one of the two has eclipsed the other sooner or later, and the case of Agra and Delhi is only an apparent exception to this general rule. These two cities, which were the twin capitals of the Mughal Empire in India, did remain on a par with each other until both cities forfeited their status in consequence of the Mughal Raj's decline and fall. However, this is not a test case; for Agra and Delhi both lie in the same region, the north-western end of the Ganges–Jumna plain, and their locations are not far apart on the scale of distances in the Indian subcontinent. The test case would have been the future of Awrangabad, the capital laid out by the Mughal Emperor Awrangzeb in the Deccan in the hope of thereby confirming his hold on the territories of the former local states in the Deccan which he had conquered and annexed. The history of the Mughal Empire's capitals might have proved to be an exception to the general rule if Awrangabad had been allowed time to show whether or not it could hold its own against Agra and Delhi alike. This regional capital for the Mughal Empire's newly-won possessions in the Deccan was laid out in the grand style. Its graceful replica of the Taj Mahal in miniature still stands to delight the visitor's eye. But Awrangabad had no opportunity for being put to the test; for this third capital of the Mughal Empire had no future. The Marathas laid the Mughal Raj low, and the British gathered in the harvest that the Marathas had reaped.

The institutional device of providing a state with more capitals than one has proved more successful in cases in which the government has made a practice of regularly residing in each of its capitals in turn, for a fixed length of time, during a particular season of each year. This practice has worked well in so far as it has served some useful purpose. Its utility may be either political or climatic. Climatic considerations prompted the annual migrations of the Ghaznevid Government in what is now Afghanistan, of the British government in India, and of the Government of Spain in recent times. Political considerations have prompted the dispersal of the Government of the Union of South Africa. The Government of the First Persian Empire in South-Western Asia was prompted by considerations of three kinds: climatic, communicational, and political.

In South Africa, since the date at which it became a united and self-governing state, the organs of government have been dispersed among the capitals of three out of the four constituent states of the Union. The administration is located at Pretoria, the legislature at Cape Town, the Supreme Court at Bloemfontein. This expedient of decentralization has been an alternative to the

United States' and Canada's and Australia's solution of the political problem of coping with the jealousies of the capitals of a number of local states that have united with each other voluntarily. Australia, Canada, and the United States have solved this problem, as has been observed already, by building for themselves new capital cities in order to avoid having to take the invidious step of singling out one of the local capitals to serve as the capital for the whole union. In South Africa the same problem has been solved by distributing the Union Government's organs among the three major capitals, instead of subordinating these to a new capital city specially created to perform this function. It may be noted in passing that in South Africa, Canada, and the United States, as in the Roman Empire, the economic capital has not become the political capital as well. In the Mediterranean world, Alexandria lost its chance of becoming the political capital of the Roman Empire when Antony and Cleopatra were defeated by Augustus at Actium in 31 B.C. In South Africa, Canada, and the United States, their respective economic capitals Johannesburg, Montreal, and New York have never been in the running for serving as political capitals—not even as the local capital of the constituent state or province of the union in which the economic capital of each of these unions happens to lie.

In South Africa the problem of local jealousies could be solved by distributing the government's organs between three of the local capitals out of the four. In the First Persian Empire, on the other hand, the Imperial Government had to divide its time between three capitals. It had to spend some part of every year in each of the three.

The founder of the First Persian Empire, Cyrus II, like the founder of the Second, Ardeshir, began his career as the local ruler of an out-of-the-way highland principality that was under the suzerainty of an imperial power, and each of them won his new empire by audaciously challenging, overthrowing, and supplanting his suzerain. Ardeshir made his political fortune by overthrowing the Parthian imperial regime, and Cyrus II made his by overthrowing the Median. The Achaemenian Persian royal house, of which the empire-builder Cyrus II was a scion, had split, before

Cyrus II's day, into two branches, one of which—namely Cyrus's —appears to have ruled in Luristan, while the other ruled in Fars (Parsa). Cyrus's original style and title was 'King of Anshan', and Anshan, whether the name stands for a district or for a town or for both, seems to have lain—its exact location is unknown—somewhere near the River Kherkah's exit from the Luristan highlands into the great alluvial plain (in what are now south-eastern 'Iraq and south-western Iran) that has been laid down by the silt-laden waters of the Euphrates, the Tigris, and the Eulaeus (now known as the Kārūn River).

The ruler of a local South-West-Asian state who dreamed of one day making himself master of the whole of South-West Asia was bound to strive, as a first step towards fulfilling this ambition, to gain a footing somewhere on the great alluvial plain, even if only in one of its far corners. In the division of the territorial spoils of the Assyrian Empire among the victors after the fall of Nineveh in 610 B.C., Babylonia, whose home territory extended over the major part of the alluvial plain, acquired the rest of it by annexing the lowland portion of Elam, the latest of Assyria's victims. When Cyrus II completed his conquest of South-West Asia by annexing the whole of the Babylonian Empire, at one stroke, in 538 B.C., Cyrus moved his seat of government to Susa, the extinct Kingdom of Elam's former capital.

Susa was the nearest of the more important cities on the plain to the Persians' homelands in Fars and Luristan; but, though Susa did lie on the plain, its location had two drawbacks for Persian rulers of an empire embracing the whole of South-West Asia and extending, beyond it, into the valleys of the Nile and the Indus. In the first place, Susa did not lie on any of the principal South-West Asian highways; its corner of the great plain was a cul-de-sac; its location was like Peking's location in the northernmost corner of the great North China plain. Susa's sole geographical merit was that it lay at the nearest point on the plain to the imperial people's reservoir of manpower. Susa's second drawback was that in summer its climate was intolerably hot for an imperial people whose homeland was a relatively cool highland country. Susa was thus unsuitable on two counts for serving as the Persians'

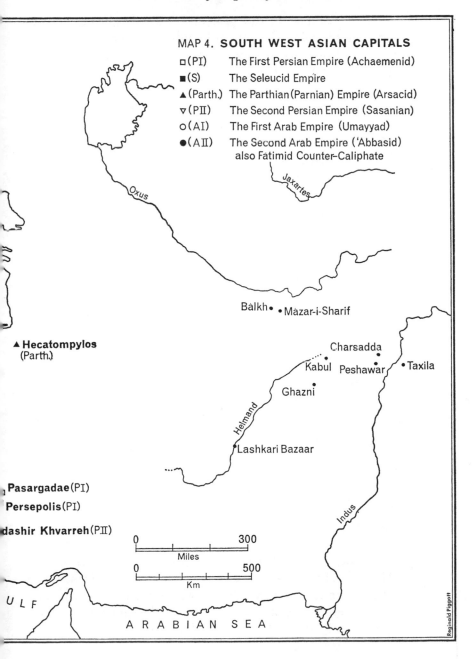

MAP 4. **SOUTH WEST ASIAN CAPITALS**

□ (PI)   The First Persian Empire (Achaemenid)
■ (S)   The Seleucid Empire
▲ (Parth.) The Parthian (Parnian) Empire (Arsacid)
▽ (PII)   The Second Persian Empire (Sasanian)
○ (AI)   The First Arab Empire (Umayyad)
● (AII)   The Second Arab Empire ('Abbasid)
          also Fatimid Counter-Caliphate

Oxus

Jaxartes

Balkh ● Mazar-i-Sharif

▲ **Hecatompylos**
(Parth.)

Charsadda
Kabul Peshawar ● Taxila

Ghazni

Helmand

● Lashkari Bazaar

Pasargadae (PI)
Persepolis (PI)

dashir Khvarreh (PII)

Indus

0 _____ 300
Miles

0 _____ 500
Km

ULF

ARABIAN SEA

Reginald Piggott

imperial capital year in and year out. Accordingly the Persian Court took to making an annual round of seasonal residences in three cities. In the cool season of the year the Court divided its time between Susa and Babylon, which was a greater city than Susa and was also better located for both communications and supply. In the hot season the Persian Court repaired to Ecbatana (Hamadan), the former capital of the Median Empire. Hamadan stands on the Iranian plateau at about the same altitude as the high-lands of the Persians' home province Fars, and it is on the great north-eastern road that runs from the alluvial plain of Babylonia and Elam to the upper basins of the Rivers Oxus and Jaxartes.

This seasonal change of the Persian Imperial Court's seat of government also served a political purpose. The First Persian Empire was a parvenu power which had suddenly risen to great-ness from humble origins by overthrowing previous empires and annexing their territories. Two ex-imperial peoples in particular, the Medes and the Babylonians—the two powers that had once jointly overthrown the Assyrian Empire and had partitioned its dominions—resented their unexpected subjugation by a small people that had previously been under the Median Empire's suzerainty. Both the ex-imperial peoples had revealed the fierce-ness of their resentment in the energy with which they had played their leading parts in the great rebellion of 522–1 B.C.—a general revolt of the Persians' subject peoples, to the east of the Euphrates, which only just failed to bring the Persian Empire to the ground. If, after the re-subjugation of the Medes and the Babylonians, there was any Persian gesture that might reconcile them, it would be the selection of their former capitals to serve as seasonal capitals of the vaster empire in which the former Median and Babylonian empires had now been incorporated.

The Babylonians proved to be irreconcilable. They continued to revolt, and, when the Persian Empire in its turn was overthrown by Alexander, he was welcomed by the Babylonians as a liberator. The Medes, on the other hand, seem to have been appeased by the Persian Government's practice of spending the summers at Ecba-tana, and the Elamites seem to have been positively flattered by the imperial status to which their national capital, Susa, had been raised by the Persian supplanters of their previous Assyrian and Babylonian masters. For the Persian Imperial Government, this reconciliation of two subject peoples in the heart of the Empire was worth an annual trek. Babylon yielded the government welcome supplies, and Ecbatana brought it welcome partners. The Persian Empire's Achilles' Heel was the inadequacy of the imperial people's manpower for holding so huge an empire—not to speak of the Persians' abortive attempt to enlarge this empire beyond all bounds by trying to annex to it the whole of the populous and far-flung Hellenic World. In inducing the Elamites and the Medes to enter into partnership with them, the Persians were strengthening their regime by broadening its demographic basis, and this partnership was the reward of the Persian Government's statesmanlike policy of dividing its time between three capitals, not one of which lay in the Persians' own homeland.

The British Indian Government's and the Spanish Government's practice of spending the summer at Simla and at San Sebastian respectively was dictated by climatic considerations alone. Neither of these summer residences had previously been the capital of a local state; Simla is nothing but a hill-station, San Sebastian nothing but a seaside resort, and the Spanish Government's use of San Sebastian as a seasonal seat has no more reconciled the surrounding Basque population to Castilian rule than the Babylonians were reconciled to Persian rule by the Persian Emperor's annual period of sojourn in Babylon.

Calcutta and Delhi are both as torrid in summertime as Susa was, and the British rulers of India came from a country with a still cooler climate than the highlands of Fars. The highlands of Afghanistan, however, are, in wintertime, even more inclement than Persepolis and than the Isle of Thanet, and consequently the Ghaznevids' climatic problem was to escape, not the summer heat of the lowlands, but the winter cold of the highlands. The Ghaznevids were not concerned for themselves or for their human troops; these were hardy; and they could have braved highland Ghazni's winter snows if the maintenance of their rule had depended on their enduring these rigours. Actually, however, the Ghaznevids' master-weapon was not their soldiery; it was their elephants; and, for the elephants' sake, the Ghaznevid Court decamped, in the autumn, from Ghazni to Lashkari Bazar, far down the course of the Helmand River, where the winter climate is almost as genial as it is in the elephants' native Hindustan. For the same reason, the Seleucidae had located their military head-quarters at Apamea-above-Orontes, a city on a ridge overhanging the northern end of the Great Rift Valley. The Seleucidae, like the Ghaznevids in a later age, relied on elephants as a weapon; they too imported their elephants from sultry Hindustan; and the winter climate of the Seleucids' end of the Rift Valley was as congenial to their elephants as the unvarying equatorial climate of the valley's southern end is to the Masai's cows.

Manifestly there are merits in the practice of keeping a govern-ment on the move between two or more seasonal residences, but this practice also has some grave disadvantages. It is costly and inefficient in all circumstances, and it may become dangerous if a government loses its grip on regions, officially under its sover-eignty, that it has to traverse in the course of its annual round.

The inefficiency is a more serious drawback than the cost, considerable though this is bound to be. A migratory imperial administration will have to suspend the conduct of its public business for an appreciable part of every year, each time that it is packing, trekking, and unpacking, and this process will have to be gone through at least twice annually. The trek itself will be time-consuming if the seasonal capitals are far apart from each other, as they ought to be if they are to serve their psychological purpose, and if the vehicles are ox-carts and the backs of elephants, donkeys, and horses. (The horses will not be able to move faster than the ox-carts' snail-like pace.)

In the Mughal Empire the trek will not have lost the govern-ment an inordinate amount of working time when it was only a question of travelling between Delhi and Agra; but the Mughals, like the British, were natives of a country with a cool climate. The dynasty's founder, Babur's, original principality had been Farghanah, in the upper valley of the River Jaxartes (Sir Darya) in what is now Soviet Central Asia, and, when he had been dis-lodged by Shah Ismā'īl Safavi from his last footholds in the

Oxus–Jaxartes basin and had been compelled to take refuge on the south side of the Hindu Kush, he had established himself provisionally at Kābul, where he was still in a region with a temperate climate. Babur's sojourn at Kābul had been only provisional because, congenial though its climate was to him, its resources were inadequate for his needs. As soon as Babur had recruited sufficient military strength, he had descended on the plains of Hindustan and had conquered an empire there which his son Humayan had lost but which his grandson Akbar had recovered. However, Babur's descendants never felt altogether at home in India. In Babur's own memoirs there are complaints about the tastelessness of India's tropical fruits by comparison with the taste of the fruits of the temperate countries in which he had spent his childhood and his early manhood. Babur appreciated the revenues of Hindustan, but resented having had to acquire them at the price of forfeiting the amenities of Central Asia.

Consequently, whenever the Mughals' dominions in Afghanistan were united politically with their dominions in Hindustan under the rule of the same member of the imperial house, the Mughal Court used to trek from Agra or Delhi to Kābul at the approach of the hot season. At Peshāwar, where the Mughal imperial convoy used to camp for a spell to brace itself for, and on the return journey to recover from, the strenuous physical exertion of making the passage of the Khyber Pass, the meadow on the other side of the great trunk road from the city, which used to be reserved for accommodating the Mughal imperial encampment, was still being preserved from being built over in 1960 when I was a visiting professor on the University of Peshāwar's campus. The size of this meadow gave the measure of the size of the imperial convoy, and the meadow's extent was impressive.

Thus the administrative inefficiency that was due to sheer loss of time will have been considerable; but a more serious cause of inefficiency in the working of a migratory government will have been the difficulty, and in fact the impossibility, of transporting, not only the migratory administrators' personal belongings, but the public records relevant to current public business. Administration cannot be conducted efficiently if the administrators do not have constant access to the documents that have an immediate bearing on the business in hand. This is true of the conduct of business affairs of any kind, public or private. I know this from personal experience both as a temporary government official during each of the two World Wars and, in peace time, as an officer of the Royal Institute of International Affairs and, since my retirement, as a free-lance writer. Business cannot be transacted properly without access to back files, and even that extensive meadow on the outskirts of Peshāwar cannot have been capacious enough to accommodate all the ox-carts and elephants that the Mughal Government would have needed to mobilize if it was to carry round with it all the back papers that it ought to have had at call in order to carry on the current business of the day. The Mughal Chancery made its records on paper, as all the World makes them nowadays, and the First Persian Empire's Chancery presumably made its records on papyrus—an almost equally handy material—in so far as it made them in the Aramaic alphabet. However, the bulk of the First Persian Empire's records, at least in its earlier days, were made in the Medo-Persian, Elamite, and Akkadian languages, and these were conveyed in the cuneiform script punched on clay tablets. This writing-material was formidably bulkier, heavier, and more brittle than either papyrus or paper, and the effect of the Persian Imperial Government's annual trek on its administrative work must therefore have been paralysing.

Moreover, all the migratory governments except the present-day government of Spain—for instance, the Mughal and British Governments in India, the Persian Government in South-West Asia, and the Ghaznevid Government in Afghanistan—went out of action before the portentous increase in the volume of public business that has accompanied the advent of the 'welfare state' in our time. Before that, government activities did not impinge directly on the private lives of a government's subjects outside the two fields of taxation and the administration of justice, and even in these two fields, as well as in the field of local government, the central government delegated much of the necessary administrative work to locally appointed (or self-appointed) local authorities. The government's own principal direct concerns were the maintenance of internal security and the provision for external defence against attack from abroad or for waging external wars of aggression on its own account. Even so, the public records that were relevant to current public business were far too bulky for it to have been possible to transport them *en bloc* two or three times a year. *A fortiori*, it would be totally impossible to move the records of present-day ministries of health, pensions, and insurance.

It is significant that the Indian regime that has now succeeded the British regime in India has abandoned the British practice of transferring the seat of government from Delhi to Simla in the hot season. One motive for this change from migratoriness to stationariness has been financial. The present Indian Government of India has, reasonably, cut out of its budget a debit item which can be dispensed with now that the personnel of the Government of India consists of native inhabitants of the country who have been inured from birth to enduring the Indian summer heat. A more cogent reason, however, is that the functions of the Government of India have now become the multiple functions of a present-day 'welfare state', and the physical scale of the apparatus of administration has expanded proportionately. Visit New Delhi today; measure the area now covered there by the Government of India's administrative buildings; calculate the total figure of their cubic content; watch the locust-like hordes of civil servants bicycling slowly, twice a day, between those administrative buildings in the centre of New Delhi and the new governmental housing-estates on the outskirts in which they and their families live; note the building-activities in these housing-estates that are providing ever more living-space for an ever-increasing host of government employees. When you have completed this reconnaissance of present-day New Delhi, you will realize that, even if the Government of India were to be endowed miraculously with the revenue of the Government of the United States, no amount of money would avail to carry New Delhi to Simla and to fetch it back. Even if the move could be financed, it would not be able to get under way. The quantity of conveyances required would choke all the roads and railways on the route, and magic carpets are not obtainable in the prosaic present-day world. The twice-a-day flow of bicyclist commuters between the centre of New Delhi and its suburbs is already almost overwhelming.

Thus the practice of making an annual trek, which has always cost a high price in terms of loss of efficiency, would bring public administration to a complete standstill in most of the states of the present-day world, and it seems unlikely that this practice can be maintained for very much longer in Spain. Moreover, even in the old days when the inefficiency caused by seasonal migration was mitigated by the comparative smallness of the volume of public business, the evil of inefficiency might be aggravated by the evil of insecurity in an empire over which the Imperial Government had lost its grip. Before the First Persian Empire fell under the blows dealt to it by Alexander, its authority had already declined to a degree at which the Emperor had to pay a toll to the highlander Elamites (the Uxii)—nominally his subjects —for the right of passage through their country between Susa and Persepolis, whenever the Emperor wanted to make one of his occasional visits to the ceremonial capital of the Persian Empire in the Persians' own homeland.

The Emperor could make his regular annual trek between Susa and Ecbatana by keeping to the great north-west road and the great north-east road, which crossed each other in the plains to the east of the River Tigris near the point where the Tigris and the Euphrates approach the nearest to each other. Presumably this route was more or less secure until the Persian Empire's last days; for the guards and patrols on the Empire's trunk roads will have been the units of the Empire's internal police force that the government will have made the greatest efforts to keep in being. However, this route was a circuitous one; and, if the Emperor preferred to travel between Susa and Ecbatana direct, he had to pay a toll to some wild highlanders here too—in this direction, to the Cossaeans (Kassites). In 331 B.C. the Uxii paid in lives for their temerity in demanding the customary passage-money from Alexander, when Alexander was on the march to Persepolis after having stepped into the last Darius' shoes. In 317 B.C. Antigonus One-Eye, who, at the moment, was the dominant figure among Alexander's competing successors, had to pay in lives to the Cossaeans for his temerity in taking the direct route from Susa to Ecbatana without having agreed to pay in·money.

In the case of the First Persian Empire the cumulative price of making an annual round of several seasonal capitals thus came to be almost prohibitive. Yet, all the same, the Arabs would have been well advised to adopt this Persian practice when, in the seventh and eighth centuries of the Christian Era, a thousand years after the First Persian Empire's fall, the Arabs made themselves masters of an empire that was approximately conterminous with the First Persian Empire in its extent.

The Arabs' rise to power was as unexpected and as rapid as the Persians' rise had been in the sixth century B.C. Like Cyrus II, Muhammad started his political career as the ruler of a tiny statelet. The nucleus of Muhammad's and his successors' dominions was the oasis of Yathrib, now known as Medina, meaning 'the City', i.e. the City of the Prophet. Muhammad lived to bring the whole of the Arabian Peninsula under his rule, and, after his death, his successors emulated Cyrus's feat of overthrowing two great empires and annexing their former dominions. The Arabs conquered the whole of the dominions of the Second Persian Empire, which had succeeded to the Parthian Empire's rule over 'Iraq and Iran; the Arabs also conquered the most valuable of the Roman Empire's dominions: Palestine, Syria, Mesopotamia, Egypt, and North-West Africa. After that, the Arabs pushed their way across the Oxus into what is now Soviet Central Asia, and also across the Straits of Gibraltar into Spain.

It quickly became evident that the government at Medina had put Medina out of business by acquiring an empire of this extent. Medina lay on the caravan route between the Yaman and Syria via Mecca; but Medina was too distant from the demographic and economic centres of gravity of the Second Persian Empire and of the southern half of the East Roman Empire for it to be feasible to govern the combined area of these huge territories from there. The capital of an empire embracing the southern half of the East Roman Empire as well as the whole of the Second Persian Empire would have to be located somewhere in 'the Fertile Crescent' if it was to be a single fixed capital from which the government of the new Arab super-empire would attempt to administer the whole of its enormous domain. In the event, the capital of the Arab Empire was transferred, *de facto*, from Yathrib to a point in 'the Fertile Crescent' in A.D. 657, and this by the Prophet Muhammad's cousin, son-in-law, and fourth successor, 'Ali, and the capital of the Caliphate remained within the limits of 'the Fertile Crescent' through all its subsequent changes of location till the last remnant of the Caliphate itself was obliterated by the Mongols in A.D. 1258. From 'Ali's residence at Kufah, or the 'Iraqi side of the Crescent's inner edge, the capital was transferred to Damascus, on the Syrian side of the same edge, in A.D. 661. In A.D. 750 it was re-transferred from Syria to 'Iraq, and here, in A.D. 762, a new city, Baghdad, was laid out to house the capital at a point on the east bank of the Tigris not far upstream from the site of Ctesiphon —the city that had served as the capital of the Parthian Empire and of the Second Persian Empire in succession. Thenceforth the capital remained at Baghdad till the end, except for occasional retreats upstream to Sāmarrā in the ninth century of the Christian Era.

However, none of these successive single capitals of the widespread Arab Empire was well enough placed to enable an imperial government, seated there, to maintain its control over all the outlying parts of the Empire simultaneously. Damascus lay too far to the west to allow the Umayyad dynasty of caliphs, who had established their capital there, to control North-East Iran (the province of Khurasan) effectively. In A.D. 747–50 the Umayyad dynasty was ousted by the 'Abbasid dynasty, and the 'Abbasids were carried into power by a Khurasani Muslim army composed of Arab settlers and local native Iranian converts. Baghdad, where the 'Abbasids located their capital in A.D. 762, was as well placed for keeping them in touch with their reservoir of military manpower as Ctesiphon had been for keeping the Arsacid rulers of the Parthian Empire in touch with the same region, which had been known as Parthia before it had come to be called Khurasan. Baghdad, however, lay too far to the east to allow a government, seated there, to control the Far West of the Islamic World. The 'Abbasids never succeeded in extending their authority over the Muslim territory in Spain; Morocco severed its connexion with the 'Abbasids almost immediately; Tunisia soon followed suit; and the viceroys whom the Baghdad Government sent to Egypt had a way of founding local dynasties of their own while continuing to pay a nominal allegiance to their sovereigns in distant 'Iraq.

The truth is that the Arabs never succeeded in welding their ex-Persian and ex-Roman dominions together into a genuine political unity. The fission of South-West Asia and the Mediterranean basin into an Iranian and a Roman portion was overcome by the Arab empire-builders only superficially. The historic dividing-line came to the surface again in A.D. 657, when 'Ali at Kufah was confronted by Mu'awiyah at Damascus. The Muslim Arab cantonment at Kufah had been planted close to Hirah, which had been the headquarters of the Second Persian Empire's Arab marchmen; Mu'awiyah at Damascus had stepped into the shoes of the Ghassanids, who had been the Arab marchmen of the Roman Empire. The historic fission reappeared in A.D. 747-50 when the Arab cantonments along the desert edge of Syria were confronted by the insurgent Khurasanis. In the modern age the same fission reappeared in the sixteenth century of the Christian Era when the Ottoman Turkish East Roman Empire was confronted by the Safavid Turkish Third Persian Empire.

Could this fission have been overcome by Arab statesmanship? Conceivably it could have been if the Arab Caliphate had adopted the First Persian Imperial Government's practice of making an annual round of seasonal capitals located in cities that previously had been the capitals of the empires that the new empire-builders had conquered and annexed. The Arabs were more mobile, in virtue of their way of life, than the Persians had been. The Persians had been highlanders; a majority of the Arabs were pastoral nomads, who were already broken in to migrating, twice a year, between their winter and their summer pastures; the urban minority of the Arabs were hardly less mobile; they were caravaneers; and this had been, in particular, the profession of the

Quraysh, the mercantile community, operating from Mecca, which was Muhammad's and 'Alī's and the Umayyads' and the 'Abbasids' clan.

Moreover, the Caliphate's civil service could have trekked with a minimum of impedimenta; for their records were not punched on cumbrous clay tablets; they were inscribed first on papyrus and later on paper. The Arabs monopolized the source of the supply of papyrus when they conquered Egypt; they learnt the art of making paper from the Chinese when they came into contact with them as a result of conquering Transoxania. If the Arabs had been aware of the First Persian Empire's practice and had been alive to its advantages, they might perhaps have followed this precedent. They might have transferred their capital from Medina, not to any single fixed point, but to a set of seasonal capitals located in well-placed cities that had already played historic roles and had thereby accumulated prestige. If the Caliphate had decided to spend part of its time every year at, let us say, Ctesiphon, Antioch, and Alexandria, it might perhaps have been successful in the attempts that it made to incorporate the rest of the Roman Empire in its dominions, and at the same time it might have averted the revolt of the Khurasanis in A.D. 747–50—a revolution that gave the Caliphate a shock from which it never completely recovered.

6: The Choice of Capitals for Strategy

THE literal meaning of the word 'strategy' is 'policy in making war', and this has also been the original usage of the word, but it can also be applied to policy in non-military fields of activity, e.g. in the location of capital cities—the field of strategy that is the subject of the present chapter. Of course the strategical considerations that have determined the location of a capital can be military, and often have been; but they can also be demographic or cultural. Strategic locations of capitals that have had these non-military considerations in view are also taken into account in this chapter. The several fields of policy cannot be insulated from each other; for, even where one consideration—say the military one—has been paramount, others—e.g. the demographic or the cultural one—may also have played some part.

If we start by surveying those strategic locations of capitals in which military considerations have been paramount, we can distinguish several different military strategies for the location of capital cities.

One military strategy is the negative one of sheer evasion. Note has already been taken of the removal of the Royal Government, at the outbreak of the Civil War in England, from Westminster, which was within point-blank range of the puissant hostile City of London, to Oxford, up the Thames valley, on the far side of the natural barrier of the Chiltern Hills. In China, the Chou dynasty, after the sack of their capital Hao (Chung-chou), 'within the passes', by barbarian assailants in 771 B.C., retreated in 770 B.C. to a new capital at Loyang, on the far side of the Yellow River gorges. After the Kin barbarians' capture, in A.D. 1126, of Kaifêng, the original capital of the Sung dynasty at the administratively convenient point where the Grand Canal of that day made its junction with the Yellow River, the Sung established a new capital for themselves at Hangchow in Chekiang. This was not a convenient location for administering even Southern China alone, but here the Sung were shielded by a network of waterways, including the lower course of the Yangtse, from attack by northern barbarian cavalry which had found a favourable terrain for itself on the North China plain. In the western half of the Roman Empire in A.D. 404, Honorius abandoned Milan, his conveniently located but militarily exposed capital out on the North Italian plain, for Ravenna, which was screened by a girdle of marshes in the plain's far south-eastern corner.

In the Islamic World the Umayyad dynasty took refuge in Andalusia, and established a new capital for itself there at Cordoba, after it had lost to the 'Abbasids and the Idrisids the whole of its former Asian and African dominions, including its previous capital, Damascus. In A.D. 836 the 'Abbasid Caliph Al-Mu'tasim withdrew upstream on the Tigris from Baghdad to Sāmarrā, as Charles I withdrew up the Thames from Westminster to Oxford, and the 'Abbasid dynasty did not move its capital back to Baghdad till 892. The aggressor whom Al-Mu'tasim was evading was not a contumacious parliament nor a rival dynasty nor a foreign invader from beyond the frontiers of his dominions; it was his own turbulent Turkish guards. Like the Caliph Al-Mu'tasim and King Charles I of England, the prince-bishops of Köln transferred their residence and seat of government upstream on the Rhine to Bonn, to escape the turbulence of Köln, a city-state whose citizens were restive under a monarchical regime. In the Islamic World at the opening of the modern chapter of its history the Safavi dynasty, whose ancestral home lay in Azerbaijan and who had made Tabriz, the provincial capital of Azerbaijan, into the capital of an empire in which they had incorporated the whole of Iran and 'Iraq, transferred their capital from Tabriz to Isfahan, far to the south-eastward on the Iranian plateau, in order to place themselves beyond the reach of their 'Osmanli antagonists when these had demonstrated the superiority of their military strength by temporarily occupying Tabriz and permanently annexing 'Iraq. The Safavis masked the humiliating truth that Isfahan was a refuge-capital by making it an architecturally magnificent one, and Louis XIV resorted to the same device for covering his with-drawal from Paris to Versailles. We must not let ourselves be hoodwinked by the sumptuousness of the palace at Versailles; its significance lies in its distance from Paris; for this gives the measure of the King's fear of his kingdom's proper capital—a fear that was justified posthumously by what Paris did to Louis XVI.

In the history of the decline and fall of the Roman Empire, Ravenna, behind its marshes, proved to be a less effective refuge-capital than Constantinople on its peninsula. Constantinople was a capital city for sixteen centuries from its foundation in A.D. 324 till it was supplanted by Ankara in 1923, and in the course of those sixteen centuries Constantinople was taken by storm only twice, and capitulated only once, out of the many times that it was besieged.

The Venetians and their accomplices the French 'Crusaders', to whom the city had capitulated in 1203, took it by assault in 1204, and the 'Osmanlis in 1453, but in 626 it survived a concerted assault by the Avars from the European side and the Persians from the Asian shore of the Bosphorus; in 674–8 and again in 717–18 it was besieged, each time with disastrous consequences for the besiegers, by the Arabs when these were at the height of their power and were potent on sea as well as on land; in the Romano-Bulgarian war of 913–27, Tsar Symeon of Bulgaria was baffled twice—in 913 and again in 924—by Constantinople's land-walls when he approached them as an enemy after having received his education within their shelter. Symeon's attempts on Constanti-nople were, indeed, less promising than the Persians' and the Arabs' attempts had been, for in Symeon's day the East Roman navy held undisputed command of the sea, and Constantinople's Anatolian hinterland was under the East Roman Government's control and could furnish the city with supplies that the Bulgars could not intercept—as, during the Atheno-Peloponnesian war of 431–21 B.C., the Peloponnesians could not intercept the city of Athens' sea-borne supplies by invading and devastating the countryside up to the Long Walls that linked Athens with her ports. The Russians attacked Constantinople four times by sea—in 860, 907, 941, and 1043—and the first of these attacks was the

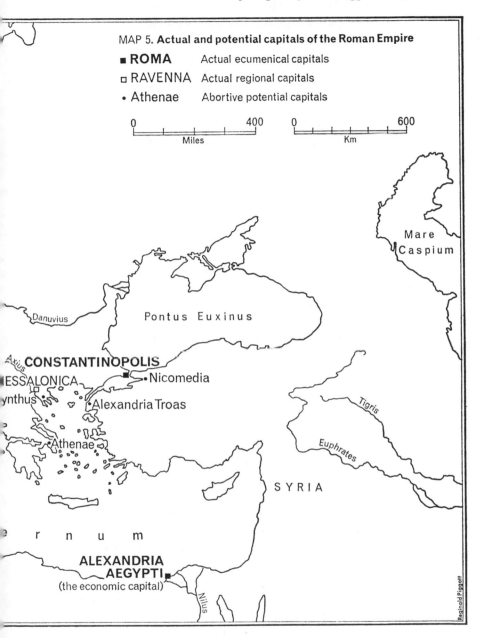

MAP 5. **Actual and potential capitals of the Roman Empire**

■ **ROMA** Actual ecumenical capitals

□ RAVENNA Actual regional capitals

• Athenae Abortive potential capitals

most dangerous of all, since it came as a bolt from the blue, and this at a moment when the East Roman army was on campaign on the Roman-Arab frontier in Eastern Anatolia. Yet this first attack and its three successors all miscarried. Even after the 'Osmanlis had encircled Constantinople by crossing the Dardanelles in 1355 and making themselves masters of the East Roman capital's European as well as its Asian hinterland, Constantinople held out for nearly a century as a still unconquered enclave in the territory of the ever-expanding Ottoman Empire.

The convenience of Constantinople's location for serving as the capital of an empire embracing the Mediterranean basin and for importing sea-borne supplies from distant sources has been considered already in an earlier chapter of this book. The topography of the site lent itself admirably to the fortification here of a city of refuge that was all but impregnable before the invention of artillery and the more recent invention of bomber planes. The fortified area could be, and was, progressively expanded from the original narrow limits of the Hellenic colonial city-state, Byzantium, at the tip of the peninsula between the Sea of Marmara and the Golden Horn. The area of Byzantium was already dwarfed by the area of Constantine's city. Constantine's land-wall, running from the Marmara to the Golden Horn, enclosed a considerably smaller area than the still surviving triple wall, which was built in 413 in the reign of Theodosius II. The sea-walls were built by the Prefect of the City, Cyrus, in 439; and, though these could not compare with the land-walls in massiveness or in elaboration, they were not escaladed with ease in 1204 by the Venetians and the French.

Moreover, the walls surrounding the City itself were not the principal fortifications by which it was defended. The peninsula between the Sea of Marmara and the Golden Horn is an excrescence on a larger peninsula between the Sea of Marmara and the Black Sea, and in either 507 or 497 the provident Emperor Anastasius I—remembering the overrunning of the European hinterland of Constantinople by the Goths during the century beginning in 378—built a 'Long Wall', from Selymbria on the Marmara to a point on the Black Sea between Podima and Lake Derkos, which had its own permanent garrison under a commandant who was apparently also, *ex officio*, the civil governor of the area between the 'Long Wall' and the Theodosian land-wall of the City of Constantinople itself. Anastasius's foresight vindicated itself when, at the collapse of the Empire's European frontier defences after the death of Justinian I in 565, the Slav Völker-wanderung swept over the Balkan Peninsula from the lower Danube southward right down to Laconia. Within the shelter of the 'Long Wall' the Roman Imperial Government at Constanti-nople remained secure; and it is no accident that in 1912–13, when the East Roman Empire's Ottoman avatar's residual Euro-pean dominions were overrun, still more swiftly, by the armies of the Ottoman Empire's Balkan successor states, the Turkish army managed to arrest the Bulgarian army's impetuous advance along a line—the Chatalja line—which approximately coincided with the tracée of the Anastasian Wall.

The degree of the enemy pressure on fortress-Constantinople in the seventh century B.C. can be gauged by the remarkable facts that in 618 or 619 even the heroic Emperor Heraclius was with difficulty deterred from evacuating it, and that in 662 Heraclius's grandson the Emperor Constans II did transfer the Empire's capital to Syracuse. However, after Constans' assassination at Syra-cuse in 668, the capital immediately reverted to Constantinople; and it reverted again in 1261 from Nicaea—the seat of the refuge-capital of the principal surviving fragment of the East Roman Empire after the capture of Constantinople and the seizure of the major part of the Empire's European dominions by the Venetians and the French in and after 1204.

A capital city has been diverted from playing its proper role if it has been made into a hiding-place for a government that has ceased to defend and administer its dominions outside the fortress-capital's walls; but a fortress-capital has a possible alternative function. It can serve as a bulwark for the government's other dominions, and this positive service was performed by Constan-tinople more often than not. The uniquely felicitous location of Constantinople as a meeting-place of maritime and overland lines of communication has already been noticed in this book, and it has been noted in that context that, in addition to its convenience for administration and supply, this location had a strategic value in the literal military sense at the date at which the capital of the Roman Empire was placed there. Located, as it was, between the two sections of the Empire's frontier that were under the heaviest pressure in and after the fourth century—namely the lower course of the Danube and the middle course of the Euphrates—Constantinople was in a position to serve as a rear base for the defence in depth of both these frontiers simultaneously; and, though, after the year 565, the defence of the lower Danube broke down, Constantinople, within the Anastasian Wall, did serve thereafter as a European bridgehead for the Empire's Anatolian core. It shielded this core against invasion from Europe at a time when the Empire was concentrating all its remaining military strength on defending Anatolia against invasions from Asia; and, after this pressure from Asia had passed the peak of its intensity, fortress-Constantinople played the strategic role of a sally-port from which the Empire's former dominions in the Balkan Peninsula were progressively reconquered.

Constantinople became the East Roman Empire's European bridgehead, as well as its capital, contrary to the Roman Imperial Government's intentions and expectations. It became a frontier-fortress because the Empire's former dominions in South-Eastern Europe had been overrun by barbarians up to the western face of the Anastasian 'Long Wall'. In Pharaonic Egypt the capital was deliberately moved from Thebes in the interior to Ramses at the north-east corner of the Delta in the thirteenth century B.C. to serve as a bulwark for Egypt itself when the Egyptian Empire's glacis that had been won by the Pharaohs of the Eighteenth Dynasty was being lost progressively to the Hittites. In the second decade of the twelfth century the last remnants of the Egyptian Empire in Asia were swept away by the Völkerwanderung of the 'Sea Peoples', whose advance was not halted and repulsed till they had reached the coast of the Delta. Ramses continued to be the capital of Egypt so long as Egypt continued to be under pressure from Asia. In the eleventh century B.C., the role was taken over from Ramses by the neighbouring city of Tanis, but the capital did not revert to Thebes.

In the Chinese World the series of capitals that were located in close proximity to each other in 'the Land within the Passes'—the successive capitals, in this district, of the Western Chou, Ch'in, Prior Han, Sui, and T'ang dynasties—were frontier-fortresses over against the Eurasian nomad barbarians. That is to say, their strategic role was the same as Constantinople's during the century and a half beginning in A.D. 565. In later chapters of Chinese history there have been two occasions on which the capital of China has been planted at Nanking—a convenient location for both administration and supply—but has then been transferred to Peking, at the extreme northern corner of the North China plain, and on both occasions the motive for the move has been strategic. The third emperor of the Ming dynasty, Yung Lo, moved his capital from Nanking to Peking in A.D. 1421 in order to guard, from this frontier city, against the risk that the previous Mongol rulers of China, whom Yung Lo's father had expelled, might attempt to return. Again, after the overthrow of the Kuomintang regime in Continental China by the present Communist regime in 1949, the Communists transferred the capital to Peking from Nanking, where the Kuomintang had located it. On this occasion, too, the move to Peking was, we may guess, a precautionary measure, and the dangerous neighbour on whom the Government of Continental China wanted to keep a watch at relatively close quarters was presumably the Soviet Union, which has replaced the Eurasian nomads as China's northern neighbour.

The same strategic consideration that led the Emperor Yung Lo and Chairman Mao to move the capital of China from Nanking to Peking led the Incas to keep their capital at Cuzco, the original capital of the nucleus of the Inca Empire. When the Incas had expanded this nucleus into an empire embracing all the lowlands, as well as all the highlands, of the Andean World, Cuzco, standing as it did on the extreme eastern edge of the Inca Empire, on the Atlantic side of the Pacific-Atlantic watershed, became very inconvenient for both administration and supply. The lowlands, not the outer edge of the highlands, were the Andean World's demographic and economic centre of gravity. However, before the unexpected and unpredictable arrival of the Spaniards via the sea, the dangerous frontier of the Inca Empire was not the Pacific coast; it was the jungle-clad *montaña* sloping down to the Amazonian forest. This was the quarter from which the Andean World had been invaded by barbarians in the past, and from which it was threatened with further invasions in the future. Cuzco, like Peking in 1421 and in 1949 and like Constantinople after 565, was a fortress-capital which served as a bulwark for the Empire on the most vulnerable of its frontiers.

Peking, as has already been noted, was chosen as the site for the capital of China by barbarian conquerors—first the Kin from Manchuria and then the Mongols—before it was adopted by the indigenous Chinese Ming dynasty; and when, in A.D. 1644, the Ming were replaced by a new band of barbarian conquerors, the Manchus, the Ch'ing (Manchu) dynasty kept the capital of China at Peking, to which it had been re-transferred by the Ming. The Ch'ing dynasty's strategic motive was, however, the opposite of the Ming's motive; it was the motive that had moved the Ch'ing's barbarian predecessors, the Kin and the Mongols, to make Peking their capital and had moved the Hyksos conquerors of Egypt to locate their capital at Avaris. The Ming had established themselves at Peking with a view to preventing the northern barbarians from re-conquering China. The Kin and the Mongols had placed the capital at Peking, and the Ching kept the capital there, in order to confirm the hold over China of a band of barbarian conquerors by ruling China from a peripheral point at which the alien rulers were still in close proximity to the 'reservoir' (Owen Lattimore's expressive term) from which they drew reinforcements of barbarian military manpower.

All alien empire-builders—whether barbarian or 'civilized' in their own self-esteem—depend on such military 'reservoirs' for the maintenance of their rule over their subjects, and accordingly, in a number of cases besides the Chinese case, the requirement of accessibility to a 'reservoir' has been a governing consideration in the location of the capital of an empire. The Hyksos Asian conquerors of Egypt placed their capital at Avaris, at the north-eastern corner of the Delta, within reach of their 'reservoir' in

Palestine and Syria. The Umayyads placed theirs at Damascus, a city which was, and is, the principal desert port on the inner rim of 'the Fertile Crescent', and which was therefore easily accessible for the nomadic Arab tribes on whose military manpower the Umayyad Empire depended for its maintenance and its expansion. The Umayyads' supplanters the 'Abbasids' reservoir of military manpower was not Arabia; it was Khurasan in North-Eastern Iran, so they planted their capital at Baghdad on the left bank of the River Tigris, where they were not cut off from Khurasan by a river-barrier. For the same reason the Arsacid builders of the Parthian Empire, who, like the 'Abbasids, had started out from Khurasan, had placed their capital at Ctesiphon, a short distance lower down the Tigris on the same bank of the river as Baghdad.

Ctesiphon was the east-bank suburb of the west-bank Greek city, Seleucia, which had been the original capital of the successor state carved out of the First Persian Empire's Asian dominions by the founder of the Seleucid dynasty, Seleucus I Nicator; but Seleucus himself, as has been noticed already, soon built a second capital at Antioch-on-Orontes, and this Antioch reduced Seleucia-on-Tigris to playing a secondary role, though Seleucia was much more conveniently situated, for both administration and supply, than Antioch was. Antioch prevailed over Seleucia nevertheless because Antioch was close to the eastern shore of the Mediterranean and was therefore far better placed than Seleucia for drawing a supply of military manpower from Greece. The Seleucid successor-state of the First Persian Empire in Asia had a rival in the Persian Empire's Ptolemaic successor-state in Egypt; the two powers were competitors in the market in Greece for mercenary soldiers; each of them had to import its mercenaries by sea; and the Ptolemaic Empire's capital Alexandria-on-Nile, at the north-west corner of the Delta, was still better placed than Antioch for this purpose, though its location was still more eccentric (in the literal sense) than Antioch's position for the purposes of administration and supply. The sea-routes across the eastern basin of the Mediterranean, which were the military life-lines of the Ptolemaic and the Seleucid Empire, have had modern counterparts in the sea-routes—first round the Cape of Good Hope and then through the Suez Canal—that were the military life-lines of the British Empire in India, and accordingly this empire's first regional capitals were located, like the Ptolemic Empire's capital, in seaports, namely Calcutta, Madras, and Bombay.

An extreme case of the deliberate choice of a peripheral site for a capital is Peter the Great's transfer of the capital of the Russian Empire from Moscow, the capital that the Empire had inherited from its historical nucleus, to St. Petersburg, (now Leningrad), a new city which Peter conjured up *ex nihilo* in the swamps at the mouth of the River Neva. St. Petersburg's location in Russia is comparable to Alexandria's in Egypt; St. Petersburg, too, was laid out at the extreme north-western corner of the populated and cultivated area of the country whose capital it was to be; the attraction of the site was the same; it was a window on the sea; and, like Alexandria and Antioch, St. Petersburg served two different strategic purposes simultaneously. One of its functions was military; Peter built it and made it his capital as a move in his design to wrest the naval command of the Baltic from Sweden; at the same time he used this window on the sea as an opening for the importation into Russia of the culture of the Western World; and, in this point too, St. Petersburg was a counterpart of Alexandria and Antioch; for the Seleucids' and Ptolemies' imports from Greece were not solely military. The Seleucids, at any rate, were eager also to import Hellenic culture, and in fact, under their regime, Hellenism gained a hold on most of the non-Greek peoples under their rule, with the two notable exceptions of the Jews and the Persians (in the limited sense of the people of the province of Fars).

7: Capital Cities:
Melting-Pots and Powder-Kegs

IT has been noted already that capital cities, like cities of other kinds, have to pay for their imports of food by producing exports of equivalent value, and that, if they cease to pay their way, they suffer an insolvent city's inevitable fate: they become impoverished, their population dwindles in numbers (as Constantinople's population dwindled during the quarter of a millennium A.D. 1204–1453), and they decay till they eventually become derelict.

It has also been noted that a capital city's exports are peculiar. A capital does not export ordinary manufactured goods that will be marketable in the capital's economic hinterland. A capital's characteristic manufactures are luxury goods produced for a privileged élite: the ruler, the members of his court, and his military and civil officials—with priority for those among them whose place of service is the capital itself. So far from thinking of these costly luxury goods as being a possible source of profit for the privy purse or for the public revenue, the ruler and his courtiers are apt to regard them as being tokens of honour whose prestige-value would decline if they were to be distributed prodigally, and still more if the Court were to be so vulgar-minded as to put them on the market.

It is true that a luxury-industry that has been called into existence originally to supply a court may eventually capture the world-market for some particular kind of luxury goods. Till recently, London tailors set the fashion for luxurious men's clothes, and Paris dressmakers the fashion for luxurious women's dress, as far afield as Western fashions of dress prevailed, and the origins of these two industrial empires can be traced back to a stimulus provided in the past by the Courts at St. James's and at the Louvre. In general, however, the exports with which capital cities have paid for their imports have been, as has already been suggested, not luxury goods, but military and administrative services. In physical terms, capitals have exported mandarins, gendarmes, and soldiers. Capitals have provided government and security (against both domestic and foreign threats to peace), and these services, like a capital's luxury-products, have not been placed on the free market. They have been imposed on all the subjects of the ruler throughout his dominions, and, as often as not, they have been unwelcome services for many of their compulsory recipients. It will be seen that a capital city does pay its way, as a city of any kind must, but that its balance-sheet is peculiar. It will therefore not be surprising to find that a capital's social and cultural role has been peculiar likewise. Capitals have been cultural melting-pots and they have also been social powder-kegs.

Capitals have played the role of melting-pots because they have drawn into themselves immigrants of diverse places of origin, diverse mother-tongues, diverse manners and customs, and diverse social classes. They have drawn in these heterogeneous recruits in the first instance from the provinces of the state that is under the rule of the government seated in the capital, but they have also drawn them in from regions beyond this state's frontiers. The immigration into a capital has in some cases been compulsory and in other cases voluntary. The population of a capital may be recruited both from deportees and from adventurers, and both these kinds of immigrants may make undesirable settlers in a city whose inhabitants are able, by their mere presence, to affect the fortunes of the government that is seated there, and consequently to affect, indirectly, the fortunes of all their fellow subjects throughout the territories that are under this government's rule.

One category of compulsory or only semi-voluntary immigrants into a capital city is the provincial nobility, including the members of formerly sovereign local royal families that have been deposed or subordinated. Ch'in Shih Hwangti, who has been the most radical and most ruthless of all empire-builders so far, is said to have deported to his imperial capital, Hsien Yang, the nobility of all the six other local Chinese states that he had liquidated when he had conquered them and had annexed their territories to Ch'in. This was one of the high-handed measures that provoked a general revolt, after his death, against the regime that he had inaugurated. In Japan in a later age the Tokugawa regime instituted the same practice in a form that was more moderate and was therefore ultimately more effective. The Tokugawa shoguns did not liquidate the local principalities which they had brought under their control when they had made this control effective over the whole of Japan. They did, however, compel the local daimyos to reside, for a period in each year, in the Tokugawa regime's headquarters, the city of Yedo (the present Tokyo). They also compelled the daimyos to leave members of their families in Yedo as hostages for their good behaviour during the periods in which the daimyos were resident in their own respective principalities. Moreover, the regime deliberately sought to cripple the daimyos financially by playing on their *amour propre*. A daimyo would be put out of countenance if in Yedo he did not live in a style that was beyond his means.

In bringing the provincial nobility to the capital by compulsion, Ch'in Shih Hwangti and the Tokugawa shoguns were doing what the governments of the medieval Italian city-states did when they compelled the rural nobility of their respective territoria to acquire houses in the city and to spend some of their time there. In France in the reign of Louis XIV, the same result was produced by a lighter-handed method. The children or grandchildren of provincial nobles who had had the local power to make the *fronde* were transformed into courtiers who had become so intimately wedded to the amenities of life in Paris and at Versailles that, if they had been banished to their provincial estates, they would have felt this to be, not release, but exile. In England, the acquisition of town houses in the City of Westminster by provincial nobles and bishops seems to have been voluntary. Being the seat of the Court and of Parliament, Westminster was the seat of power, and a provincial magnate who aspired to have some share in this power would be out of the running if he did not provide himself with a metropolitan *pied-à-terre*.

Another category of immigrants into capital cities has been the élite of the artists and artisans in the provinces and abroad, who have been good enough masters of their various arts and crafts to be capable of working in the capital's luxury industries. Artists and artisans, like nobles, have in some cases been deported to a capital compulsorily. The deportees to Assyria from the liquidated Kingdom of Israel and the subsequent deportees to Babylonia from the liquidated Kingdom of Judah were made up of these two categories. However, the fund for expending on luxury consumer goods that flows into a capital from the provinces is ample enough also to offer a prospect of lucrative employment for highly skilled voluntary immigrants, and these adventurers may come from far afield on the chance of being able to make their fortune. A striking example, already cited in this book, is the Parisian goldsmith, William Buchier, whom King Louis IX of France's envoy Friar William of Rubruck found practising his art in the Mongol Khaqan's capital Qāraqōrum.

A third category, and this a numerous one, of immigrants into capital cities is the great army of employees in domestic service— one of the commonest of all forms of employment before the rise and progress of mechanized industry and of office-work made it more profitable, as well as less disagreeable, to find employment in this new and rapidly expanding field. Domestic servants might be imported forcibly as slaves. The huge metropolitan households of the Roman nobility, and the superlatively huge household of the Emperor after the inauguration of the imperial regime, were recruited almost exclusively from slaves and freedmen, and these also played in 'Abbasid Baghdad and in Ottoman Constantinople the same prominent part that they had played in Imperial Rome. In states in which slavery has, long ago, ceased to be legal, economic necessity continued, till the Second World War, to provide a copious supply of domestic servants, and the *de facto* status of these in Victorian London is revealed in the insulting word 'slavies'.

There is a fourth category of immigrants into capital cities that has been influential out of all proportion to its numbers. The missionaries of proselytizing religions have frequently made for the capital of the state whose inhabitants they have been planning to convert. They have reckoned that, if they could gain the ear of the ruler or of some of his principal counsellors and executants, these political authorities would do the rest of the missionaries' work for them. The conversion of the North-European barbarian peoples to Eastern Orthodox and Western Christianity was mainly achieved by this short cut. Celebrated examples are Saint Augustine's mission to the Kentish Court of Canterbury and Saint Constantine-Cyril and his brother Saint Methodius's mission to the Court of Great Moravia.

Missions to monarchs have not always achieved this degree of success. Constantine-Cyril's mission to the Court of the Khaqan of the Khazars missed fire. By that time, the Khazar Court was embracing Judaism in preference to both Christianity and Islam. The Jesuits' series of apparently promising visits to the Mughal Emperor Akbar's Court was foiled by Akbar's catholicity (in the generic meaning of the word). Akbar preferred to launch a syncretistic religion of his own devising. As for the Jesuits' apparently still more promising mission to the Court at Peking, this survived the replacement there of the Ming dynasty by the Ch'ing in 1644, but was brought to naught by the jealousy of other Roman Catholic Christian missionary orders. All the same, even those religious missions that have failed to achieve their aim have nevertheless influenced, in some cases, the culture of the capital cities in which their missionary labour has been lost. They have left a mark on non-religious facets of their unconverted mission-field's life.

The cultural effect on a capital city of the influx of exotic immigrants can be far-reaching. Horace, writing at the time of the stabilization of the Roman imperial regime by Augustus, was correct in declaring that the military conquest of Greece by Rome had resulted in a cultural conquest of Rome by Greece. Juvenal, writing about a century later than Horace, was not exaggerating when he put into the mouth of one of his characters the dictum that Rome had become a Greek city, and he was certainly expressing one current of contemporary Roman opinion when he made this character exclaim that he could not bear this and that he was consequently leaving Rome for good. Greek became, in truth, the common lingua franca of the miscellaneous hordes of immigrants that flocked into, or were herded into, Rome after she had imposed her military and political domination on the whole of the Mediterranean basin, and it is possible that more Greek than Latin could be heard being spoken on the streets of Rome from before the close of the second century B.C. until after the opening of the third century of the Christian Era.

When 'the Orontes discharged itself into the Tiber', the City of Rome became an alien body in its native Latium. It is not surprising that the Roman Government made repeated efforts to reverse the current. It is also not surprising that these efforts were failures. Rome was not re-Latinized till the government of the Roman Empire moved away from the city by which the Empire had originally been created. It was only then that the Orontes' flow was diverted from Rome to Milan and Ravenna and Nicomedia and finally to Constantinople. Meanwhile, no appreciable permanent effect was produced on the course of daily life in the City of Rome by the persecution of religious sects, from the Bacchanals to the Christians, or by the expulsion of Greek philosophers either individually or *en masse* or by discrimination against some particular school. 'You may throw out Nature with a pitchfork but she will come back at you every time.' It is the nature of a capital city to be cosmopolitan; and, whatever the government whose seat it is may do, a capital will continue to be cosmopolitan unless and until it loses its status.

While it is not surprising that Imperial Rome should have been overwhelmed by Hellenism, it is remarkable that Imperial Vienna should have succeeded in setting her own cultural impress on the host of immigrants that flocked into her from all quarters of the Danubian Habsburg Monarchy of which she was the capital. Vienna has been a melting-pot in which non-German-speaking and even non-Western incomers have been transmuted into German-speaking Westerners bearing the special Viennese cultural imprint. If you turn the pages of the Vienna telephone directory, you will find that German surnames are in a minority; Czech, Slovak, Polish, Magyar, Russian, Slovene, Croat, and

Serb surnames are collectively preponderant. This preponderance is not surprising, considering that the German-speaking inhabitants of the Monarchy, within its latter day frontiers, amounted to only about a quarter of the Monarchy's total population. If, however, you were to call upon one of the exotically-named subscribers to the Vienna telephone service, you would find that he was as thoroughly Viennese as any Schmidt or Schulz—and this even if his surname reveals that his family originated in one of those non-German-speaking regions of the former Monarchy in which local nationalism was up in arms against the German-Austrian or the Magyar ascendancy at the date when this present-day Viennese or his ancestors migrated to the city whose stamp he now bears.

Vienna has been unusually successful among the capitals of multinational empires in assimilating the aliens whom her role as a capital has gathered in within her gates. Many imperial governments have been alarmed at finding themselves surrounded, in their own seat of government, by an immigrant urban population that is alien to them or, worse still, has become alienated. Today, the Federal Government of the United States—a country whose population is predominantly European in race—now finds itself chained, by the United States constitution, to a city in whose population the Negro element has come to be in a majority. These Negro residents in Washington, D.C., are American citizens, and racial integration is the policy of the United States Government and of a majority of the nation, so there is nothing that the Administration at Washington can do to change the city's present racial complexion. The President and Congress of the United States are not free, even if they had the wish, to resort to the expedients of persecution and expulsion that were tried in the City of Rome by the Senate and the Emperor.

In any case, these expedients were ineffective, as has been noted already. One reason why they were ineffective is because they were negative. A positive expedient by which an imperial government has sought to provide for its own security against the population of its own capital city has been to enlist an armed guard. The government can recruit this guard from among its own nationals or it can recruit it from alien sources, and each of these alternatives is double-edged, as history has already shown.

If the guards are natives they will perhaps be willing to use their arms against the capital's cosmopolitan populace in the event of an *émeute*. At the same time they may also be a menace to their employer; for they will be conscious that they, like him, are representatives of the imperial people, and they may therefore feel no inhibitions against playing the profitable and gratifying role of king-makers. This is how the Italian-born praetorian guards at Rome behaved in the last decade of the second century of the Christian Era, and how the French Crown's French Guards behaved when, at a crucial early stage of the French Revolution, they went over to the revolutionaries' side.

The alternative is to recruit foreign mercenaries from so remote a source that they will feel themselves to be strangers even among the cosmopolitan population of the capital. Their imperial employer may then hope that they will be loyal to him so long as he is a generous and punctual paymaster. These considerations have moved imperial governments to opt for a foreign mercenary guard more often than not. Augustus hired a guard of Germans from the North-European forests. His East Roman successors in the ninth and tenth centuries of the Christian Era hired Khazars from the Steppe and Khwarizmians from Central Asia, and later they replaced or supplemented these by Scandinavians and by Englishmen (the 'Varangians'). The Khazar Khaqan, who was a Jew himself, hired Muslim Khwarizmians. The 'Abbasids at Baghdad bought Central Asian Turkish slaves. The refugee Umayyad regime in Andalusia bought Slav slaves (hence the word 'slave') from Frankish slave-dealers. The Ottoman Padishah conscripted a slave-household from among the children of his Christian subjects and used these ex-Christian slave-converts to Islam as his instruments, not only for guarding his own person, but for administering his empire, to the exclusion of his freeborn and Muslim-born co-religionists. The French Crown and the Papacy hired Swiss Guards.

In a majority of cases, these alien guards have pierced the hand that has leaned on them. They have been as perfidious as Louis

XVI's French Guards and as the Emperor Pertinax's praetorians. The Khazar Khaqan's Muslim Khwarizmians had a habit of dictating stiff terms to their employer at moments of crisis. The 'Abbasids' Turkish slave-guards made life in Baghdad so intolerable for their masters that they drove the Caliphs into taking refuge at Sāmarrā. The Ottoman Padishah's slave-household became so capricious and so turbulent and at the same time so unmartial that in 1826 Mahmud II got rid of them by massacring them. The East Roman emperors' guards of three nationalities are exceptional in having no damaging endorsement on their record, and the French Crown's Swiss Guards are unique in having sacrificed their lives, after the French Guards had changed sides, for a paymaster who was too pusillanimous to allow them to defend either him or themselves. The Papacy's Swiss Guards have not been put to the test; for when, in 1870, the Italian Army reached the threshold of the Vatican, it did not try to cross it.

The record of the majority of the guards hired or purchased to protect the rulers of empires in these rulers' own capital cities shows that a melting-pot can easily turn into a powder-keg. This can happen all the more easily because the imperial guards are not the only explosive ingredient in a capital's population. There is also an urban proletariat in the sump beneath the capital's glittering upper-works. This proletariat is recruited from immigrants who have come, or have been brought, to the capital to perform some of the menial services that are in demand there, and who have sunk (and these will be the majority) to the bottom instead of succeeding in making their way upwards.

A metropolitan proletariat will find little opening for earning a livelihood. In a pre-mechanization-age capital there are three remunerative professions: the civil service, the armed forces, and the arts and crafts that produce luxury goods for the 'establishment'. The proletariat is ineligible socially and culturally for the two first-named of these professions, and technologically for the third, since the production of luxury goods requires skilled workmanship. The proletariat's only bargaining asset is the potential nuisance-value of its presence in large numbers in the immediate neighbourhood of the Court and the government offices. A mass revolt of the metropolitan proletariat might take the imperial government by surprise and bring it suddenly to the ground, whereas, in the pre-mechanization age, a provincial insurrection will not have such a swift effect, even if it is on a greater scale and even if the provincial insurgents are more determined and more persistent than the metropolitan proletariat is likely to be.

It has therefore, in a number of cases, seemed to an imperial government to be worth its while to pay its metropolitan proletariat a dole as a *douceur* for keeping quiet. This dole will be likely to be minimal, since it will be the last charge on the imperial revenues after provision has been made for the upkeep of the Court and for the civil service's and the armed forces' pay. On the whole the policy of buying the metropolitan proletariat off cheaply has been surprisingly successful. Insurrections of metropolitan proletariats have been rare, and, when they have occurred, they have seldom been successful. In order to overthrow the existing 'establishment', a metropolitan proletariat needs the support of the metropolitan middle class and of those armed forces that happen to be on the spot. In the French Revolution the brief alliance between these three forces carried all before it; but either the bourgeoisie or the armed forces alone, or, *a fortiori*, the two in combination, have usually got the better of the metropolitan proletariat when this has fallen out with them. That was the denouement, in Paris, of the French Revolution and also of its aftermaths there in 1848 and 1871. In the 'Nika' insurrection in Constantinople in 532, the Emperor Justinian I's throne, and perhaps his life as well, was saved, not by his guards, but by a small force of veteran field-troops.

8: Holy Cities

EVERY city—or, it might be more accurate to say, every city before the present age of mechanization—has been, among other things, a holy city in some degree. Religion is an intrinsic and distinctive element in human nature as I see it, and it is unquestionable that, until not more than about two hundred years ago, every city has had a religious aspect among others. No city at any time or place before the outbreak and spread of the Industrial Revolution has ever been either a commercial, an industrial, a political, a military, or a religious city exclusively. Cities have differed from each other in being concerned with one or other or several of these activities predominantly only, never exclusively. They have always been seats of the other activities as well. The mechanized city, which made its first appearance in eighteenth-century Britain, has been peculiar, so far, in either lacking the traditional religious facet of a city altogether or retaining it, if it has retained it, only in a vestigial form.

In the traditional city the most prominent public building was the principal place of worship of the prevalent religious community: a cathedral, mosque, church, or temple. It is only within the last two centuries that the principal architectural landmark in a typical city has ceased to be a minaret, or spire, or pagoda and has become a factory chimney, or a high-rise hotel or block of offices or flats. This typical present-day urban skyline may be only temporary. As I have declared, I myself believe—though I am aware that this belief is controversial—that religion is a fundamental and ineradicable element in human life, and that it is therefore likely to re-assert itself in visible material form in the coming World-City that is going to be mankind's future habitat.

In the past, religion has normally been an element in urban life, and indeed the most prominent element, in virtue of the paramount importance of religion among the various kinds of human activities. The Sumerian cities are the earliest from which contemporary records survive, and their records show that each of these cities was juridically the property of a god or goddess—a power that had originally symbolized one or other of the forces of Nature, but had been conscripted subsequently to serve the different purpose of symbolizing the collective power of the human community incorporated in a city-state.

At the earliest date from which we have surviving Sumerian records, the Sumerian political communities were city-states whose heads of state were laymen, but the continuing juridical sovereignty of a god or goddess, together with the continuing role of the tutelary divinity's priesthood in the community's economic life, suggests that originally the Sumerian communities must have been, not city-states, but temple-states. This guess—and it is no more than a guess—is supported by at least two historically attested cases in which sedentary civilization was introduced by ecclesiastical corporations into an environment—physical, economic, and social—which was as unpropitious for urban life and for agriculture as the jungle-swamp of the lower Tigris-Euphrates basin must have been before it was drained and irrigated by Man.

In both these cases, the communities that performed this feat were monasteries. In Ireland, life had been pastoral till the foundation there, in the sixth century of the Christian Era, of Christian monasteries that became the growing-points for towns. In Mongolia, life had been not only pastoral but nomadic pastoral till the conversion of the Mongols to the Tantric form of Buddhism in A.D. 1576–7 and the subsequent conversion of their kinsmen and western neighbours, the Calmucks, *circa* 1620. This originally Bengali form of Buddhism had struck root in Tibet. The missionaries who converted the Mongols and Calmucks were Tibetans; the conversion was followed by the plantation, on the high eastern half of the Eurasian steppe, of Buddhist monasteries of the Tibetan type; and every Mongol or Calmuck boy who became a novice also became, in the act, a convert from the nomadic way of life to the sedentary way.

In Mongolia, as in Ireland, the economic and social revolution produced by religious conversion was radical and arduous, and this difficult feat was performed by dedicated and organized ecclesiastical corporations. It seems reasonable to guess that the same high degree of dedication and organization will have been required to move the ancestors of the citizens and peasants of the Sumerian city-states to perform the long-sustained team-work demanded for transforming jungle-swamps into irrigated fields. These pioneers were working on the grand scale for distant ends. They can hardly have expected to live to enjoy the fruits of their labours for themselves. It seems unlikely that they would have persisted if they had not been inspired and organized by ecclesiastical corporations that lived by a faith which they were able to communicate to the laity.

The introduction of the sedentary way of life into Mongolia is not the only case in which monks have defeated their own original purpose by becoming pioneers instead of continuing to be anchorites. In their search for solitude they have ensconced themselves in inhospitable fastnesses: the Cistercian abbeys—Rievaulx, Byland, Fountains, Jervaulx—among the hills of Northern Yorkshire; the rocky peninsula culminating in Mount Athos with its ironbound coast lashed by the waves of the Aegean; the chilly summit of Koya San in Japan; and—greatest *tour de force* of all—the precipitous pinnacles of Metéora ('Up Aloft') in a north-western recess of Thessaly. The discipline and diligence that are two of the cardinal monastic virtues have made these wildernesses blossom, and the monks' heroic presence there has attracted worldly visitors who would have shunned these intractable regions if those monastic heroes had not previously opened them up. In an age of faith, laymen resort to these monastic retreats as pilgrims; in an age of scepticism they continue to resort to them as tourists; and their visits set the monks a tricky moral problem.

If the monks welcome lay visitors, they will be allowing themselves to be overtaken and re-absorbed by the world from which, at the cost of such travail, they have striven to withdraw. On the other hand, if the monks rebuff the laity, they will be renouncing a possibility of spiritual influence and a certainty of financial revenue (and even monks—still being human, as they still are—cannot subsist on the chameleon's legendary diet of air). Consequently, a monastic sanctuary that has survived the advent of public security and private agnosticism tends to become transformed into a secular settlement. At Metéora today, most of the stylite monasteries have been evacuated, and those few that are still tenanted and visited are now shackled to the profane world by telephone wires—a necessary concession to the requirements of the tourist trade but a posthumous frustration of the physical and spiritual feat of the first monks who scaled those perpendicular precipices—no one today knows how—in order to win for themselves an inaccessible asylum there. If the economic development of the wilderness by the monastic pioneers has been a success, the penalty for the monks may be the expropriation of so tempting a prize. The success of the Cistercian pioneers in Northern Yorkshire in developing the mining and sheep-farming potentialities of the formerly forbidding Cleveland Hills was their undoing when the country that they had opened up was overtaken by the Reformation.

In a Sumerian city-state the corporation of priests who managed the tutelary god's or goddess's affairs also managed *ex officio* the city's economic life; and, in cities that have come to be holy cities first and foremost, religion and economics have usually retained their original association with each other. This is illustrated by the cases of Mecca and Assisi.

For anyone today, Muslim or non-Muslim, Mecca is primarily a holy city in virtue of its having been the home town of the Prophet Muhammad—the town in which he was born and brought up and in which he conducted his prophetic mission before his migration to Yathrib (Medina). Yet Mecca had been a holy city long before Muhammad set his seal on its holiness. Muhammad enhanced Mecca's already established holiness by being a Meccan citizen born; by eventually giving his blessing to the worship, in the Ka'bah, of one of the Ka'bah's gods; and by also giving his blessing to the annual pilgrimage to Mecca, which, in virtue of the Ka'bah's long-since established sanctity, had already become a pilgrimage-resort.

Moreover, the prestige of Mecca's sanctuary, and the annual pilgrimage that was a tribute to this prestige, were indissolubly associated with Mecca's economic role as a commercial centre for a zone in Arabia that extended far beyond the frontiers of the Meccan city-state. Mecca, like its forerunners Petra and Palmyra and unlike Ta'if and Yathrib, was not an agricultural oasis. It did possess a spring, the famous Zamzam. The site would have been uninhabitable without that. But Mecca had to earn its living by trade; in the anarchic world that Arabia was in almost all ages before the creation of the present Sa'udi state, commercial travelling was practicable only if and when there was a temporary truce; the only sanction for a truce in traditional Arab society was a religious one; and the annual fair, attended by commercial travellers from distant parts, which was the mainstay of Mecca's economy, could be held only on condition that this fair was also a religious festival and that, in consequence, the commercial travellers who attended the fair at Mecca could count on enjoying a temporary immunity from attack in virtue of their being pilgrims as well as business men. Muhammad himself was a typical Meccan of his day in having earned his living as a conductor of caravans between Mecca and Damascus before he became first a prophet and then a politician as well, and it is possible that one of the subconscious inspirations of his prophetic mission may have been the incidental acquaintance with Judaism and Christianity that he had made in the course of his journeys abroad on commercial business.

Similarly, for anyone today, Christian or non-Christian, Assisi is primarily a holy city in virtue of its having been the home town of Saint Francis and the principal scene of his activities both before and after his revulsion from the contemporary medieval Western bourgeois way of life. But the reason why Saint Francis had been brought up in the way of life that he came to reject so vehemently was because Assisi was a city-state with a wide range of economic activity. Saint Francis's father, Pietro Bernardone, was an Assisan cloth-merchant who had made a fortune by operating, from his headquarters in Assisi, as far afield as France. The name Francesco, which Pietro gave to his son, was a token of gratitude to the country in which Pietro had made his money. His spoiling of his son Francesco by giving him a princely allowance and encouraging him to spend it on faring sumptuously was a vicarious form of 'conspicuous consumption' on Pietro's part. Francesco's eventual violent reaction against the affluent way of life for which his father had destined him is perhaps the earliest recorded example, in Western social and spiritual history, of a revolt of the rising generation against what is now known as 'the American way of life' (i.e. the way of the present affluent eighty per cent of the people of the United States). In the United States in 1969 this revolt is rampant among the rising generation in 'white-collar' American families that have been rich enough for long enough for their children to be satiated and nauseated by a wealth that they take for granted because they have never had any direct experience of poverty.

The particular cases of Assisi and Mecca raise the general question of how cities that have become holy cities have acquired this status. In some cases their holiness has been conferred on them by their association with some holy human being, or by some particular crucial event or events in a holy human being's life. Assisi would never have become a holy city if it had not been Saint Francis's home town and the headquarters of his religious activity till the end of his life. On the other hand, Mecca would have been a holy city, even if Muhammad had never been born or if, till the end of his days, he had continued to live and work in Mecca as a typical Meccan business man. It is true that, but for Muhammad's career, Mecca's field of religious force would never have expanded beyond the limits of the city's field of commercial activity. It would never have come to embrace the vast area of the present-day Islamic World. Yet, within the pre-Muhammadan limits of the radiation of Mecca's commercial and religious influence, the Ka'bah—still tenanted by a trinity of goddesses as well as by a unique male god styled simply 'God' ('Allah', which means literally '*the* god' *par excellence*)—would have continued to enjoy religious prestige and to attract visitors who were both pilgrims and commercial travellers.

Bethlehem owes its status as a holy city solely to the tradition that Jesus was born there, and Nazareth solely to the historical fact that he was brought up there and presumably also worked there in his family's craft, carpentry, before he set out on his religious mission. In Nazareth, Jesus's mission was a failure. His fellow townsmen took offence at the spectacle of one of their own number speaking in a tone of independent personal authority that would not have been assumed by even an eminent rabbi who had received a rabbi's conventional schooling. Jesus conducted his mission mainly in the towns and fishing villages on the shores of the Sea of Galilee, and it was there that he won a following; yet these lake-shore scenes of Jesus's mission have not become holy places for the Christian Church. More logically, the tree at Bodh Gaya, under which Gautama won his enlightenment, and the Deer Park at Sarnath, which was frequently the scene of his subsequent preaching, have become the principal holy places and pilgrimage-resorts for the Buddhist World, whereas Kapilavastu, the city-state in which Gautama had been born and brought up, and to whose throne he had been the heir-apparent, has received comparatively little veneration.

This is natural, considering that the Buddha not only repudiated his heritage, as Saint Francis did, but fled from Kapilavastu, as Muhammad fled from Mecca and as Jesus apparently shunned Nazareth after his hostile reception when he had presented himself there in the novel role of prophet. The Buddha was eventually reconciled with his fellow-townsmen, including his father their king, as Muhammad was eventually reconciled with the hostile majority of his fellow Meccans. But neither the Buddha nor Jesus nor Muhammad continued, after each of them had entered on his mission, to operate from his home town, as Saint Francis did continue to operate from his.

Yathrib, like Assisi and like Bethlehem, would never have become a holy city if a charismatic personality had not come to be associated with it. Yathrib, unlike Mecca, was, like Ta'if and like Jericho, a self-sufficing city-state in which the city drew its food supply from the fields and palm-groves of an oasis. Yathrib did not have to live, as Mecca had to, by commerce conducted under the umbrella of religious sanctity. Yathrib would never have become a holy city if it had not become 'the City of the Prophet' (*Madinat-al-Nabi*) in virtue of its having been the scene of the successful second stage of his career and the site of his tomb.

Being a charismatic personality's birth-place or being the scene of his subsequent mission are not the only forms of local association with such a personality that can make a city holy. A city can also become holy through having been the scene of a transcendent spiritual experience, whether authentic or legendary. For instance, Jerusalem is a holy city for Muslims because the Prophet Muhammad believed that this was the place where, on 'the Night of Power', he had ascended into Heaven and re-descended to Earth. The most tragic of all possible events in a prophet's life is martyrdom, and the holiness of the scene of a martyrdom is enhanced if the martyr has been buried in the same place. The crucifixion and burial of Jesus in Jerusalem are the two events in Jesus's history that have made Jerusalem a holy city for Christians. The reputed martyrdom and burial at Rome of the Apostles Peter and Paul have made Rome a holy city, second in rank to Jerusalem alone, for Roman Catholic Western Christians. Before the Reformation, Canterbury, to the embarrassment and annoyance of the English Crown, was a holy city and a pilgrimage-resort for English Christians—and for other Western Christians too—in virtue of its having been the scene of the martyrdom of Thomas Becket and the site of his tomb. Karbalā and Mashhad are holy cities for Shi'i Muslims as the respective scenes of the martyrdom and sites of the tombs of Muhammad's grandson and 'Ali's son Husayn and of the Imam Riza.

'Ali himself was assassinated at Kufah, but the city that he has hallowed by his martyrdom is Najaf, where he is buried. At Najaf the city of tombs of Shi'is whose bodies have been brought there to be buried near to 'Ali's stretches away and away into the desert beyond the horizon. Qazimayn—the third of the Shi'ah's holy cities in 'Iraq—has been hallowed by the mere burial there of the two Imams Qazim and Musa. The tomb of Saint Antony at Padua, and the reputed tomb of Saint James the Apostle at Compostela, in the far north-western corner of Spain, have drawn pilgrims from all parts of the Catholic Western Christian World. So powerful can be the attraction of a saint's tomb, even if the charismatic personality whose body has been buried there has not died a martyr's death on that spot.

Neither a martyrdom nor a tomb is indispensable for the making of a holy city; the belief that the place has been the scene of a miracle can be equally efficacious. At Wu-t'ai, 'The Mountain of the Five Terraces' (actually peaks), in the Chinese province Shansi, a play of light—deemed to be supernatural because unusual—was interpreted as being an aura of the Bodhisattva Monju (Mañjuśri). This belief generated a cluster of monasteries—a veritable monastic city—that became a pilgrimage-resort for devout Buddhists from as far afield as Japan. One of these, the Japanese monk Ennin, has left a record of his visit to Wu-t'ai in A.D. 840.[1] His rapture there consoled him for the hardships and perils of his journey.

Twice already in the history of Western Christendom, a village perched on the plateau that crowns the 'spur' of Italy has become a lode-stone for pilgrims. The grotto at Monte Sant'Angelo, in which bishop Laurentius of Siponto is said to have seen an apparition of the Archangel Michael at about the year 490, had become, by the eleventh century, the third most popular pilgrimage-resort in all Western Christendom after Rome and Compostela. In that century Monte Sant'Angelo made military and political history by attracting to South-Eastern Italy an advance-guard of the Normans who subsequently conquered the East Roman and South Lombard territories there and went on to carve out the Kingdom of the Two Sicilies. Pilgrims still resort to Monte Sant'Angelo at the present day, but in my lifetime it has been outbidden by its neighbour San Giovanni Rotondo, in virtue of the imprint of the stigmata on the hands of the local parish priest, Padre Pio di Pietralcina (1887–1968). The array of hostels for pilgrims at San Giovanni in Monte Gargano is as astonishing as it is at Fatima in Portugal, where three young shepherd children

---

[1] See *Ennin's Diary*, translated by Edwin O. Reischauer, pp. 214–60, and *Ennin's Travels in T'ang China*, by Edwin O. Reischauer, pp. 26–8 (both volumes: New York 1955, Ronald Press).

saw six apparitions of the Virgin Mary on and after 13 May 1917. Fatima and San Giovanni are still in their early days. They have not yet had time to rival, if they ever will, the prestige and popularity of the grotto at Lourdes in which, on 11 February 1858, a shepherdess, Bernadette Soubirous, saw an apparition of the Virgin, which was repeated. Lourdes is at present the most highly frequented Catholic pilgrimage-resort in the Old World.

In the New World the grotto of Lourdes has a counterpart in the Basilica of Guadalupe, on the north-eastern outskirts of Mexico City, at the spot where, in December 1531, an Indian convert to Roman Catholic Christianity, Juan Diego, saw three successive apparitions of the Virgin. At Guadalupe, according to the story, the goddess appeared to her Indian devotee in Indian skin-pigmentation and in Indian dress and imprinted a likeness of herself on his cloak, as Jesus's countenance is reputed to have been imprinted on the mandylion which he is said to have sent to a contemporary King Abgar of Osrhoene and on the kerchief with which Saint Veronica is said to have wiped the sweat from his brow on the Via Dolorosa.

The miraculous cures and rescues attributed to the Virgin of Guadalupe rival those attributed to the Virgin of Lourdes, and the primitiveness and sincerity of the naïve pictures of the experiences, painted and dedicated by grateful beneficiaries, are deeply moving. At Guadalupe the Virgin has made secular history, as the Archangel has made it at Monte Sant'Angelo. A common devotion to the European goddess who made her epiphany to an Indian convert in Indian guise has fused together the European conquerors of Mexico and their native victims into a Mexican nation in which the differences of physical race have been transcended by intermarriage and, still more potently, by a union of hearts that has made intermarriage here psychologically acceptable. In Mexico, economic and social inequalities and the resulting political conflicts do not coincide with differences in physical race.

The Virgin Mary has been able to conjure up other holy cities without making an epiphany in person. At Walsingham in the county of Norfolk in East Anglia a statue of the Virgin that was deemed to shed tears drew to Walsingham a stream of pilgrims from many parts of Western Christendom who have left their mark down to this day in the size and splendour of the parish churches along the pilgrims' road. These churches could not ever have been built on this scale by the local population out of its own funds nor ever have been filled by the local congregations, even when the population of East Anglia was at its numerical peak. They are monuments to the piety of the pilgrims *en route* for Walsingham who left alms for the parish churches that lay on their road. As for the little Italian town of Loreto in the Marche, it owes its existence to the presence there of the Casa Santa—reputed to be the Virgin Mary's house which stood originally in Nazareth but which, according to the legend, was transplanted to Western Christendom by the hands of angels, after the fall, in 1291, of Acre, the Crusaders' last foothold in Palestine. The angels are said to have deposited the Santa Casa provisionally on the eastern side of the Adriatic and then to have moved it, four years later, to its present resting-place in a laurel grove on the Italian side. The pilgrims whom the Santa Casa has attracted to Loreto have called into being a little holy city there.

However, the living Christian holy cities in Western Europe and in Middle America that have been enumerated, so far, in this chapter are surpassed in splendour by the now deserted ruins of Qal'at Sam'an, the vast labyrinth of ecclesiastical buildings in Northern Syria whose nucleus is the base of the column—three times increased in height—on whose summit Saint Symeon Stylites lived from A.D. 412 till his death in 459. Here I speak for the most part as a first-hand witness, for I have visited, besides Qal'at Sam'an, all the Western Christian sites that I have mentioned except Compostela, Loreto, and Lourdes. I should like to live to visit Compostela, but I long, still more eagerly, to see Dayr Sam'an (Telanessos), the group of hostels—a whole city in itself—that lies at the foot of the hill on whose brow Qal'at Sam'an stands. The two places are within only about ten minutes' walk of each other, and they were linked by a paved sacred way, but this is now a wreck, and, on the date—22 April 1957—of my wife's and my visit to Qal'at Sam'an, the rain was so heavy and the mud was so deep that low-lying Dayr Sam'an was inaccessible.

If such was the weather on this chilly spring day, what must it have been like during the forty-six winters that Saint Symeon passed on the summit of the column that was three times raised for him to an ever dizzier and ever bleaker height?

Qal'at Sam'an is an example of those sites of historic events in a charismatic personality's life, and sites of reported miracles, that have not been the scenes of previous historic events of which any memory has survived and have also not been occupied previously by any important human settlement. There is no manifest historical reason why Saint Symeon's column should have been erected at Qal'at Sam'an, or why the Virgin should have appeared to the three shepherd children on a bush in the pasture-lands of the village of Fatima and to Juan Diego at Guadalupe, or why San Giovanni Rotondo should have been the village in which the local priest received the stigmata, or why the tree at Bodh Gaya should have been the one under whose shade the Buddha attained enlightenment. In such cases the settlement that gathers round the site of the numinous occurrence may never develop beyond its original form, which will be an array of hostels for housing pilgrims—and pilgrims are, by definition, a floating population, not a permanent one.

Olympia, which shared with Delphi the role of serving as the Hellenic World's international religious and cultural centre, was the locale of a quadrennial gathering which, like the annual gathering at Mecca, was made practicable in an anarchic society by the observance of a festival-time truce under the auspices of the local tutelary gods and goddesses. The festival at Olympia was celebrated once in every four years, with only a few lapses, over a period of more than eleven centuries running from at least as early as the year 776 B.C. to the year A.D. 393. Yet the permanent population at Olympia never grew beyond the limits of a skeleton staff of priests and caretakers. On the other hand, Delphi was already a city-state, though a politically insignificant one, before its oracle and its festival gave it its eminent international status; and the Delphians had to pay for this status by having to let the control of their oracle and their festival be taken out of their hands by an international body—the Amphictyonic League—which originally represented twenty-four of the peoples of Central and North-Eastern Greece and which eventually came to represent all of the most important Hellenic states to the east of the Straits of Otranto.

Mecca, like Delphi, was a city-state which, in becoming a holy city, rose to a religious eminence that was out of scale with its political and economic importance. The Meccans, however, have been more successful than the Delphians were in keeping the control over their shrine and their pilgrimage in their own hands. They did not suffer the Delphians' ironical fate till the annexation of the Hijaz to Saʿudi Arabia in 1926.

What were the sets of monumental buildings constructed by the Maya in Northern Guatemala and in Yucatán? Were they counterparts of Olympia or counterparts of Delphi and Mecca? On this question there is no consensus among the archaeologists and no written record to give the answer.

The location at Bodh Gaya of the tree under whose shade the Buddha attained enlightenment was perhaps fortuitous, but the Buddha's subsequent choice of the Deer Park at Sarnath as a frequent locale for his preaching may have been determined by the previous history of Sarnath and its neighbourhood. The Deer Park was a sanctuary for wild animals because it was already consecrated ground before it acquired its sanctity for the Buddhist World from the Buddha's practice of preaching there; and, on this analogy, we may guess that Loreto, the Laurel grove in the Italian Marche, had likewise been consecrated ground, and that the Casa Santa had been the shrine of an indwelling pre-Christian *genius loci*, before the Casa was identified with the Virgin Mary's house in Nazareth and was deemed to have been deposited in the laurel grove by the hands of angels.

We have next to ask ourselves why the Buddha should have picked out Sarnath, in particular, from among all the consecrated sites that were scattered over the vast plain of Hindustan. We may guess that the determining consideration in the Buddha's mind was that a preacher at Sarnath would have a good chance of attracting a large audience. This audience would be within reach because Sarnath is within a short walking-distance of Benares, and, before the Buddha repaired to Sarnath, Benares had become what it is today: the principal holy city, and the most highly frequented pilgrimage-resort, in the whole of India. This was not, however, the earliest chapter in the history of Benares. Before it had become a pre-eminent holy city, Benares had been the political capital of a petty state, the Kingdom of Kasi. Before the Buddha's day this little kingdom had lost its identity through being swallowed up by the expanding Kingdom of Kosala. By then the political chapter of Benares' history was already over; the subsequent religious chapter had already begun, and this brilliant religious chapter has eclipsed the previous obscure political one.

Benares is one of a number of ex-capital cities that have made their fortunes as holy cities after they have lost their original political function. Other cities whose history has followed this course are Yathrib (Medina), Canterbury, Lalibela, Rome, and Jerusalem.

Yathrib was, as has already been noted, the political capital of the original Islamic state for hardly longer than a third of a century, but it has been a holy city for more than thirteen centuries already, and it will retain the exalted status of being one of the two Haramayn for as long as Islam continues to be one of the World's principal living religions.

Canterbury is today the see of the Primate of All England because in A.D. 597 it was the capital of the Kingdom of Kent. This Jutish kingdom was one of the smallest of the barbarian successor-states of the Roman Empire in Britain, but it was also the nearest of them to the Straits of Dover and the one that had the closest political and cultural connections with the continental kingdom of the Franks; and for this reason the Roman Christian missionary Augustine and his companions made for Canterbury, where King Aethelberht of Kent and his Christian Frankish wife Bertha held their court. The Kingdom of Kent lost its separate political identity before the end of the eighth century through being merged in the Kingdom of Mercia; and Mercia, after being partitioned between the Danish invaders of Britain and the Kingdom of Wessex, was eventually merged, in its turn, in the

Kingdom of England into which the Kingdom of Wessex grew. But, through all these political changes, Canterbury continued to be the ecclesiastical capital of England in virtue of its once having been the political capital of Kent.

In Ethiopia today the village of Lalibela is visited, not by pilgrims, but by tourists. The attraction there is the set of churches hewn out of the living rock; and the reason why so much labour and art was lavished on Lalibela is that this village was the capital of Ethiopia from 1137 to 1270.

Rome is a holy city for Roman Catholic Christians today because the Apostles Peter and Paul are believed to have died and to have been buried there. The two Apostles were drawn to Rome by the same consideration that drew the Roman missionary Augustine to Canterbury: it was the political capital of the state whose population they aspired to convert. Indeed, for the Apostles, Rome was the capital of the Empire whose subjects the Apostles were. In their day, Judaea, Galilee, Antioch, and Tarsus all lay within the Roman Empire's frontiers. Thus Rome is a holy city today thanks, ultimately, to the military and political achievements of a series of Roman soldiers and statesmen who had transformed a small Italian city-state into the capital of the whole Mediterranean World in the course of the four centuries ending at the dates at which Peter and Paul arrived there.

The political first chapter of Rome's history is at least on a par with the ecclesiastical second chapter in point of historical importance. On the other hand, Jerusalem's history has been like Yathrib's (Medina's) and like Canterbury's. Jerusalem has become immeasurably more important as a Jewish, Christian, and Muslim holy city than it was either in its first political role as a Canaanite city-state or in its second political role as the capital of the little Kingdom of Judah which was liquidated in 587 B.C. by the Babylonian empire-builder Nebuchadnezzar. All the same, Jerusalem would not be a holy city now if it had not been the capital of Judah for about four centuries ending in 587 B.C.

Why is Jerusalem a holy city for Muslims today? Because it was a holy city for the Prophet Muhammad; and it was holy for him because of its long-since-established holiness for Christians and Jews—'the People of the Book' who enjoyed religious prestige in Muhammad's eyes in virtue of their having been previous recipients of divine revelation. This is why Muhammad originally instructed his followers to face towards Jerusalem when they were saying their prayers, and it is also why, in his mind, Jerusalem was the place from which he ascended to Heaven and to which he re-descended on 'the Night of Power'.

Why is Jerusalem a holy city for Christians today? Because it was a holy city for Jesus. It was holy for him because he was an orthodox Jew, and he was observing the Jewish Law, as this stood in his day, when he went from his native Galilee to Jerusalem to celebrate the Passover there in the year in which he was crucified and was buried outside Jerusalem's city-wall.

Why is Jerusalem a holy city for Jews? Because King Josiah of Judah (*circa* 640–610 B.C.) centralized in Jerusalem all acts of worship in his kingdom and put all other places of worship there out of commission. Why did Josiah carry out this act of cultural synoecism (to use an Hellenic term of constitutional art)? Because Jerusalem was the capital city of the Kingdom of Judah in Josiah's day. Why was Jerusalem the capital of Judah? Because, at an early date in the tenth century B.C., David had conquered and annexed the Canaanite city-state of Jerusalem and had made this city the capital of his kingdom, which included not only Judah but Israel. After the irruption of the Israelites and Judahites into Palestine *circa* 1200 B.C., this Canaanite city-state had maintained its independence for about two hundred years in between the Israelite invaders to the north of it and the Judahite invaders to the south.

It will be seen that the holiness of Jerusalem is paradoxical. It was the last piece of Canaanite territory to be acquired by the Judahite worshippers of Yahweh, yet it became the only place in Judah where the worship of Yahweh was allowed, and it acquired this cultural monopoly because, after its annexation to Judah, it had been made the capital of the Judahite state.

Thus a number of ex-capitals have become holy cities after having lost their previous political status, and in some of these cases the religious consolation-prize has been more splendid than the city's former political role. There have also been several cases in which an empire that has disintegrated has left some vestiges in the shape of temple-states.

In Egypt after the expiry of the New Empire and the infiltration of Libyan barbarians in the tenth century B.C., the only enclaves of Egyptian territory that certainly remained free from occupation by the new intrusive Libyan military caste were four temple-states that were centred respectively on the shrines of Amon-Re at Thebes, Ptah at Memphis, Re at Heliopolis, and Horus at Letopolis. It seems unlikely to have been just a coincidence that the three first-named of these four cities had been political capitals of Egypt previously at one time or another.

Similarly the Hittite Empire, which was overwhelmed by the Phrygian Völkerwanderung *circa* 1200 B.C., left vestiges, which still survived in Augustus' day, in the shape of two temple-states, both named Comana, one in Pontic Cappadocia and the other in Inland Cappadocia, which are described by the Anatolian geographer Strabo of Amaseia. The cities bearing the Greek name Hierapolis or Hieropolis, which are to be found here and there on the post-Alexandrine map of Anatolia and Northern Syria, must once have been temple-states likewise, even if some of them were eventually transformed into secular city-states by Greek and Roman imperial propagators of the city-state form of local political organization.

In the Western World the Roman Empire of the German Nation disintegrated even more gradually than the Egyptian New Empire. The process of disintegration here took more than half a millennium, running from the collapse of imperial authority in the thirteenth century to the juridical dissolution of the Empire on 6 August 1806. A number of the fragments into which the Empire fell apart took the constitutional form of prince-bishoprics, and these survived till those of them that lay on the left bank of the Rhine were annexed by Revolutionary and Napoleonic France and till the more extensive ecclesiastical states on the right bank were annexed by their secular neighbours, in pursuance of the *Reichsdeputationshauptschluss* of 1803, to compensate them for left-bank territories of their own which France had also annexed.

My list of these prince-bishoprics begins with the three—Köln, Mainz, and Trier—whose prince-bishops had the status of electors of the Emperor—and the list also includes Liège, Münster, Osnabrück, Paderborn, Hildesheim, Fulda, Bamberg, Würzburg, Passau, Eichstett, Salzburg, and Trent. I should be surprised if this list of mine proved to be complete.

This proliferation of ecclesiastical principalities in the disintegrating Roman Empire of the German People is what was to be expected on the precedent of the sequel to the disintegration of the New Empire of Egypt. It is, however, surprising to find an ecclesiastical principality making its appearance in a more closely knit medieval Western state, the Kingdom of England.

From the date of the Norman conquest of England onwards, the English royal crown's power was waxing while the German imperial crown's power was waning. Yet the English crown delegated the military defence of England's northern border, over against Scotland, to the bishop of Durham; in return for the performance of this military service, the Palatinate of Durham was granted a considerable measure of administrative and jurisdictional autonomy; and some relics of this autonomy survived till the last of them were extinguished by the passage of the Municipal Reform Act of 1835. The emblem on the bishop of Durham's seal is still an armour-plated knight galloping into action on his charger; and the choice of this particular see to serve as the Kingdom's northern march was judicious. The City of Durham stands far enough back from the Border to be a well-placed base for defence in depth against Scottish raiders. Durham Cathedral crowns a hill which falls steeply to the River Wear. Like Chittor in Rajasthan and Machu Picchu in Peru, Durham is embraced by its river on three sides; and on the fourth side, where Nature has not provided a moat, the cathedral is shielded by the castle. Thus Durham was the Palatinate's virtually inevitable location, and the Palatinate's privileges were the virtually inevitable reward for its services.

An example of a secular capital giving birth to a holy city is to be found in Japan. The ancient city of Nara, which was the political capital of the Japanese Empire from A.D. 710 to A.D. 784, has been deserted ever since, in the latter year, the capital was transferred to Kyoto. In recent years this ancient city of Nara, whose site fortunately lies in what is now open country, has been partially excavated by the archaeologists. During ancient Nara's brief spell of existence as the capital, a number of religious foundations were planted, outside the city's bounds, at the foot and on the slopes and in the recesses of the nearest hills. The most famous of them are the Kasuga Shinto shrine and the Todaiji Buddhist temple with its gigantic statue of the Buddha. When the city of Nara was abandoned and was allowed to revert into rice-paddies, the shrines and temples that Nara had called into existence in its neighbourhood continued to be maintained and to be frequented by pilgrims and latterly by tourists as well, and a modern city of Nara has sprung up round these religious vestiges of the old city. Between the old city and the new city, the shrines and temples are the historical link.

I have hazarded the guess that the Sumerian city-states had been temple-states originally, and the evidence presented by the histories of Pharaonic Egypt, the Kingdom of Judah, the Roman Empire, and the medieval Western Roman Empire of the German People shows that political capitals may turn into holy cities and that disintegrating empires may leave vestiges in the form of temple-states. The history of Nara shows that religious foundations that are legacies of a defunct capital city may generate a new secular city; and history can take a still longer series of twists and turns than this.

After the City of Rome had ceased to be the capital of its own empire, it became one of that empire's outlying provincial cities; in the medieval age of Western history it became one of the city-states of Central Italy; in and after the fifteenth century it became a prince-bishopric ruling over a miniature empire stretching across Peninsular Italy from sea to sea; since 1870 Rome, except for an enclave round St. Peter's and the Vatican, has been the secular capital of an Italian national state; since the Lateran Agreements of 1929 between the Holy See and the government of the Italian state, the Vatican enclave has become a temple-state of the same type as the two Comanas and as the temple-states of Egypt under Libyan occupation and of Germany during the disintegration of the Roman Empire of the German People.

The history of the City of Jerusalem since the liquidation of the Kingdom of Judah has been as kaleidoscopic as the history of Rome since the disintegration of the Roman Empire. When, in 538 B.C., the Babylonian Empire was liquidated in its turn by the Persians, Jerusalem became a non-sovereign temple-state, and it retained this status under the successive Persian, Ptolemaic, and Seleucid regimes till the second quarter of the second century B.C. A Hellenizing party among the Judaean Jews then attempted to transform the Jerusalem temple-state into a city-state on the Hellenic pattern. This led to a domestic Judaean Jewish conflict between Hellenizers and conservatives, and to a consequent collision between conservative Jewish religious and political nationalists and the Seleucid Imperial Government. The break-up of the Seleucid Empire enabled the Hasmonaean leaders of the Jewish nationalist movement to turn the Jerusalem temple-state into a Palestinian Jewish miniature empire of the kind that Pope Martin V and his successors carved out in Central Italy in and after the fifteenth century of the Christian Era. The Hasmonaean Empire was cut back to the dimensions of its nucleus, the Jerusalem temple-state, by the intervention of the Roman war-lord Pompey in 63 B.C. The sequel was a head-on collision between the Palestinian Jewish community and the Roman Empire; the destruction of Jerusalem by the Romans in A.D. 70; the foundation, on the vacant site, of a Graeco-Roman city, Aelia Capitolina; and the eviction of the Jews from all parts of Palestine except Galilee.

At the moment of writing, in October 1969, a new Jerusalem, outside Aelia Capitolina's western wall, was the capital of the post-Second-World-War state of Israel, while the Old City—which contains the Jewish, Christian, and Muslim holy places—was a piece of Jordanian territory under the Israelis' military occupation. Since 1929 it has looked as if the relations between the Vatican City, the rest of the City of Rome, and the Italian national state have become stabilized; but in 1969 the future of the two parts of the City of Jerusalem was still unpredictable.

9: Mechanized Cities

I₅ the increase in the size of cities in the course of history is presented visually in the form of a curve, this curve will be found to have the same configuration as a curve presenting the increase in the potency of technology. In each of these two curves the first stretch is by far the longest so far, and this long stretch is almost horizontal. If it has a gradient, this is hardly perceptible. In both cases, again, the second stretch of the curve contrasts dramatically with the first stretch. The curve, which has been horizontal for so long, suddenly takes a sharp turn upward. Its ascent is not continuous; it mounts in a series of rises, separated from each other by intervening periods of relative stagnation; but each successive upward thrust surpasses its predecessor, and, if this second half of the curve is smoothed out, its adjusted shape is an upward movement of increasing steepness. In this second half of the curve the size of cities is growing in a geometrical progression, and so is the acceleration of this explosive growth's pace.

Thus the respective configurations of the two curves are strikingly similar, but their respective time-scales are, of course, utterly different. The curve of the increase in the potency of technology is coeval with humanity itself. The duration of its horizontal first stretch is perhaps as long as 1,000,000 years, and the duration of the second ascending stretch perhaps as long as 30,000 years. The corresponding time-spans in the curve presenting the increase in the size of cities are about 5,000 years and 200 years respectively. This curve is coeval, not with humanity, but only with civilization.

The first million years of mankind's history do not enter into the urban curve at all; nor does the Upper Palaeolithic part—which is by far the longest part of the latest 30,000 years. Even the Neolithic Age, which dawned, on the longest reckoning, not more than about 10,000 years ago, is represented—at least in the present state of our archaeologists' knowledge—by only two cities, Jericho and Lepenski Vir. In spite of the surprising discovery, at Lepenski Vir, of a contemporary and counterpart of Jericho in Jugoslavia, it looks as if, in the Neolithic Age, cities were very exceptional rarities. The characteristic form of human settlement in the Neolithic Age was the agricultural village community; and in this there was not the division of labour—characteristic of urbanized societies—between artisans and traders working in the built-up areas and peasants—at the start, perhaps mostly peasant women—working in the fields. The true beginning of the urban curve is contemporaneous with the third spurt in the ascending second half of the curve of technological advance, not with the first spurt that begins with the Upper Palaeolithic refinement of stone-chipping, and not with the second spurt, which begins with the Neolithic Age's achievements of producing ground-stone tools, inventing the arts of agriculture and weaving, and adding the domestication of a number of animals to the previous domestication of the dog.

The urban curve starts at the time of the invention of metallurgy, of water-control for drainage and irrigation, and of the art of writing. With the exception of Jericho and Lepenski Vir, the oldest of the rest of the World's so far known cities were created not more than about 5,000 years ago; and, for far the greater part of these latest 5,000 years, the curve of the increase in the size of cities is as horizontal as the curve of the increase in the potency of technology during the first million years of mankind's existence. Goethe's Weimar was the same kind of city as Abraham's Ur or, indeed, as the lowest stratum of the *tell* at Jericho. These three cities resembled each other not only in size but in structure and—what is more important—in the kind of life that was lived by their inhabitants. Indeed, all the cities examined in previous chapters of this book except for capital cities—and these have been as exceptional as Jericho and Lepenski Vir—were variations on the original type. It is only within the last 200 years that a new type of city—the mechanized city—has sprung up: a type that differs from all its predecessors, capital cities included.

The differences between the mechanized cities that are coeval

with the Industrial Revolution and all the cities of earlier types
are differences of degree, not of kind, though these differences of
degree are so great as virtually to amount to differences of kind in
effect.

For instance, the mechanized cities have not been the first urban
mushroom growths. Some of the capital cities that have been
called into existence in the past by a political fiat have been created
still more rapidly. Even in our day Brasilia—a capital conjured up
out of the virgin wilderness—has outstripped the industrial and
commercial titan São Paulo in the speed of its growth. But
Brasilia, Alexandria, Constantinople, and Ch'ang-an have been
rare *tours de force*, whereas São Paolo is not unique; the modern
mechanized titanic cities are legion.

One of the salient features of the mechanized cities is that they
are hives of manufacturing industry and marts of trade; but it has
been noted in this book, at the outset, that manufacture and trade
are characteristic activities of all cities—and necessarily so, if a
city is correctly defined as being an area which cannot, within its
own limits, produce sufficient food to feed its inhabitants, and
which must therefore produce other things—things that food-
producers will be willing to accept in exchange for their surplus
food-production, supposing that they do produce a surplus. It has
been noted that capital cities, which might seem, at first sight, to
be parasitic, actually export services in exchange for their imports
of food. It has also been noted that holy cities, which at first sight
might seem to be uneconomic, actually make their living from
the pilgrim traffic, and that pilgrims are in many cases traders as
well. The economic aspect of the life of all holy cities is illustrated
particularly clearly in the classical case of Mecca. The capacity of
Mecca's home territory for producing food is minimal. Mecca
has always had to make its living by serving as a mart for an
extensive region beyond its own bounds; and, since the date of
our earliest records of Meccan life—records which antedate the
Prophet Muhammad's lifetime—Mecca's function as an annual
pilgrimage-resort has been an indispensable support for the annual
fair that is held in Mecca during the pilgrimage-season.

Thus trade and industry, which are one of the salient features of mechanized cities, are not peculiar features of cities of this new type, and mechanization itself is not a peculiar feature of them either, though the role of mechanization in their life is so dominant as to justify the use of this word as a descriptive label for them. Mechanization may be defined as a harnessing by human beings, to serve human purposes, of the physical forces of inanimate nature, in contrast to the employment of the muscle-power of human beings and of domesticated animals. If mechanization is defined in these terms—and this definition is surely correct—it is coeval with the third spurt in technology's advance, the spurt which began at the dawn of civilization about 5,000 years ago. One of the inventions that were made at this date was the harnessing of wind-power to propel boats by catching the wind in sails. At least 1,300 years ago, wind-power began to be applied to the new purpose of driving mills; and windmills, originally devised for grinding corn, had come, before the outbreak of the Industrial Revolution, to be used in Holland for the different purpose of pumping up water. The harnessing of water-power for driving mills was invented more than 2,000 years ago, and—again before the outbreak of the Industrial Revolution in the North of England and on Clydeside—water-power had already been turned to account for mechanizing the iron industry in Sussex. The last substantial product of the Wealden iron industry was the ring of iron railings round Saint Paul's Cathedral in London which was forged when the Cathedral was re-built after the Great Fire of 1666; but the Sussex 'hammer ponds' still retain their name after having been out of action by now for about a quarter of a millennium. This name is evidence that machinery driven by water-power antedates the Industrial Revolution; and water-power was the mechanical power that was used in the Industrial Revolution's first phase.

The new departure that justifies the term 'Industrial Revolution' was neither the invention of the harnessing of water-power nor the use of water-power in place of handicraft (which is, of course, the literal meaning of the word 'manufacture'). It was the sudden great increase in the scale of the use of water-power for industrial production; the extension of the range of industries in which water-power was used (notably the application of the use of it to the textile industry); and the subsequent rapid supplementation of water-power—and its replacement for most purposes except the generation of electricity—by the successive harnessing of coal, steam, coal gas, mineral oil, natural gas, and nuclear energy, either for direct use or for indirect use in, for example, the generation of electricity. In the light of the accelerating increase in the number of the sources of energy that had been harnessed within the immediately preceding 200 years, it seemed in 1969 to be improbable that the harnessing of nuclear energy would be the last of Man's victories (this latest one has been a pyrrhic victory) in Man's progressive conquest and domination of his natural environment.

This progressive harnessing of natural forces after the outbreak of the Industrial Revolution opened the way for an increase in the size of cities—and this to an extent that is limited only by the limits of the habitable portions of the Earth's land-surface. For the first five thousand years of the history of cities, their size had been restricted by two features. One of these was the need for, and the practicability of, protecting a city by surrounding it with static fortifications. The other factor was the shortness of the distance that could be traversed twice in one day by urban workers going to and fro between their homes and their work-places (supposing that the home and the work-place were not housed in the same building). The great majority of urban workers were pedestrians, and there was only a small privileged affluent minority that could afford to own or hire a horse or donkey to ride.

The circuit of curtain-walls, reinforced at intervals by towers, by which cities had been defended effectively till the turn of the fifteenth and sixteenth centuries of the Christian Era, was made ineffective by the invention of explosives. However, the traditional practice of surrounding a city with static fortifications died hard. Walls built of stone or kiln-baked brick or sun-dried brick were replaced by earthworks as a retort to cannon-balls and, later, to shells. The construction of the ramparts of Paris in the years 1840–4—mentioned at an early point in this book[1]—was the last

[1] On p. 13.

major work of this kind; and those nineteenth-century ramparts did not save Paris from falling in 1871 and would not have saved her from falling again in 1940, supposing that they had not been levelled, as they had been, after the end of the First World War. The invention of aeroplanes capable of dropping bombs, and the further invention of nuclear bombs, culminating in hydrogen bombs, reduced *ad absurdum* the time-honoured device of trying to protect a city by surrounding it with a ring of fortifications on the ground. But the newfangled mechanized cities had already broken out of their antique walls and ramparts before the invention of bombing from the air.

The second age-old limitation on the growth of the size of cities—namely the shortness of the distance traversable on foot or on the hoof—was swept away by the invention, not of bombing-planes, but of mechanized means of locomotion for peaceful economic purposes. In this branch of mechanization the break-through was achieved by the harnessing of steam-power for driving locomotives hauling trains along rails. This invention of railways opened the way for revolutionary changes not only in the size of cities but in their lay-out and in their location.

Before the invention of railways the most convenient way of life for a commercial or an industrial worker had been to live, with his family, in the same building in which he did the work by which he earned his family's living. For trading on any appreciable scale, the shop with living-rooms above it had to be in a city, but one major industry—the textile industry—could be carried on, before it was mechanized, in cottages dispersed over the countryside, and it could be operated by families who combined spinning and weaving with agriculture and animal husbandry. The urban worker was able, as a second-best alternative, to do his work in a shop or workshop that was ten or fifteen minutes' distance away from his home if he made the journey on foot or on donkey-back. The maximum possible distance between home and place of work was increased, suddenly and greatly, by the invention of vehicles running on rails: first trains drawn by steam-driven locomotives along a specially constructed 'permanent way', and then trams running on rails laid in a city's

streets. The original horse-drawn trams were eventually superseded by electricity-powered trams, and these by petrol-powered
omnibuses liberated from rails.

One effect, on the lay-out of a city, of this revolution in the
means of conveyance was to articulate the city into separate
areas—residential, commercial, and industrial—and, in the process,
to enlarge the area of the city out of proportion to the increase in
the size of its population. In pre-Industrial-Revolution cities the
population had been congested by the necessity of confining the
city within a circuit of walls and by the limitation of the means of
locomotion to animate muscle-power embodied in legs, feet, and
hooves.

In the history of the evolution of cities so far, the peak of
density has been reached in the Phoenician cities that were perched
on islets and peninsulas in the last millennium B.C. The average
density of population at night-time in the conurbation which
today sprawls over the North-Eastern United States, from Boston,
Mass., to Washington, D.C., inclusive, is much lower than the
density at all hours of night and day in ninth-century-B.C. Tyre
or fifteenth–century-A.D. Florence or eighteenth–century-A.D.
Frankfurt-am-Main. In the Boston–New York–Philadelphia–
Washington conurbation today, by far the greater part of the area
is suburban or recreational and very many of the inhabitants are
commuters. An aeroplane-passenger's-eye view, as the viewer
soars over this megalopolis, will give him the illusion that the
greater part of it is open country, though, if he then traverses the
same area on mechanized wheels, he will find that it is not
genuinely rural, considering that it is being used now, not for the
raising of crops or of livestock, but for the suburban housing and
recreation of people who earn their living in the built-up industrial and commercial patches of this megalopolis's domain.

In this particular conurbation the percentage of the population
that spends its nights and its week-ends in suburbia and commutes
between home and work-place twice a day on working days is
probably greater than in any other mechanized megalopolis so far,
though, in terms of absolute figures, New York City's host of
commuters is outnumbered by Tokyo's. However, it is probable

that, in terms of percentages, commuting is at its maximum today in the Boston–New York–Washington megalopolis taken as a whole. This is probable because the average wealth of the population is greater today in this conurbation than it is in any other. But there has been a tendency for an increasing percentage of urban workers to become suburbanites and commuters in all mechanized cities since the date when the mechanization of the means of conveyance first made it possible for some of their inhabitants—of course, the richest of them—to live at far more than walking or riding distance away from their work-place and to spend their holidays far away from their city—perhaps abroad, if they have been able to afford this.

These facts bring out the truth that to think in terms of the average night-time density of the population of a present-day mechanized megalopolis is highly misleading. To arrive at the true picture, we have to think in terms of the distinction between working hours and recuperating hours and to be aware that, even in the most affluent present-day megalopolis, the section of the workers that can afford to sleep in suburbia and to commute is still a minority. In working hours the density of the population in suburbia sharply declines and the density in the commercial and industrial areas—in the commercial areas above all—rises sharply. The inhabitants of the Phoenician cities lived and worked in 'high-rise' buildings, but there is no record of there having been any buildings in, say, Carthage or Motya that were more than six storeys high. By present-day standards the Phoenician 'sky-scrapers' were dwarfs, not giants, and the density of population during working hours on present-day Manhattan Island is very much higher than it was at any time of day on fifth-century-B.C. Motya Island, though at night-time it is very much lower.

It has also to be borne in mind that, though the average night-time density of population in the total area of a present-day megalopolis is lower than it was at any time of day in Motya, Carthage, or Tyre, most of the World's present-day megalopolises contain a 'ghetto', or more 'ghettos' than one, in which the night-time density of the population is at least as high, and is perhaps even higher, than it ever was in any Phoenician city. The classification of the areas of a modern megalopolis as industrial, commercial, and residential is, indeed, as misleading, if carried no farther, as it is to think in terms of the night-time density alone. To see life in megalopolis as it really is, we have to dissect the term 'residential area' into two sections that present a painful contrast to each other. The widespread, thinly inhabited suburbia in which the richer minority of the urban workers spends its nights is at the opposite pole—both topographically and metaphorically—from the intra-urban ghetto.

The poorer part of the population of a megalopolis—and this part of it is still the majority—has to spend its nights near enough to the factories in which it earns its living in working hours to be able to travel to and fro at a cost that it can afford. It can no longer do its travelling on foot—the areas of the industrial patches of a megalopolis and of the adjacent ghettos have now become too large to be traversed on foot—but most industrial workers still have to sleep near enough to their place of work to be able to get to work and get home again by a cheap bus-ride. Commuting by suburban train is beyond the means of most industrial workers, even when the full fare for a single journey has been 'commuted' to the reduced rate charged for a season ticket. *A fortiori*, only an exceptionally highly skilled and therefore highly paid minority of the industrial workers can afford to buy and to maintain an automobile. So far, the United States and Canada are the only countries in which an appreciable minority of the industrial workers have become car-owners.

The mechanization of the means of conveyance has not only enlarged the areas of cities and changed their lay-out; it has also widened the possible choice of sites for their location. In the pre-mechanization age the means of conveyance on land were decisively inferior in terms of speed, of cost, and of convenience to water-borne transport. On land, horse-drawn or ox-drawn wagons and carriages were immobilized by mud in rainy seasons; and pack-horses, riders, and pedestrians could keep going only by keeping to high and dry ground as near as possible to the watersheds. By contrast, travel and transport by boat on navigable rivers or canals or by ship on the sea, except during the winter-time suspension of maritime navigation, was relatively swift and cheap. Consequently a commercial or industrial city had to be located on a navigable river or on a good natural maritime har-bour or, best of all, on a harbour at, or near, the mouth of a navigable river (the location of Salonica and of Marseilles).

Even after the Portuguese invention, in the fifteenth century of the Christian Era, of a new type of sailing-ship that could keep the sea for many months on end had turned the whole sea-surface of the planet into a medium for maritime traffic, the portion of the land-surface of the planet in which the transport of goods and of persons was practicable and profitable still remained confined to the immediate neighbourhood of maritime harbours and navigable rivers. As a result of the technological conquest of the Ocean, these strips of land had now become accessible, first to West-European mariners and then to others, over a world-wide range; but the accessible land-areas, though now scattered all round the globe, were still mere ribbons of territory adjacent to navigable waterways. The invention and rapid construction of railways in the nineteenth century suddenly opened up the water-ways' hinterlands.

Rail-transport made it practicable to stock and cultivate the interior of North America and of Southern South America and to convey the abundant additional supplies of foodstuffs from these new sources to the rapidly increasing populations of the rising mechanized cities. This nineteenth-century long-distance trade in foodstuffs had been anticipated in the last millennium B.C. The Phoenician and Greek industrial cities of that age im-ported grain by water—on the first stage of the voyage, down navigable rivers (Nile, Dniepr, Bug) and, on the second stage, by sea. Timber had also been floated down the Euphrates and the Tigris from the forests of Mount Amanus and of Urartu to supply the needs of the cities of Sumer, and down the Tiber from the forests of Umbria to provide building-material for the city of Rome; timber cut in the Lebanon had also been carried by sea from Byblos to Egypt; but, with these and other rare exceptions, the shipping of cheap and bulky goods was virtually confined to grain, 'the staff of life', so long as the size of ships was limited by the nature of the material—wood—of which they were built.

Most maritime cargoes, apart from shipments of grain, consisted of luxury goods that were neither bulky nor perishable. Phoenician and Greek mariners could, and no doubt would, have shipped the gold that was discovered in the nineteenth century in California and in Australia. They did ship tin, mined in Cornwall, to the Mediterranean to provide the rarer and costlier of the two components of bronze. They could not, however, have shipped meat from New Zealand or Argentina or coal from Newcastle or iron-ore from Venezuela. The long-distance transportation of cheap bulky goods and of perishable goods became possible only as a result of the nineteenth-century invention of iron-built ships and the twentieth-century development of refrigeration.

The substitution of metal for timber as the material for ship-building has removed the previous technological limitation of a ship's size. On 9 December 1967, I watched tankers of 200,000 tons' displacement being built, in steel sections weighing 200 tons each, at New Sakai in Japan. On 3 February 1963, in the newly rising industrial city of Ciudad Guayana on the Orinoco River in Venezuela, I looked down, from the air, on two mountains, each composed of almost pure iron. One of the two (the other was still intact) was being scraped off into railway trucks and being carried an eight-miles-long journey by train to be loaded, at the riverside, into ocean-going freighters which were to convey their cargoes to some port accessible for ocean-going vessels on the Delaware River. From there the ore would be carried again by train—a rather longer journey this time—to the Bethlehem steel-works in Pennsylvania. From the ground I then viewed, behind the two mountains of iron, a long row of great waterfalls that were being harnessed to yield an almost unlimited quantity of hydroelectric power, and, between waterfalls, iron mountains, and river-bank I saw a huge steel-works being constructed in order that Venezuela might use its own hydroelectric power and its own iron to make its own steel for itself, instead of continuing to export the iron to the United States and re-import from there the steel into which this Venezuelan iron was being turned by North American technology.

It is reasonable to plant a steel-mill, and to plan to build an industrial city, at a place where the raw material and the source of power are both close at hand. In Britain, in the first stage of the Industrial Revolution there, the mills had been planted first astride steeply falling streams and, in the second stage, next door to coal-fields; and, though raw cotton had to be imported from regions with a different climate, wool and iron-ore could be found in Britain close to the water-power and the coal. However, the efficiency of present-day means of transportation, even for conveying bulky materials, has made it possible for an industrial plant to be operated at a profit, even if all the essential materials are not to be found close at hand. On the wharf on the bank of the River Orinoco I saw great mounds of coke that had been unloaded from one ocean-going ship while the local iron was being loaded on to another. On inquiry I learnt that this coke had been imported from Britain. This was the nearest country that produced exactly the kind of coke that was required for fuelling the steel-furnaces at Ciudad Guayana, and it paid to bring just what was wanted, even from that distance away.

Thanks to the astonishing improvement in the size, speed, and cheapness of the means of conveyance within the last century and a half, it has now become practicable to site an industrial city anywhere in the World and to draw upon all the rest of the World for sources of raw material and for markets for finished products. Today São Paulo in Brazil is one of the most rapidly growing commercial and industrial cities in the World. Railways and roads have now enabled São Paulo to wrest the markets of coastal Brazil, including the coastal cities in the far north-east, from the West European manufacturing cities that used to supply coastal Brazil with manufactures by sea. But São Paulo's rise to economic eminence is as recent as it has been rapid. Standing, as it does, in broken country just on the inland side of the watershed between the Pacific coast of Brazil and the basin of the Paraná River, São Paulo was inhibited from playing its present role before the invention of railways and iron-built mechanically-driven ships and motor-trucks running on roads with the capacity to carry them.

Long-distance goods-traffic still has room for manœuvre, in spite of the great and constantly growing increase in its volume. The Ocean can still accommodate as many giant ships as mankind is likely to be able to build in the foreseeable future; and giant tankers, in contrast to freighters loading or unloading dry goods, do not need to dock at a quayside. They can imbibe and discharge their liquid cargoes through pipelines while the tankers themselves ride at anchor out in the open sea. However, long-distance passenger-traffic is becoming congested now that it has been decanted out of ships into planes. The quantity of air-passengers, the size of planes, and the length of runways are now increasing beyond the capacity of airports to accommodate them. Successive new airports threaten nowadays to become inadequate before their construction has been completed. When we turn from long-distance traffic between one megalopolis and another to internal traffic within any single metropolitan area, we find that, on this scale, goods-traffic, as well as passenger-traffic, has become self-obstructive to the point of being self-frustrating. In 1969 the traffic-problem is as serious a menace as the ghetto problem is to the mechanized city's future. The critical point—possibly a 'point of no return'—in the history of the internal traffic in a mechanized city was reached and passed, as we can now see in retrospect, when the railway age was succeeded by the automobile age.

A mechanized city cannot work—indeed, it cannot live—without being equipped with some efficient means for commuting. The affluent minority of the workers in a mechanized city has been commuting since the first appearance of cities of this new type; and the percentage of commuters in the total force of urban workers has been increasing and is going to go on increasing with the progressive spread of affluence from the summit of the social pyramid downwards—as affluence is going to spread, both because the progress of technology is increasing the total amount of human wealth, and because there is a growing demand for a more equitably widespread distribution of this total wealth that is becoming more abundant. In Tokyo, which is now the most populous city in the World, I was told, on good authority, in 1967 that 17,000,000 people were to be found inside the city limits during working hours, but that only 12,000,000 people spent the night within the same area. I was fascinated by the spectacle of trains, each about a quarter of a mile long and crammed full of passengers from end to end, travelling, almost head to tail, in both directions, along a railway that had eight parallel tracks.

Commuting, like manufacturing, commerce, and mechanization, is a characteristic feature of the megalopolises that have sprung into existence within the last two hundred years, but, like these other characteristics of theirs, commuting antedates the rise of the new type of human settlement in which it now plays a key part. (This historical fact has been noted at the beginning of the present book.) Commuting was invented at some date in the early centuries of the second millennium B.C. by some shepherds and cowherds who had been living on the arid fringes of lands that were well enough watered to have been turned successfully into fields and pastures. Beyond the fringes of these oases there stretched away vast regions that had never yet been turned to economic account by human beings because their aridity was too extreme to allow of their being used either for arable or for pasture by the employment of existing methods of agriculture and animal husbandry. At some date in the early second millennium B.C. some shepherds and herdsmen who had been making a living on the fringes of an oasis ventured on the experiment of cutting loose from their previous fixed base of economic operations and trying whether they could not find sufficient pasture for their flocks and herds out in the dry steppe.

These adventurers discovered that they could make a success of their new enterprise at the price of renouncing their previous sedentary life and keeping constantly on the move in a carefully-routed and precisely-timed recurrent annual migration from pasture to pasture. On the dry steppe the pasture is so thin during most of the year, except for a few lush weeks in the spring, that no tract can provide flocks and herds with sustenance for more than a brief spell at a time; but, by constantly moving on from one tract to another, according to the season, it is possible to find some sustenance, somewhere, all the year round.

It will be seen that nomadic pastoralism is a form of commuting, and that it is one that demands more skill and foresight and discipline than the present-day urban commuter is required to exercise. These two varieties of commuting differ, of course, in at least two ways: in the time-span of the cycle and in the relation between work-place and home. The urban commuter's cycle is a daily one; the pastoral nomad commuter's is an annual one. The urban commuter works in one place, sleeps in another, and commutes between the two. The pastoral commuter, like the pre-mechanization-age urban worker, works and lives in the same place, but, unlike him, he is not stationary. His work keeps him constantly on the move, and he does this mobile work by living in a tent that he is constantly shifting to a new camping-ground on fresh pastures.

In 1969, nomadic pastoralism is on the point of becoming an extinct form of economic activity, and, since it is the only way in which the surface of the more arid parts of the planet's land-areas can be coaxed into yielding a subsistence to human beings, these arid regions are now passing out of use again except where they overlie subterranean accumulations of mineral oil. The point of the comparison between this rapidly vanishing pastoral form of commuting and the rapidly increasing urban form of it is that the needy pastoral commuter has the room for manœuvre that his more affluent urban counterpart lacks. The Steppe lies as wide open as the Ocean, and, by comparison with the size of the fraction of the Earth's surface that is cultivable, the Steppe, as well as the Ocean, is vast. By contrast, the urban commuter's traffic-lanes are becoming more and more frustratingly congested.

So long as the urban commuter's means of conveyance was the suburban railway, the traffic was manageable. Railways have the merit of using a minimum amount of space for conveying a maximum amount of persons or goods, and they do not infest the city's streets. A city's internal railway-network, if it has one, runs underground. In the pre-automobile age an urban worker, commuting between his suburban dormitory and his urban office, circulated inside the city either by underground railway or by horse-drawn public transport (omnibus or cab), or else he walked.

Horse-drawn vehicles take up more space, lengthwise, than mechanized vehicles of the same size. The horse is an additional space-occupant to the vehicle that it is pulling. However, the horse makes up for this by limiting the number of horse-drawn vehicles that can be dumped on to a city's streets. A horse-drawn vehicle, unlike an automobile, cannot be parked unattended. Therefore the driver has a whole-time job, and this makes it impossible for him to be both driver and passenger at the same time, unless, in his role as passenger, he is content never to alight and so never to transact any business. The passenger who has business to transact must either walk or ride in a bus or hire a cab, *ad hoc*, if pressed for time, or, as a third alternative, he must own a private carriage; but owning a private horse-drawn carriage for use in professional work involves employing the full-time services of a coachman besides owning, feeding, and stabling a horse or a pair of horses; and this was an expense that few people were able to afford in the horse age.

A private carriage with a coachman was an unavoidable charge on the income that a private medical practitioner earned by going his rounds. My grandfather was a London doctor who was not a general practitioner but a specialist, and his consulting-room was in Savile Row while his house was in Wimbledon. He did not have to own a carriage because his patients, not he, did the travelling in town, but he did own more than one riding horse. He used to commute by the Metropolitan Railway between Savile Row and the foot of Wimbledon Hill; but he used to mount the hill in the evening and descend it in the morning on horseback, with a groom to fetch his horse and with several of his nine children, also on horseback, to meet him at Wimbledon Metropolitan Station when he came home from his work. As I have already mentioned, when I was a child the solicitor who lived opposite to us used to go to his office every day on horseback. I do not suppose that stabling a horse in the City for the inside of a working day was as difficult or as expensive then as parking a car there is now. Yet privately-owned riding-horses, as well as privately-owned carriage-horses, were comparatively rare because possessing them involved employing a groom or a coachman.

In the mechanized city of today, horses have vanished from the streets, and privately-owned automobiles far outnumber buses, taxis, and even commercial vehicles. More often than not the owner-driver is the sole passenger, though his car is built to carry five or six people, including the driver, and occupies a corresponding amount of road-space. In the operating of an owner-driven car, one of the two operating-expenses of a horse-drawn carriage is saved. The cost of feeding the horse with oats has been translated into the feeding of the car with petrol, but the coachman's wages have been eliminated. At the same time the level of real incomes has been rising. Taken together, the reduction of costs and the increase in incomes has brought the private ownership of an automobile within the reach of a very much larger number of people than were ever able to afford to own a horse-drawn carriage. The rapidly growing horde of car-owners commutes by car and travels by car inside the city in doing its business in working hours. Consequently, privately-owned automobiles are threatening to cancel, by a sheer plethora of numbers, the benefit of the mechanization of conveyances of which the automobile itself has now become the symbol in succession to the locomotive. This threat of a general paralysis of urban traffic is a threat to the life of the mechanized city itself; for, if mechanized traffic were to multiply to a quantity at which it would bring itself to a standstill, the mechanized city's heart would cease to beat.

Since I grew up as a child in London when the mechanized city was still in its railway age, and since I have lived on into its automobile age, I am in a position to draw a comparison between these two ages on the basis of first-hand experience. The mechanized city of the railway age was dirtier than its present successor. Factory chimneys and underground railways belched out smoke. I can remember the permanent blue-black fog in Gower Street station on the Underground, and the volumes of smoke, belched out by the locomotives, that used to well up through gratings into the street. The Underground had not yet been electrified, and factories had not been compelled to use smokeless fuel.

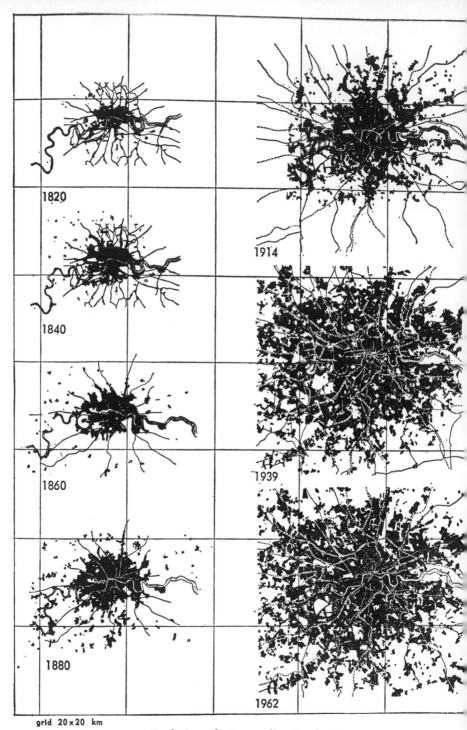

grid 20×20 km

Evolution of a Dynapolis - London

(*Taken from* CONSTANTINOS A. DOXIADIS, Ekistics - An Introduction to the Science of Human Settlemen *by permission of Hutchinson, London, and Oxford University Press Inc., New York.*)

London fogs would sometimes last for three days on end, with the gas lamps in the streets and in the houses alight all through what, in the stratosphere above, would have been daylight hours. In wet weather the streets were muddy; the mud was a noxious compound of soil and horse-dung; and the pedestrian who had to cross a street would thankfully give a penny to the crossing-sweeper who kept the crossing relatively clean. On the other hand, the worst that was likely to happen to a pedestrian crossing the street was to foul his or her boots; the pedestrian was not in any great danger of being run over by the horse-drawn traffic; its flow was so much thinner and slower than the flow of mechanized traffic is today in the self-same streets (self-same, with few exceptions, because, in a city where land-values are high and buildings are massive, the widening of a street is a difficult and costly undertaking). As for the pollution of the air, the smoke-smog has been eliminated to make way for the fumes given off by petrol-driven mechanized vehicles. Petrol fumes have now become a menace in all cities, and the degree of the menace is in proportion to the volume of the urban traffic. It is therefore greatest today on Manhattan Island and in Tokyo.

As between the anti-amenities of an archaic horse-and-coal megalopolis and an up-to-date petrol megalopolis, there is perhaps not much to choose, but the petrol megalopolis is a worse kind of city than its immediate predecessor in the vital—or lethal—point of the congestion of its traffic. However, apart from this crucial difference, the megalopolises that have sprung up in one country after another, beginning with Britain, in the course of the last 200 years have been suffering from the same self-inflicted evils throughout the two phases of their history up to the present date.

The mechanized cities have lost touch with the genuine countryside—the food-producing area, surrounding a city, with which most of the cities of the past were in intimate touch. Like the capital cities that were an exceptional kind of city in the pre-mechanization age, a mechanized city draws its food-supply from distant sources, with whose people its inhabitants are not in personal contact, and, in exchange, it sells its goods and services equally far afield. But, unlike both the pre-mechanization-age

capital city and the normal market-town of the past, the mechanized city is distressingly noisy, dirty, and, worst of all, soulless;
and, because it is soulless, it is unloved. The more highly mechanized the process of manufacture becomes, the more jejune the
spiritual satisfaction that it gives. The only countries in which it
is still 'economic' to produce goods that are works of art are
technologically backward countries in which labour is still cheap
enough for manufacture still to be literally handicraft. But these
'backward' countries are now 'developing'.

Everyone who makes money in the mechanized city uses the
money that he makes there to escape, as far and as frequently as he
can, from the inferno that is the source of his wealth. As soon as he
can afford it, he moves his home out from within the city-limits
into suburbia; he takes his holidays in what is still left of genuinely
rural country; and, when he retires, he withdraws to die on the
French Riviera or in Southern California or at Montreux or
Vevey. This is not surprising, considering that the mechanized
city is as repulsively ugly as the mass-produced manufactures that
it pours out. It is, however, a spiritual misfortune for a worker
to be alienated emotionally from the place in which he has done
his work, has earned his living, and had made his mark, for good
or for evil, on the history of the human race.

Moreover, this is a portentous reversal of the past relation
between a city and its citizens. Our surviving records of this
testify that, from the earliest date for which they provide evidence,
the normal feelings of a citizen towards his city have been pride
and love. Read the encomium of Athens that Thucydides has put
into Pericles' mouth in the Funeral Speech in honour of the
Athenians killed in the first campaigning season of the Atheno-
Peloponnesian War of 431–404 B.C. Recall the pride in his home-
town, Tarsus, that Saint Paul expresses in words that are attributed
to him in the Acts of the Apostles. Read Browning's poem, 'Up
in a Villa—Down in the City', in which this nineteenth-century
English poet enters, with convincing imaginativeness, into the
feelings of an impoverished Italian nobleman who has to econo-
mize by living in his country-house though he longs to be in a
house in the city square. Read Goethe's account, in *Wahrheit und*

Dichtung, of his childhood in Frankfurt-am-Main in the middle
years of the eighteenth century. Feel in your own heart the pain
that was felt by Thucydides and by Cicero and by Dante when
they were exiled, and by Machiavelli when he was rusticated.
Thucydides continued to love Athens and to pine for her, even
though he had a poor opinion of her democratic regime and
believed, with just cause, that he had been treated by her unjustly.
Dante's and Machiavelli's feelings for Florence were the same. In
every letter that Dante wrote after he had been exiled, he styled
himself '*exul immeritus*', but he continued to yearn to be repa-
triated nevertheless.

As for Cicero, he missed Rome even when he was away from
Rome, not under compulsion as an exile, but in one of his spells
of voluntary withdrawal to a nearby country-house, in order to
enjoy the peace and quiet that he needed for doing his literary
work. Cicero, like Thucydides, had a poor opinion of his city's
current political regime. He came from a country town; he had
thrown himself into law practice and conservative party politics
in the metropolis with a naïve belief in the probity of the decadent
Roman aristocracy of his day. He eventually became disillusioned
with his aristocratic fellow conservative politicians through a long
course of distressing experience, but he never became disillusioned
with Rome herself. This politically unedifying capital of the
Mediterranean World fascinated Cicero for the same reason that
Browning's imaginary nobleman was fascinated by his miniature
city. The boon that Cicero found in the City of Rome was a
stimulus that was exquisitely exhilarating. His expression of his
attachment to Rome is eloquent. 'The City, the City! Devote
yourself to her and live in her incomparable light. As a young man
I came to a conclusion from which I have never since wavered.
Absenting oneself in any circumstance spells eclipse and discredit
for any of us who have the capacity to add to Rome's glory by
our labours.'[1] In the next generation, Virgil called Rome 'the
loveliest thing in the World',[2] and manifestly he meant what he
said, with no reservations. Cicero's and Virgil's love for Rome is

---

[1] *Ad Familiares*, Book XI, Letter 12, § 2.
[2] Virgil, *Georgics*, II, 534.

the more impressive considering that each of them, like their fellow Roman citizen Saint Paul, had come originally from a small town of which he continued to be proud. Cicero loved his Arpinum and Virgil loved his Mantua; but each of them had a place in his heart for Rome as well. While the rare capital city was stimulating, the standard miniature city was cosy. Within the shelter of the city walls the artist and the scholar—Dürer in Nürnberg and Casaubon in Geneva—could work in peace and freedom, and these precious gifts won the beneficiary's heart for the city that bestowed them.

In painful contrast to these normal feelings of affection and devotion, the citizen of a present-day mechanized city is estranged from it, and this no less if he has made money inhumanly there than if he has been inhumanly exploited. This augurs ill for the mechanized city's future, and that is serious; for, in the age of mechanization, the future of the mechanized city is bound up with the future of mankind itself.

10: The Coming World-City

In the previous chapters of this book, glances have been taken at cities of a number of different types, but all the different types that made their appearance before the arrival of the mechanized type had one important feature in common. All of them were more or less static. The great majority of the cities that were created during the first 5,000 years of the history of the urban kind of settlement were on a small enough scale for pedestrians to be able to live and work in them conveniently, and, in this class, there is a recognizable resemblance between third-millennium-B.C. Ur and eighteenth-century-A.D. Weimar. Capital cities were exceptional in being both relatively rare and relatively large, but this class, too, remained static, on its own peculiar scale, after the first representatives of it had come into being. There is, for instance, a recognizable resemblance between Nebuchadnezzar's Babylon and Ch'ienlung's Peking, though they are separated in time by a span of twenty-three centuries.

The rise of the mechanized cities has brought with it the greatest change in the nature of cities that has yet overtaken them since they first came into being. Mechanized cities are not stationary; they are dynamically on the move, and in 1969 it is already evident that they are changing into a new type. They are coagulating into the megalopolises that are the subject of the immediately preceding chapter—a new phenomenon, of which the outstanding example in 1969 is the conurbation extending from Boston through New York, Philadelphia, and Baltimore to Washington, D.C., along the north-eastern seaboard of the United States. Meanwhile the megalopolises themselves are beginning to coalesce. In North America, for instance, the north-eastern-seaboard megalopolis and a Great-Lakes megalopolis are already stretching out tentacles towards each other, and the tips of these tentacles are beginning to intertwine. This development in North America is part of one that is world-wide. The megalopolises on all the continents are merging to form Ecumenopolis, a new type of city that can be represented by only one specimen, since Ecumenopolis is going, as its name proclaims, to encompass the land-surface of the globe with a single conurbation.

The open question is not whether Ecumenopolis is going to come into existence; it is whether its maker, mankind, is going to be its master or to be its victim. Are we going to succeed in making the inevitable Ecumenopolis a tolerable habitat for human beings? The answer to this question depends on whether mankind is going to take early enough and effective enough action to shape Ecumenopolis to satisfy human wishes and human needs, before Ecumenopolis has set hard, in a haphazard shape, as an irreversible accomplished fact. If we are to achieve this objective, we cannot afford to waste time. Within the last 30,000 years, human affairs have been getting up speed, and this acceleration has now reached a degree at which we find ourselves in constant danger of being overtaken by undesired and undesirable events. The happiness, and perhaps even the survival, of the human race is at stake in the policy—or lack of policy—of the living generation. The question is whether we are going to take action now to humanize the World-City in which our children and our children's children are going to have to live in any event, whether or not the conditions of life in Ecumenopolis are going to be endurable.

Human affairs are already being swept towards Ecumenopolis by two currents, both of which are strong and which are both flowing in the same direction. Between them, they make the coming of the World-City a certainty. One of these two currents is the present rapid growth of the World's population, especially among the economically backward and therefore indigent majority. The second current that is making for Ecumenopolis is the simultaneous migration from the countryside into the cities which is taking place in the 'developing' and the 'developed' countries alike.

The 'population explosion' that is now swelling the numbers of the poverty-stricken majority of mankind is due, as is well known, to their slowness in starting to limit, voluntarily, the number of births to offset the reduction in the death-rate—particularly in the rate of infant mortality—that has been achieved already by public health measures. In the 'developed' countries, in which the death-rate has been reduced to a still greater degree, the population has already been brought back into equilibrium by voluntary family planning, and a restoration of equilibrium by the same voluntary action is already within sight in Japan, where the population soared after the Meiji Revolution of 1868. Japan has transformed herself from a scientifically and technologically backward country into an advanced one in the course of the last century, so her approaching success in solving the population problem, too, in the 'developed' countries' way may be a portent and a turning-point for the rest of mankind. However, we cannot foresee when, or even whether, the backward majority is going to follow suit, and we therefore cannot predict the size of the planet's population in, say, the year 2000 or the year 2050.

Almost everything in human life is now accelerating, and it is therefore possible that the majority of mankind may follow the minority's example in adopting family planning unexpectedly quickly. However, the more backward that human beings are, the slower they are apt to be in making changes, and they are likely to be particularly slow in departing from traditional practice in one of the most intimate concerns of personal life. We have therefore to reckon with the certainty that there is going to be a very great increase in the World's population—and this in the largest, most backward, and poorest section of it—though we cannot estimate what the future figures are going to be.

The migration of the World's rural population into the cities, which is taking place in the 'developing' and the 'developed' countries alike, is happening, in the two kinds of country, for opposite reasons and is affecting opposite types of people. In 'developed' countries—in the State of Iowa, for example, in the United States—the application of science to agriculture and to animal husbandry has been enabling fewer hands to produce greater quantities of food, and this of better quality, per acre. This has made part of the rural population, formerly engaged in agriculture, superfluous; there has therefore been a competition for the prize of remaining in the farming business under the more lucrative but also more exacting new conditions; the more able, active, and enterprising farmers have been the winners; those who have failed to 'make the grade' from the old-style to the new-style method of farming have been forced off the land, and they have had nowhere to go except into the cities. On the other hand, in the backward countries, where the antiquated and relatively un-productive traditional methods of farming are dying hard, the people who are leaving the land for the city are the enterprising, though, as will appear, these are not in all cases also far-sighted. These enterprising rustics have realized that, in their traditional avocation on the land, they have no prospects under present conditions. Unfortunately they have no means of ascertaining in advance whether or not they have any better prospects in the city. They are migrating to the city on the reckoning, which is not invariably correct, that, at the worst, their prospects cannot be any darker there than they are in their native village.

Thus the populations of the cities are being augmented from three sources simultaneously: the population-explosion in the poorer and more backward part of their existing population; the excess of rural population created by the contemporaneous popu-lation-explosion in the corresponding section of society in the countryside; and the decrease in the numbers of the rural popula-tion for different reasons in countries of different types. In combination, these three movements are giving the population-explosion the form of an urban explosion. The population of the cities is growing at an even faster rate than the population of the World as a whole, because the population of the non-urban area of the habitable part of the Earth's land-surface is being siphoned off into the cities. Consequently the coming of the World-City is inevitable; but it also follows that the World-City is not going to cover the entire land-surface of the globe. It is going to be a World-City in the sense that all the existing local megalopolises are going to coalesce into one single world-encompassing city as a result of the expansion of their residential areas and of their industrial areas too.

In the aggregate, the coalescing mechanized cities' combined area, Ecumenopolis, is certainly going to be immensely larger than the aggregate area that was formerly occupied by the tiny, densely populated cities of the pre-Industrial-Revolution age. This immense coming increase in the absolute extent of the planet's urbanized area will be the product of two causes. In the first place there will be an increase in the total cubic content of the buildings. In the second place the average height of the buildings will be as low as, and possibly even lower than, it was in cities of the traditional type. On first thoughts, this may seem paradoxical, considering that the mechanization of cities has been accompanied by the construction of buildings of unprecedented height. It has, however, also been accompanied by the proliferation of residential suburbias consisting of low houses surrounded by gardens, and, in calculating the overall average height of buildings in the future Ecumenopolis, its villas and bungalows, as well as its 'skyscrapers', have to be taken into account.

A preview of the coming reduction in the average height of urban buildings has been given in a passage of a eulogy of the City of Rome, written by a second-century-A.D. Greek man of letters, Aelius Aristeides. In its original context, this passage is merely a rhetorical 'conceit', but the *jeu d'esprit* of eighteen centuries ago has become a sober reality of the present day. As Aelius Aristeides puts it,

Rome is not content with the extent of its built-up area, vast though this is. . . . Rome carries a whole pile of additional Romes, of equal extent, which it has hoisted up one above another. . . . If the city were to be spread out flat, so that the Romes which are now up aloft would be deposited on ground-level side by side with each other, I reckon that the remnant of Italy that is not already covered by Rome would be completely filled up. There would then be one continuous city extending [from the Tyrrhene Sea] to the Adriatic.[1]

This is, of course, hyperbole, yet it does serve a present-day purpose by giving some idea of the magnitude, in absolute figures, of the current expansion of the planet's urbanized area.

[1] Aelius Aristeides, *In Romam*, § 8.

In relative terms, on the other hand, Ecumenopolis, like the far smaller aggregate of the old-style tiny separate cities, will still cover no more than a small fraction of the planet's total land-surface.

As for the increase in the numbers of the planet's urban population, this is going to be enormous. Yet, compared with the population-density of the antique cities, the average density in Ecumenopolis will be notably lower, as it is already in each of the megalopolises that are now rushing towards each other to coalesce. The reason why the average density will be lower is because the increase in the planet's urbanized area is going to be greater, proportionately, than the increase in its urban population.

The ratio between the relative densities of the planet's urban population and of its rural population thus seems likely to remain much the same as before. The urban population will be more widely diffused on the average (though there will be glaring differences, on this point, within it, as between different income-groups). But, to offset this, the rural population will also be spread thinner.

On the other hand, in terms of absolute figures, the past distribution of population will have been reversed. From the date of the invention of agriculture at the dawn of the Neolithic Age until the outbreak of the Industrial Revolution about two hundred years ago, an overwhelming majority of the World's population was rural, and the townspeople were a small and exceptional minority. In the near future, on the other hand, the normal human being will be a townsman; all but a fraction of mankind will be living within the confines of a World-City that will occupy only a fraction of the planet's land-surface. The exceptional minority will be the inhabitants of cities and towns outside Ecumenopolis and the food-producers; and, while the food-producers will be a dwindling minority, they will be becoming progressively less exceptional in their way of life. They will be tending to become what the surviving farmers in Iowa were already in 1963. They will be becoming industrial workers employing the most up-to-date applications of science to technology—workers whose industry happens to be food-production and who therefore do their work in un-built-up areas. In other words, food-production will be urbanized. The World-City's pseudo-*rus in urbe*, suburbia, will be matched by a genuine *urbs in rure* in those patches of the great open spaces that human beings will continue to turn to economic account. In this future chapter of the story of urbanism the city—now no longer just London or just New York, but the World-City—will be 'going out of town', not to devastate the countryside, but to make it more productive than it has ever been before.

If we want to obtain a preview of this future demographic, economic, and social configuration of the World as a whole, we can find it in present-day Australia and Japan. At first thoughts it may seem strange to mention these two countries in the same breath; for they are thought of by many people as being antithetical to each other. We commonly picture Australia as being a huge country with almost unlimited reserves of unused space, and of Japan as being a tiny country in which every square yard is intensively cultivated or built up. Actually, in Japan, as well as in Australia, all but a small fraction of the population is crowded together on a fraction of the country's land-surface. Most of Australia's population lives in three large cities: Sydney, Melbourne, and Brisbane. Most of Japan's population lives in the megalopolis whose axis is the track of the super-express train between its terminals at Tokyo and at Ōsaka. The greater part of Japan consists of unused forest-clad mountains, while the greater part of Australia's vaster area consists of unused deserts and semi-deserts.

The proximate reason why, in both countries, these tracts are unused is that the cost of transforming them into economically productive areas would not bring in adequate returns. The ultimate reason is that the procurement of food—whether by gathering, hunting, fishing, agriculture, or animal husbandry—is now fast becoming one of mankind's minor economic occupations, instead of taking up all but a small margin of mankind's time and work, as it still did everywhere till about 200 years ago. In the 'developed' countries by now, the increase in productivity through the application of science to the technology of food-production has been so great that the major part of the energies of the people of these countries has now been liberated for application to non-food-producing activities.

The configuration of the coming World-City can perhaps be envisaged more clearly if we make a rapid global survey of it. There will, of course, still be other cities outside Ecumenopolis's limits, and, though these will all be dwarfed by Ecumenopolis, some of them will be large and populous in terms of absolute figures.

It has been noted already that the existing conurbation along the north-east coast of the United States has begun to coalesce with another conurbation that has been taking shape round the Great Lakes of North America. The Boston–Washington conurbation has been the first to take shape, not merely in the United States, but in the New World as a whole. In the coming World-City, however, this seems likely to be a less important component than the Great Lakes conurbation, and this for two reasons: the Great Lakes megalopolis will have greater room for manœuvre and it will have a more abundant supply of fresh water.

The Boston–Washington megalopolis's field for expansion is restricted by its location on a relatively narrow strip of lowland between the coast and the mountains (the Alleghanies and the Appalachians); the Great Lakes megalopolis has a virtually boundless field in the basins of the St. Lawrence and the Mississippi, which are spread out back to back with a hardly perceptible watershed in between. The Boston–Washington megalopolis has a water-supply, from the headwaters of the rivers descending from the mountains to the Atlantic, that would be ample by any ordinary standards of demand; but this particular megalopolis's demand for water is inordinate, and the separate urban authorities among whom its administration is divided are already competing with each other for the command of those waters, within their reach, that are still unappropriated. By contrast, the Great Lakes megalopolis has a virtually unlimited supply of fresh water in the Lakes themselves.

One of the many novel features of the mechanized city that has been on the move during the last 200 years is a huge increase in the quantity of fresh water consumed per day per head by comparison with the requirements of cities of all previous kinds. Amida (Diyarbakir) in the upper basin of the Tigris, the Acrocorinthus in Greece, and Cyrene in Libya each subsisted on a single spring from which the women of the city fetched the water in jars carried on their heads. Today, fresh water is needed in the home not only for drinking but also for baths, and the industrial use of water has made an enormous new demand on the supplies.

Already a time can be foreseen at which the water of every river in the World will have been impounded for human use before it has reached the sea, and this water will be discharged, after having been polluted, through sewers. Reservoirs of fresh water of unprecedented capacity will be created, as has been done already in one case in the 'New Territories' of Hong Kong, by sealing off inlets of the sea, pumping the salt water out of them, and then letting them fill up with fresh water from rainfall or from streams. However, giant natural fresh-water lakes, like those of North America, will continue to be the most copious, as well as the cheapest, sources of supply for a natural resource which is the principal necessity of life for any human settlement and is therefore the element that is likely to be the limiting factor in the growth of the components of the coming World-City, unless and until the advance of technology finds a way of converting salt water into fresh water, and then pumping it over long distances, at an economically acceptable cost. Meanwhile, conurbations in arid regions, such as Southern California, may have their growth checked through their finding themselves unable to increase their supply of natural fresh water beyond a certain volume.

The Caspian Sea, which is by far the largest lake in the world, is unfortunately salt. The largest fresh-water lake, Lake Superior, is less than one-fifth of the Caspian's size; Lake Victoria is only slightly smaller than Lake Superior, and, like its North American counterpart, it does not stand by itself but is one member of a chain. The African Great Lakes straddle the Equator, but they are perched on a plateau, and the altitude tempers the climate of the region round their shores. This region, therefore, seems destined eventually to come second only to the region round the North American Great Lakes in the competition for becoming the most

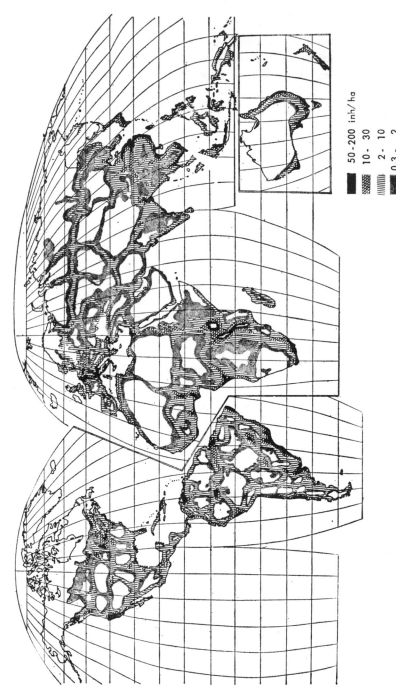

	50 - 200 inh/ha
	10 - 30
	2 - 10
	0.3 - 2

Ecumenopolis at the end of the twenty-first century

(Taken from CONSTANTINOS A. DOXIADIS, Ekistics - An Introduction to the Science of Human Settlements, *by permission of Hutchinson, London, and Oxford University Press Inc., New York.*)

populous component of the World-City. Ruanda-Urundi, on the eastern shore of Lake Tanganyika, is densely populated already.

These two groups of Great Lakes give us two definitely ascertained points in the configuration of the coming World-City. Can we forecast the rest of its shape? Its members will not, of course, be in unbroken contiguity with each other. This is impossible because the greater part of the planet's surface is covered by the sea, and, besides, the portion of the land-surface for which human beings have no use is increasing in extent, as has been noted already. The components of the World-City will be linked with each other by long-distance railways and highways and seaways and airways and telegraph and telephone lines, and radio communication between them will be conducted through the stratosphere.

How do we get from the North American Great Lakes megalopolis to the African Great Lakes megalopolis when we have made our merger of the Cleveland–Detroit conurbation with the Boston–Washington one? A mere ribbon of overland means of communication will connect this North-East North American double conurbation with a lesser one extending from the Bay Area of Central California southward to Los Angeles, and far longer sea-lanes and air-lanes will connect the North American components of Ecumenopolis with its Asian components: a Japanese megalopolis extending from Tokyo to Ōsaka; a coastal Chinese one round Shanghai and Hangchow; a larger inland Chinese one running north and south from Peking to Canton; and an Indo-Pakistani one running up the Ganges basin and then across the Panjab from Calcutta to Islamabad. There will be a single European component of the World-City which will extend westwards from the Donetz Basin through Upper Silesia, Saxony, and the Ruhr Basin to the Rhine at Düsseldorf.

At this point on the Rhine, the European conurbation will fork. One branch will run on westwards through Belgium and Northern France—the largest and the most populous nodule of the European megalopolis—and this branch will then swerve north-westwards up Britain to Glasgow. The other branch will run

up the Rhine and down the Po to the head of the Adriatic.
From there it will continue south-eastwards, skipping over the
Mediterranean and the White Nile *Sadd* by using Egypt as a
stepping-stone, to link up with the conurbation round the African
Great Lakes, while the north-western branch of the European
member of the World-City will connect with the North-East
North American branch via sea-lanes and air-lanes across the
Atlantic. The eastern end of the European conurbation is already
connected with the Peking–Canton conurbation in China by
railways and airways. It is fast coming to be connected with the
Indo-Pakistani conurbation by air and by road.

The most outlying component of the World-City will be the
South American one. This will start at Belem on the southernmost
branch of the estuary of the Amazon and will run southward from
there—netting the whole 'hump' of Brazil—through Brasilia,
São Paulo, Rio de Janeiro, Montevideo, and Buenos Aires and
thence westwards to Santiago de Chile.

This sketch of the future geographical configuration of the
World-City is, of course, only a provisional one; and, though
some of the points in it can already be predicted with assurance,
other predictions will, no doubt, fail to be borne out by the
actual course of the World-City's development, as this proceeds.
When we have allowed for these uncertainties, certain general
features of the coming World-City can nevertheless be descried
clearly. For instance, the World-City is certainly going to leap
over historic natural barriers and to sprawl across historic political
frontiers.

Ecumenopolis may not have occasion to 'abolish the Pyrenees'
—the feat of political engineering that Louis XIV fancied, mis-
takenly, that he had achieved. But Ecumenopolis is certainly going
to 'abolish' the Alps, the Rockies, the Alleghanies, and the Andes;
the Channel, the Atlantic, and the Pacific; and, *en passant*, the
Nilotic *Sadd*. It is also going, at Detroit, to spread across the
border between the United States and Canada. In its European
component it will bulldoze the electrified iron curtain by which
the Soviet Union is surrounded and insulated at the present day.
It will ignore the line of demarcation between the present Warsaw

Pact group and the present NATO group of European states; and the Franco-Belgian nodule of the European megalopolis has already, long since, abolished, for economic purposes, the frontier between France and the Habsburg Netherlands (present-day Belgium)—a frontier which Louis XIV did succeed in shifting, in France's favour, at the cost of a huge expenditure of blood and treasure.

A second predictable feature of Ecumenopolis is one that has been noted already. The average density of its population will be lower than the average in the walled cities of the past, and this average figure will be unrevealing and perhaps even misleading, because the actual degrees of density will differ widely, from district to district, in different kinds of built-up areas and at different times of day and night. This uneven distribution of the average population-density is a problem in itself, and it generates a second problem—the problem of the volume of commuter-traffic, twice a day, between dormitory and office or factory. It has already been noted that slums and traffic-jams are the two major blights of the local mechanized cities whose progressive merger is now bringing the World-City into being. In each of the still more or less separate megalopolises of the year 1969, these two evils are already as menacing as they are proving difficult to cure. They may become incurable and lethal if we allow them to be carried over into the future Ecumenopolis from the existing megalopolises that are destined to be Ecumenopolis's components.

The evil of traffic-congestion need not be enlarged upon, since it is a daily torment for everyone—pedestrian, public transport user, or owner-driver of an automobile—who lives and works, and therefore necessarily moves, in any of the World's present megalopolises. The scenes that can be witnessed at rush hours on the bridges connecting Manhattan Island with the mainland can also be witnessed in Istanbul on the Beyoğlu side of the Golden Horn in the steep and narrow streets running up from the water's edge to the Genoese Tower.

The evil of slums is perhaps less familiar, at first hand, to the privileged minority of the World's present urban population that has not yet been condemned to live in slums. The World's present-day slums—which the coming World-City is going to inherit—are of four different kinds. One kind is a 'ghetto' in the original residential area of the mechanized city before it began to hive off residential suburbs. The houses or tenement-towers in a ghetto may have been designed, from the start, for housing the poor, and therefore may have been built without the fittings that are necessities according to middle-class standards. Alternatively, this housing may have been built for, and been originally inhabited by, the rich, and have been occupied by the poor after the rich had moved out into new suburban residential areas. In either case, the housing in the ghetto is likely to be in poor material condition, to be overcrowded, and to be without modern plumbing in either good or bad repair—or at any rate without a sufficient amount of it to meet the needs of the number of inhabitants that this slum-housing now harbours. The third kind of slum is a shanty-town inserted in the interstices between the more opulent parts of the original heart of the city. The fourth kind is a shanty-town on the outskirts. The shacks composing a shanty-town are put together by squatters out of discarded rubbish: old boards, old pieces of corrugated iron, flattened-out petrol cans, or even cardboard in climates in which rain is rare or slight. A shanty-town is likely to have no sewers, no water-supply, and no street-lighting (it will have no proper streets).

In cities infested with slums of any or all of these four kinds there is a cold war—sometimes heating up into physical violence—between the slum-dwellers and the more well-to-do minority of the urban population. Like many wars in the conventional meaning of the word, this is a war for the possession of territory. Both within the original city-limits and on the expanding mechanized city's outskirts, the bourgeois are trying to keep the proletariat out of residential areas, whether urban or suburban, that have hitherto been preserves for middle-class families, while the proletarians are struggling desperately to find some kind of shelter, however sordid, unhealthy, and uncomfortable, for their families and themselves.

In this class-war in which the objectives are zones of residential housing, the proletarians have the advantage over the bourgeois.

Their plight is more desperate, and therefore they are more active, more determined, and more persistent, whereas the bourgeois will yield ground more readily because their greater resources give them a wider choice of options. If they are inhabitants of an urban residential area that is being invaded by proletarians, they can move out to a suburb, and, if the proletarians follow them there, they can move again to another suburb still farther away from the commercial and industrial quarters of the city in which rich and poor alike do their work and earn their incomes. The rich can afford to retreat, because they can afford to commute over distances that the proletarians cannot afford to travel.

Ghettos consisting of housing that was originally built for the poor or that has been evacuated by the rich are to be found in every mechanized city that is on the move. It is notorious that, in such cities, the inner residential area tends to be inhabited by families with lower and lower incomes, and therefore tends, *pari passu*, to become more and more distressingly dilapidated physically. The shanty-towns, urban and suburban, are not quite so widespread a phenomenon.

Rio de Janeiro and Carácas are classical examples of the city in which shanty-towns (in Rio these are called *favélas*) have been inserted in the interstices between opulent quarters. The landscape of Rio lends itself to this intermingling of slums and luxurious buildings at close quarters. The properly-built well-to-do part of Rio is broken up into sections strung along a series of bays that are separated from each other by mountains which fall steeply to the shore. At least one of these mountains, the famous Sugar Loaf, is too precipitous for it to be physically possible to perch human dwellings of any kind on its flanks. Others, which are too steep-sided to allow proper house-foundations, roads, sewers, and water-mains to be installed on them except at prohibitive cost, have been left vacant by the architects and builders and have therefore been seized upon by destitute squatters. The layout of the housing in Rio is, however, as unusual as the landscape is. The more usual location of the shanty-towns is not in the city's heart but on its outskirts, where the shanty-towns compete for space with the bourgeois suburbs. This is the lay-out at Brasilia, Brazil's new capital, at Buenos Aires and Rosario in Argentina, at Arequipa in South-Eastern Peru, and at Baghdad in 'Iraq.

The city lures the peasant, even in the increasingly rare cases in which the peasant has prospects in his native village but has none in the city to which he has migrated.

The most irrational example that I have seen at first hand is the drain of 'Iraqi peasants off the land into a ring of shanty-towns round Baghdad, because, in 'Iraq, the prospects for the peasantry on their ancestral land are exceptionally promising. 'Iraq is one of the two countries (Egypt is the other) in which the highly productive irrigational method of agriculture was first put into operation by draining and canalizing the waters of a jungle-swamp. In Egypt, irrigational agriculture has continued, without a break, to be a going concern ever since its inauguration there about 5,000 years ago. In 'Iraq, where irrigation was inaugurated at approximately the same date as in Egypt, the system was allowed to deteriorate in successive stages, beginning in the fourth century B.C., till, in the thirteenth century of the Christian Era, it was virtually put out of action. 'Iraq's network of irrigation canals and provision of dykes to keep out flood-water and of basins to contain it have been in process of restoration since the close of the First World War. The 'Iraqis can therefore look forward to seeing their country become once again, when this rehabilitation-work has been completed, a counterpart of Egypt as a food-pro-ducing area; and it is certain that there will be a market for 'Iraq's surplus food-produce when the current population-explosion has doubled or trebled the present numbers of the World's population. Yet, in spite of this certainty, for the 'Iraqi peasants, of a pros-perous future at home as tillers of the soil, they are streaming into shanty-towns round Baghdad—a capital with no large-scale industries and therefore with hardly any employment to offer to newcomers.

The drift of peasants to Arequipa is hardly less irrational. This Peruvian city, situated about half-way up from the coast to the Altiplano, is the urban centre of an oasis that lives by agriculture.

The only industrial establishment of any importance in Arequipa is the workshops of the Southern Railway, and the oasis's agricultural production is restricted rigidly by the limit of the amount of water obtainable for irrigation. Thus the squatters on the outskirts of the city have no prospects of local employment. The municipal authorities try to explain this to them, and they implore them to go home to their villages on the Altiplano. Some of the squatters actually own land there which they have abandoned without having forfeited their ownership. These therefore have a means of livelihood at home, though their plots of land may be small and in any case the climate of the Altiplano is bleak. Their prospects at home are, however, at any rate less bleak than they are in a shanty-town on the outskirts of Arequipa. Yet they cannot be persuaded to return. Nor can the squatters on the outskirts of Buenos Aires who have trekked to there from the still bleaker Altiplano of Bolivia or from the tropical lowlands of Paraguay and have rigged up their shanties on the fringe of the great modern city in the vain hope of finding for themselves there the Eldorado that Buenos Aires has been in truth for nineteenth-century British middle-class immigrants.

If the World-City is allowed to come into being haphazard, the whole of the World's additional population, beyond its present figure, together with the increasing portion of the World's present rural population that is abandoning the countryside, is going to silt up in urban slums of one or other of the four kinds that have been distinguished in the present chapter. In fact, the result of *laisser-faire* will be that by far the greater part of the World-City's area will consist of slums which will be inhabited by the greater part of its population—and this will be the greater part of the population of the World itself. In this welter of slums, there will be, here and there, patches of a different composition which will be as small and as rare as walled cities used to be in the age before the outbreak of the Industrial Revolution. These patches will be of two sorts. There will be clusters of factories and business offices, and there will be suburban middle-class housing estates. These suburbias will be as afraid of being overwhelmed by the surrounding slums as the antique walled cities were of being overwhelmed by the surrounding countryside. Each suburbia may, indeed, revert to the antique practice of insulating itself within a ring of fortifications. The up-to-date equivalent of a curtain-wall reinforced, at intervals, by towers is an electrified barbed-wire fence equipped at intervals of every few hundred yards with miniature eiffel towers that will be manned by watchmen. There is already a model for this on the grand scale in the iron curtain that runs round the whole vast perimeter of the Soviet Union.

The middle-class suburbs of the present-day megalopolises have not yet insulated themselves militarily. They have, however, already insulated themselves juridically and fiscally. In the United States in recent years, one middle-class residential suburb after another has incorporated itself separately from the city in which the suburb's residents make their living, and the taxes payable on the value of the residents' houses are then paid, not to the city, but to the separately incorporated suburban municipality. Of course, the breadwinner who commutes between the incorporated suburb and the city will pay tax—and this at a higher rate than on his suburban residential property—on the office space in the city in which he does his work and earns his family's living. He will pay direct if he is the owner of the business, and indirectly if he is an employee. However, the amount of the tax that can be levied on the residential part of the built-up area of the city, inside its administrative limits, will have appreciably declined; for, as the former middle-class residents have moved out progressively into newly-incorporated suburbs, their evacuated houses will have been occupied by new residents, in lower income groups, and the valuation of this property for tax will have declined. In a city in which, as in Rio and in Rosario, there are shanty-towns in the city's heart, the squatters presumably pay no taxes to the city at all. Yet, out of this declining revenue, the city still has to pay for a host of municipal services—keeping the roads and sewers and the gas and electricity networks in repair, and maintaining a police-force for security and for traffic-control—and the residents in separately incorporated suburbs still get the full benefit of the urban municipal services, as they did when they used to pay taxes to the city on residential property as well as on business property.

The point has been put forcefully by Professor Jean Gottmann. The interests of commuters

thus diverge from those of the less well-paid employees who both live and work there [i.e. inside the city limits]. An opposition of interests grows between those who live and those who only work in the central cities. The business function of the city, of course, depends on both groups. Such trends towards opposition of interests cannot go on indefinitely without deeply disturbing the social and economic co-operation that must somehow be maintained between the various groups in Megalopolis.[1]

When rich and poor meet, there is bound, even in the least bad of all possible circumstances, to be some friction between the two parties, and this friction will be proportionate to the width of the gap between the two income-scales. If the gap is wide, the poor will feel resentment against the rich, while the rich, on their side, will seek to avoid contact with the poor. This is because a difference in scale of income is apt to be accompanied by a difference in degree of education—in the broad sense of this word in which it includes breeding and cultivation as well as the acquisition of intellectual knowledge. It is this unhappy cultural consequence of poverty that moves the rich to shun the society of the poor; and poverty and lack of cultivation promote each other in a vicious circle. The poor cannot afford to give as good an education as the rich can to their children, and consequently the children of the poor are handicapped at the start in their struggle to escape from poverty. In the United States this coincidence between lower levels of income and of education is likely to be found in the average immigrant into a city, whether he comes from overseas or comes (as the unsuccessful Iowan farmer comes) from the native American countryside.

If poverty is accompanied by inferiority in degree of cultivation, as it is likely to be, and if this pair of interacting handicaps also coincides with a difference in physical appearance which gives the difference between different income-groups a conspicuous

[1] Jean Gottmann, *Megalopolis: The Urbanized Northeastern Seaboard of the United States* (New York, 1st ed. 1961, 2nd ed. 1962, Twentieth Century Fund), p. 720.

visual image, this cumulation of coinciding differences between two groups of human beings may aggravate their antipathy towards each other to a degree at which it will turn a cold war into a shooting and killing war. In recent years this has been happening in some of the major cities of the North-Eastern United States as between American citizens of African and of European physique. A similar mutual antipathy, associated with differences of physique, has recently been revealing itself in Britain as between natives and immigrants.

Racial antipathy is saddest and most discouraging in cases in which it still persists after its usual initial accompaniments of poverty and lack of cultivation have been overcome by the party that is the victim of it. Several years ago, on my way from the city of Denver, Colorado, to its airport, I found myself passing through a suburban area that was attractive enough to move me to ask who had laid it out and what kind of people were living there. I was told—as if this were bad tidings—that it had been built and been originally inhabited by members of the 'white' middle class, but had recently been evacuated by them because some of the houses had been bought by Negro families that could afford this suburban housing thanks to their having risen in the world. The whole of this suburb was now inhabited by Negroes exclusively. Three points struck me. First, the new-comers were not only sufficiently well-off, but also sufficiently cultivated, to take pride and pleasure in the good new housing that they had now acquired. The doors and window-frames were freshly painted, the roofs were in good repair, the lawns were neatly mown, and the borders planted with flowers were trim. My second thought was that any West-European middle-class family would feel itself fortunate if it owned as good a house and garden as one of these in such agreeable surroundings. My third thought was the sad and discouraging one. The actual inhabitants of this suburb were still second-class citizens, in spite of their economic prosperity and the high level of cultivation that they revealed in the way in which they were using their money. They were still second-class citizens nevertheless, because their replacement of the previous 'white' inhabitants was evidently regarded as a misfortune by the 'white' majority of their fellow-townsmen and fellow-citizens. Their acquisition of good housing that had once been 'white' was resented by the 'whites', though, to all appearance, the change of ownership had not resulted in the new owners allowing the standard of upkeep to deteriorate.

Evidently the juxtaposition of people with different levels of income, different manners and customs, and different physiques produces more exasperating psychological effects in an urban environment than in a rural one. In a city, life is more tense than it is in the countryside, and nerves are more highly strung. If this is so in any city, it is so *a fortiori* in a megalopolis, and in the coming World-City the increasing strain seems likely to result in a catastrophe unless effective action is taken in time to forestall and avert this. Traffic-congestion, which is the other major evil of the mechanized city, likewise needs to be dealt with drastically before the arrival of the World-City, which is now fast bearing down upon us, aggravates this evil, also, to a degree at which it, too, might become irremediable.

The catastrophes that we may be going to bring upon ourselves are evident, but these are possibilities only; they are not inevitable dooms. Whether the possible catastrophes will be incurred or will be averted will depend on what we do today to cope with them in advance, before they have had time to become accomplished facts. What are the principal measures of social and technological preventive medicine that we ought now to explore and to put into effect if, on examination, they appear to be promising?

One of the indispensable preventive measures is manifestly a set of changes in the structure of the World's public administration. Urban life is more complex than rural life; social relations in an urban environment are more delicate; and an efficient technology is a more imperatively required condition for urban human welfare. This is another way of saying that a city—above all, a World-City—needs a skilful and powerful municipal administration; and the municipal administration of a World-City is just another name for a world-government. No state on any geographical scale that falls short of the global scale can contain and administer a World-City whose geographical ramifications are going to be global by definition. The coming of the World-City is a certainty, but the creation of a world-government is not; and, if we allow ourselves to be overtaken by the arrival of the World-City without having set up, to manage it, the world-government that it requires, we shall bring catastrophe on ourselves for certain. We have therefore to act before we find ourselves confronted with the terrifying prospect of the World-City's coming to birth in an administrative chaos.

This means, in the first place, that the 125 sovereign independent states that now divide between them the land-surface of our planet will have to reconcile themselves to entering into a world-wide federation. A number of the present local states are, themselves, federal in their internal structure, and these local federal states have come into being through the voluntary self-subordination of states that are now components of these sovereign federal states but were once each severally sovereign and independent. The fact that federation has already been achieved on a less than global scale is fair evidence that it can also be achieved on a global scale, if mankind recognizes the necessity for this further step forward and summons up the will to take it. The United States was brought into being by the voluntary union of thirteen states that had previously been connected politically with each other only by the indirect link of their having been respectively subject to the sovereignty of the British Crown. The spirit which moved the thirteen states to federate in the eighteenth century could move the United States and the 124 other local sovereign states of the present day to federate now in their turn.

The coming of the World-City is going to make a global federation of all the now existing local sovereign states a necessary condition for the survival of mankind; but, necessary though this is, it is not going to solve all the problems that the World-City's arrival will bring with it. In the comment on the sketch of the geographical configuration of the coming World-City that has been made at an earlier point in the present chapter, it has been observed that some of the most important of the conurbations that will be the components of the World-City already straddle international frontiers (the Franco-Belgian conurbation is an instance), and that, as the World-City takes shape, the non-correspondence between historic administrative territorial units and new urban territorial units is going to become more common, more conspicuous, and more awkward.

How are we to deal with this administration problem? The new World-City will require new administrative areas and authorities to fit the new configuration that it will have given to the distribution of human settlements over the land-surface of our planet. These requisite new areas and new authorities are likely to be incommensurate with the territories and the governments of the World's present 125 sovereign states; but these existing states cannot be erased from the map; their juridical roots go too deep and, what is still more decisive, their hold on their citizens' emotions is too strong. Their citizens may perhaps be persuaded to subordinate them to a new federal world-state; but to attempt to erase them from the political map, as Prussia has been erased, and to re-draw this map *in toto*, would not be practical politics.

In this administrative dilemma we shall be wise to seek light from the history of the Boston–New York–Philadelphia–Washington megalopolis, which is the oldest of all the megalopolises that are now coming into existence. It has been pointed out by Professor Gottmann, in the book of his that has already been cited, that the area of this particular megalopolis is partitioned between the administrative domain of 'ten state governments plus the committees of Congress that administer the District of Columbia or are concerned with the National Capital metropolitan region'.[1] Even the youngest of these ten states had been in existence for nearly a quarter of a millennium before the Boston–Washington megalopolis began to take shape; for this megalopolis, like its younger sisters, is the product of the age of automobiles with owner-drivers, and this age had hardly dawned before the interval between the two world-wars. Moreover, the ten states over whose territories the Boston–Washington megalopolis then began to sprawl had, by that time, been built into the federal structure of the United States for nearly a century and a half. It is manifest that the problem of giving this megalopolis

[1] Op. cit., p. 740.

the administrative organization that it requires could not have been solved, and cannot be solved, by sweeping away the administrative structure of the United States and its constituent states, as the physical structure of a slum can be swept away by a bulldozer. A parvenue megalopolis cannot abolish an old-established administrative structure for its own administrative convenience; it has therefore to provide for its own new administrative needs by some new administrative device that can be accommodated to the existing political structure. This problem has been solved in the Boston–New York–Philadelphia–Washington megalopolis in at least one case that is of major importance both in itself and as a model for similar administrative engineering in similar situations.

One of the oldest-established 'state lines' in the area now covered by this megalopolis is the boundary between New York state and New Jersey down the thalweg (i.e. the median line) of the channel of the Hudson River in the lowest reach of its course. At the date at which an administrative boundary was sited along this line, the lower course of the Hudson was a conspicuous 'natural frontier', and there were no awkward consequences for maritime trade, since the principal port then serving this region was, not New York, but Albany at the head of navigation on the Hudson for ocean-going sailing-ships, and at Albany both banks of the Hudson and the whole of its channel are inside the single state of New York. The state line running down the middle of the Hudson's lowest reach began to become awkward for maritime business when New York superseded Albany as the principal maritime port on the Hudson, and when the number and the size of the ships berthing there increased to a degree at which the docking-space in New York State territory along the western edge of Manhattan Island could no longer accommodate all the traffic. The port then overflowed from the New York side to the Jersey side of the lower Hudson, and this economic development created administrative and fiscal complications, because the port business on the New Jersey side was under a different state jurisdiction with differing laws and regulations.

The administrative impediment to the conduct of business was disadvantageous to both the states that were concerned, as well as to all American citizens, engaged in the port business, who were domiciled in either New York State or New Jersey. Accordingly, in 1921, the two states set up jointly a new administrative organization, the Port of New York Authority. This new public body was given the task of administering the whole of the actual area of the port of greater New York, in New Jersey as well as in New York State. Since then, two new forms of transportation, mechanized road-traffic and aviation, have developed enormously; and these, like maritime traffic, straddle the boundary between the two states. The administration of road-bridges and tunnels and of airfields in the greater New York area has therefore been added to the Port Authority's duties, and this is a promising extension of the Authority's powers.

The Authority's field of action might, with advantage to the public interest, have been extended still farther to include railways used for commuting and subways, but unfortunately the Authority has avoided being saddled with responsibility for these economically and socially indispensable but at present financially unprofitable means of conveyance.[1] Even so, the creation of the Port of New York Authority and the extension of its field of operations, even if this extension has not been carried so far as logic and the public interest demand, points the way to a solution of the world-wide problem of reconciling the administrative need for creating new public bodies, corresponding to the coming World-City's structure, with the political necessity of preserving the pre-existing territorial units of administration and the historic boundaries between them—and this whether these units have already subordinated themselves, as New York State and New Jersey have, to a local federal state or whether, like France and Belgium, they are today still politically sovereign and independent. The fact that the problem created by the spread of the mechanized city has been solved substantially, in an important case, by co-operation between two states members of the United States is evidence that the same problem can be solved on a world-wide scale—always supposing that mankind consents to provide

[1] See Gottmann, op. cit., p. 665.

the inevitable World-City with its political counterpart in the shape of a federal world-government.

On this condition—though on this condition alone—the territorial units of administration and the corresponding organs of government that were in existence before the World-City began to arise, can co-exist with the radically new pattern of human settlement that the rise of the World-City has been bringing into being, and with the new organs of administration that this new pattern requires. We must resign ourselves to accepting the co-existence of these two disparate administrative maps, one representing the administrative demands of the future, and the other the administrative legacy of the past. This expedient appears to be the most promising device for reconciling the future's dynamism with the past's inertia in an age in which the pattern of human settlements is being changed rapidly and radically. Even so, the adjustment of administrative structures to the new facts of life is unlikely to be easy. The sinews of administration are revenues; under democratic political regimes, revenues are allocated by elected legislators; and, in the United States, the redrawing of the map of electoral districts is already a contentious issue because this map has been manipulated, by the representatives of the rural districts, to preserve or secure for them an over-representation that is unfair and inexpedient. The crux is the resistance of the countryside—whose economic and demographical importance is diminishing—to conceding a larger share of the total community's public revenues to the cities, though the cities are contributing a continually increasing percentage of the total revenues in consequence of their increasing economic predominance.

A classic case is the financial plight of São Paulo, which is one of the most productive, and therefore one of the most rapidly expanding, cities in the World today. São Paulo has been capturing the domestic market of Brazil from the overseas Powers that have dominated this market in the past. It might almost be said that Brazil has escaped from her former economic thraldom to Western Europe only by exchanging a foreign master for a native one. Brazil has now become São Paulo's economic colonial empire instead of Britain's and Germany's; but the Paulistas' fellow-countrymen have used the traditional administrative and financial map of Brazil to take their revenge on São Paulo for the revolutionary economic map that the Paulistas have imposed on them.

Politically, Brazil has a three-tier structure: it is a federal polity composed of states comprising subordinate units, rural and urban; and, in the allocation of public revenues, the federal and the state governments receive, by law, the lion's share, while the municipal administrations are starved. São Paulo's economic productivity yields a notable proportion of Brazil's total public revenue, and São Paulo needs to receive back an ample share of her substantial contribution for financing her own urban development. A productive city is inevitably also a growing city, and a growing city needs to be adding constantly to its costly equipment of municipal services—not merely sewers and subways, but parks and hospitals and universities and museums. Yet the law of the land keeps the municipal administration of São Paulo poor though São Paulo's population is rich—and earns its riches by its economic energy and efficiency. This ironical plight of São Paulo illustrates the difficulty of doing justice to the new map of human settlements by giving present-day São Paulo and the coming World-City the quotas of political representation and public revenue that they ought to receive.

Evidently the old order is going to put up an obstinate resistance to the new order's demand for a fair share of the public revenues. This resistance will have to be overcome; for the new order will not become viable if it does not obtain the financial resources that it needs, and the effective establishment of the new order, side by side with the old one, is imperative. It is called for imperiously by the new distribution and the new way of life of the World's population. This makes it all the more important that the revenues which the administrative organs of the World-City do acquire shall be allocated equitably; this requirement, in its turn, calls for an equitable mapping of the World-City's administrative units; and this means that the toleration which will have to be given to the administrative *ancien régime* must not be extended to the World-City's own unhealthy territorial and administrative by-products, as if these, too, were sacrosanct. The most undesirable of these are the new separately-incorporated suburbs, occupied by well-to-do middle-class emigrants from the heart of the mechanized cities that are the World-City's local nuclei and growing-points. This new administrative device has been draining the mechanized cities' life-blood. In contrast to the old-established local states, these mushroom-like suburban municipalities are neither venerable nor estimable, and consequently they are not inviolable. They have no political, economic, or financial justification and have not ever had any. They stand for nothing but the sly collective selfishness of an excessively privileged minority. They are inimical to mankind's public interest, besides being geographically out of scale with the World-City's territorial structure. They ought therefore to be liquidated, and their areas ought to be added to the domains of the cities that their inhabitants have been exploiting illegitimately. This internal administrative and financial reform is a long overdue act of justice. It will not be enough, by itself, to solve the World-City's financial problems, but at least it will ease them.

Besides requiring a special new administration geared to its own new structure and new needs and adequately financed, the World-City will require physical installations of a number of different kinds: for instance, buildings, conveyances, and artificially constructed traffic-lanes of various kinds to carry traffic of various types. In looking ahead to the provision of the World-City's material requirements, there is one simple consideration which is obvious even to laymen and which ought to be constantly in the professional planners' and technicians' minds. The World's population is increasing at an unprecedented rate and is going to be stabilized—if mankind succeeds in stabilizing it—at a figure that will certainly be several times, and may be many times, as great as its present magnitude. Consequently the living generation's children, and perhaps the younger age-classes of the living generation itself, will need an immense increase in the quantity of the World's material installations and equipments.

From this it surely follows that we ought to be chary of scrapping any of the equipments and installations that we now possess, however inadequate or dilapidated some of these may be. It would be a grave error to imagine that we can afford to scrap because the advance of technology has increased our productivity. We need the maximum of production and the maximum of conservation as well. This is worth saying, because the now prevailing inclination, among laymen and experts alike, is to scrap assets that are not bringing in a financial return at the present moment, and even to scrap assets that are still in fair condition but happen to have fallen out of fashion—for instance, last year's model of this or that make of automobile, or last century's prime means of communication, the railway-train, in contrast to the present favourite—which is, of course, the mechanized road-vehicle.

Current fashions in the means of conveyance are as irrational and as arbitrary as fashions in dress have ever been; but the straits to which we may reduce ourselves by heedlessly following the fashion in the field of transportation may be more dire than the extravagances of the Parisian *merveilleuses'* costume after the end of the Terror. Money wasted on following fashions in dress is marginal and is therefore expendable without disaster. On the other hand, we are courting disaster by scrapping existing installations for means of transportation because these have become unfashionable, although they have not become inefficient and although they also represent an enormous past capital investment which, once sabotaged, can never be replaced. In indulging in this folly, we are deliberately exposing ourselves to the danger of bringing our successors—and perhaps ourselves, in the case of those of us who in 1969 are still young—to a pass at which a large part of mankind will find itself immobilized. The fact that most of the World's railways are now being run at a loss is not the decisive consideration. This financial loss is a temporary consequence of a fashion for travelling by automobile or by plane; but all fashions are ephemeral, and this fashion will eventually be terminated forcibly by the progress of the population-explosion and the automobile-explosion if these two inevitable and imperious events do not result in the fashion's being voluntarily abandoned. To keep the World's existing railway-network in being by operating it at even a large annual financial loss for twenty or thirty years or even for half a century will be, on a long view, a remunerative investment of mankind's current savings. In making this investment now, we shall be safeguarding mankind's future ability to travel.

Another asset that we are inclined to scrap but ought to conserve is our slums. We cannot spare either the slums or the railways, however grim the slums and unfashionable the railways may be. A leaking roof is better than no roof, and travelling by train is better than being unable to travel at all.

For as far into the future as we can yet see ahead, the total resources of mankind's construction industry ought to be applied exclusively to productive work. We should build new houses and recondition old houses; we should not deliberately deprive ourselves of the maximum possible amount of housing by directing any of our resources to the perverse activity of pulling existing buildings down—especially if we pull down houses inhabited by the poor in order to clear the ground for additional houses for the rich. Grander new houses on old sites will, of course, bring in higher rents and higher tax-yields, but the evicted previous indigent occupants may have nowhere to go—or, at least, no alternative housing that is within their slender financial means. Demolition should be sanctioned only if it is proven that the condemned house is in so insanitary a condition that it is a genuine and immediate danger to public health; a dilapidated house should be reconditioned before it has reached the degree of decay at which it needs to be condemned, but, except for such imperative salvage work, even reconditioning should be a second priority to new building—and this even if the reconditioned houses are to be rehabilitated and adapted, not in order to increase the housing options of the rich, but still to house the poor, while improving the material conditions of life for them. Housing that is habitable as it stands is a valuable asset, however poor its quality, so long as there are still people who are living under threat of being left without shelter of any kind.

Of course slums are unquestionably deplorable. They not only breed physical sickness; the overcrowding and the privation of the elementary material decencies of life can be demoralizing. World-wide slum-clearance at the earliest expedient date ought to be one of mankind's highest priorities in its agenda of economic objectives; but the earliest expedient date will not arrive until the World's now exploding population has come near enough to re-stabilization for it to become possible for demographers to estimate approximately the permanent number of houses that will be required in a World whose population—whatever its number may then be—will be kept at a stable figure by universal family planning. When we have built as many new houses as will be required for housing that number of families and have done this building on the standard that will be considered, at this future date, to be the obligatory minimum of decency, then we can, and should, start to clear away the slums of all kinds in all locations; and we can go on to replace them, not with new houses for the rich, but with Parthenons and Taj Mahals in the cleared areas in the heart of our cities, and with Boboli Gardens and Bois de Boulogne on the cleared sites of what is now the outer ring of shanty-towns.

This huge programme of constructive work could, of course, be carried out quicker and better (i.e. on a higher standard) if mankind were to compel its present sovereign local governments to devote to construction, and eventually to slum-clearance as well, the tax-money that the governments are now spending on fantastically costly competitive armaments that are threats to mankind's survival and on fantastically costly feats of spacemanship that make no contribution to human welfare or happiness.

Meanwhile, some of our now existing shanty-towns will not merely have survived temporarily *faute de mieux*; they will have been performing a positively useful social function. There is nothing to be said for the shanty-towns on the outskirts of Arequipa and of Baghdad. It has been pointed out already that the ex-peasants who have squatted round Arequipa have no prospects there, and that the peasants who have squatted round Baghdad have good prospects in the villages that they have deserted. On the other hand, the shanty-towns that have sprung up round Brazil's new capital, Brasilia, make sense.

When the decision to build Brasilia was announced, tens of thousands of workers from the over-populated poverty-stricken 'hump' of North-Eastern Brazil trekked to the designated site across hundreds of miles of wilderness in order to earn wages by building the great and grand new city. They did do the building, and, presumably, while they were being employed on this by the federal public authorities, they were housed in camps. But where were they to go when the work had been finished and they had been paid off? Unlike the squatters round Baghdad, or even the squatters round Arequipa, the discharged labour-force at Brasilia had no prospects awaiting them in their original homes. On the other hand, their prospects at Brasilia were as promising, if they could manage to stay on there, as the Baghdad squatters' prospects would have been if they had had the foresight to stay on in their native villages. The urban prospects at Brasilia are as good as the agricultural prospects are in rural 'Iraq, because Brasilia is the capital of one of the largest countries in the World— a country with a great and rapidly increasing population and with still untapped reserves of valuable natural resources. In such a country a new capital city is bound to boom, even if the country itself is suffering economically from having over-strained its present economic strength in creating this new capital *ex nihilo*. Consequently there are bound to be, in Brasilia, increasing opportunities of remunerative employment in the future, even though the building-work on the layout of the central part of the new city has been completed.

The immigrant ex-building-workers' resolve to stay on at Brasilia was therefore shrewd; but where were they now to live? The monumental centre of Brasilia, which they had already built, was not for them; nor, indeed, were the satellite towns which the professional planners of Brasilia had been intending to build, as the second stage of their operations, for housing the surplus of the 'white-collar' population of the new national capital when the population of the completed part had risen to the figure that they considered to be ideally the maximum. At this stage, however, the planners were forestalled and outmanœuvred by their discharged labour-force. Before the planners had started to lay out their projected ring of satellite towns, their ex-employees had put up a ring of shanty-towns and had squatted in their improvised ramshackle home-made—and home-making—shacks. In this race, the squatters were bound to win, for 'do-it-yourself' work on unplanned shanty-towns outpaces monumental work planned and designed and executed by professionals.

On a visit to Brasilia on 21–25 August 1966, I took care to look in on one or two of the shanty-towns that, in the planners' eyes, are unintended and regrettable blots on their exquisitely-designed townscape. I had only a passing glimpse of Brasilia's non-planned slum suburbia; but this was enough to inform me that the material setting of life in Brasilia's ring of shanty-towns is sordid but that the slum-dwellers themselves looked happy. I guess that my impression of their happiness may have been correct, because I suspect that life in these shanty-towns may be jollier, because it will be less formal and less oppressively inhibited by regulations, than it can be in Brasilia's almost too well-planned central area.

In the painful material contrast between slums and middle-class residential districts there seems to be a redeeming psychological compensation. The higher the income and the better the roofing and the plumbing, the lower the standard of neighbourliness. It is well known that the poor give to each other far more spontaneous unremunerated mutual aid than the rich give to each other. Indeed, without a high standard of neighbourliness, the difficulties and hardships of slum life would be insuperable. The slummier the slum, the higher the standard of neighbourliness is apt to be. In the world of 1969, neighbourliness is probably at its maximum in the *favélas* in Rio. Neighbourliness is demanding, but it is rewarding too. Its reward is sociability and the zest for life that sociability brings with it. However, this credit-entry in the balance-sheet of slum life is manifestly far outweighed by the formidable sum of all the dreadful debit entries. These are, as has been noted, not only material; they are spiritual as well; and we must therefore re-house the World's present slum-dwellers in decent new housing as rapidly as possible, even at the spiritual risk that the ex-slum-dwellers may acquire a middle-class unsociability in their new middle-class material setting.

If new housing, on hitherto vacant sites, is to be built for the World's slum-dwellers, it will have to be located in a zone beyond the zones already occupied by middle-class suburbs. This means that the workers who are now living comparatively near to their places of work, either in the hearts of the cities or in shanty-towns on their immediate outskirts, will have to be turned into commuters. This will swell the present host of middle-class commuters to a many times larger multitude, and the new majority of commuters will be having to commute over longer distances on smaller incomes. This prospect puts a premium on the provision of the cheapest possible means of transport in the largest possible volume, and this portends that railway-traffic will recapture the primacy that it held for nearly a century ending less than half a century ago.

The progressive mechanization of life since the outbreak of the Industrial Revolution has inflicted woes on mankind but has also conferred benefits, and one of its signal benefits has been the invention of trains running on rails and hauled by inanimate motive-power—steam, electricity, or oil—instead of by the muscle-power of human beings and domesticated animals.

In the first chapter of this book, it has been noted that, during the five thousand years or so that elapsed between the invention of sailing-ships and the invention of steam-trains, transportation by water was incomparably quicker and cheaper than transportation overland. The only limitation on the speed of navigation by sail was the caprice of the winds; the only limitation on a wooden sailing-ship's size was the limit on the size of tree-trunks; and these handicaps to navigation in timber-built wind-propelled ships were slight compared to the handicaps on overland transport, even after the invention of the wheel. Muscle-power, even when efficiently harnessed, is puny by comparison with the power of inanimate physical forces, and the amount of effective muscle-power that can be harnessed to a wheeled vehicle is narrowly limited.

When a one-horse wheeled vehicle is replaced by a two-horse one to which the horses are yoked side by side, the traction-power of muscle is doubled; but additional horses, beyond the first pair, bring in diminishing returns, and the diminution dwindles almost to zero if the number is increased to a dozen. One trace-horse on either side of the original pair may contribute appreciably to the total haulage-power, though these two trace-horses will not be able to pull the same weight as the middle two; but an extra set of trace-horses or an extra span of horses harnessed in tandem will be relatively ineffective. The limits of the effective use of muscle-power for overland traction were reached, before the dawn of the age of mechanization, in the coach-and-four and in the horse-artillery gun and limber drawn by six horses harnessed in three pairs in tandem, with a postillion mounted on one of the horses in each pair to flog his mount and its companion into making exertions beyond their strength.

The performance of overland transport was suddenly enhanced —and this to a sensational degree—by the invention of the steam-driven locomotive. This could haul a train of dozens of coaches or waggons far more swiftly than the fastest and strongest and most efficiently harnessed team of horses; and the weight and volume of goods or cattle or human passengers that a single steam-train could draw was also far greater. The speed and traction-power of a single steam-driven locomotive were, in fact, so vastly greater than those of the largest effective team of horses that trains, which could not have been moved an inch in the horse-age, now became practical possibilities.

Stand at a window in the Imperial Hotel in Tokyo from which you can look down on eight parallel tracks of railway-line. Watch the mechanically-hauled passenger-trains, each about a quarter of a mile long, and each chock-full of passengers, moving swiftly, almost head to tail, in both directions, with none of the eight tracks idle for longer than a minute or two at a time, and you will realize what the invention of mechanically-hauled trains has done for passenger-traffic. Stand on the left bank of the Rhine at Bad Godesberg; watch the freight-trains (these are even longer than the Japanese passenger-trains) travelling, likewise almost head to tail, along the railway on the opposite bank of the river; and remember that there is another railway, carrying perhaps an equal volume of traffic, just behind you, on the side of the Rhine on which you are standing, and you will realize what the invention of mechanically-hauled trains has done for goods-traffic.

If this invention had not been made, the World's cities, which had been static for the first five thousand years of their history, would never have been able to get on the move. Since the invention and construction of railways, cities have merged with each other to form the clusters that we have labelled 'megalopolises', and in our generation the World's megalopolises are coalescing into a single World-City.

Mankind has committed itself to the World-City by the application of science to the technology of medicine and of agriculture —two technological advances that have produced the current population-explosion and the contemporaneous migration into the World-City from the countryside. We cannot revert to the pre-mechanization way of life. This could be done only at the price of genocide; for the antediluvian system of economy would support only a fraction of the number of human beings that this planet is going to carry by the time when its population has been re-stabilized. In this situation, in which we are irretrievably caught whether we like it or not, it is suicidal to scrap our railways—the invention that has made the already existing megalopolises and the coming World-City possible. Of course we are right in also developing to its full capacity the more recent invention of road-borne mechanized vehicles; but these are supplements to railway-trains, not substitutes for them, and it is already becoming apparent that they are going to be marginal supplements only.

The attractions of mechanized road-vehicles are manifest. They have two advantages over railway-trains. A passenger-automobile or a motor-propelled commercial road-vehicle (in Unitedstatesese, 'truck'; in Unitedkingdomese, 'lorry') can be driven from door to door; a train of railway-coaches or trucks cannot, since it has to run on rails laid on a special kind of permanent way. The driver of an automobile or a lorry can start his journey at any hour that he chooses, and can stop, and can make detours, likewise at his own choice, at any point and any moment on his way. The user of a railway, like the user of any other form of public transport, has to conform to a timetable, set, not by him, but by the management, for both passenger-service and goods-service, and he can entrain and detrain, load and unload, only at a passenger-stop or a goods-yard. It is the attractiveness of these two advantages, taken together, that has made mechanized road-transport popular and railway-transport unfashionable.

However, the first of the two disadvantages of railway-transport has been partially overcome for the railway-carriage of goods, though not of passengers, by the recent invention of containers that can be transferred, without breaking bulk, between a railway-truck and a road-truck or a ship. The use of containers makes it possible to combine the advantage, possessed by road-traffic, of being able to collect and deliver from door to door with the advantages, possessed by rail-transport, of being able to apply mechanized traction to a train of vehicles, as against the necessary limitation of mechanized road-transport to single vehicles, supplemented, at most, by a single trailer—and this is the equivalent of a railway-train consisting of only two units, including the locomotive.

A train consisting of more than two units necessarily has to run on rails; a longer train than that would run off a rail-less road in attempting to round the road's bends; and, even if the rail-less road were to be aligned absolutely straight, a long train travelling along it could not move at high speed, because the rearward units of the train would then sway from side to side to an extent at which they would leave the road and would bring the whole train to grief. Thus the rails, that are an essential feature of mechanized train-traffic, are its strong point as well as its weak point. They are the railway's weak point inasmuch as they make rail-traffic rigid, both in the route that has to be followed and in the timetable to which the traffic has to keep. This is, however, a small price to pay for the railway's strong point, and its strength lies in the supremely important fact that the railway can, whereas the rail-less road cannot, take full advantage of the immense potential increase in haulage capacity that has been brought within mankind's reach by the change-over from muscle-power to mechanized power as the means of traction. Rails make it possible for an engine to haul a long and heavy train of vehicles—a feat that is beyond the power of muscles—whereas an engine of the same power as a railway-engine could not haul a train along a rail-less road; it is debarred from doing this by an insoluble problem of dynamics.

The significance of the railway's advantage over the rail-less road—the advantage of making it possible to haul trains and not just single vehicles—lies, above all, in its bearing on the future, when the numbers of the World's population are going to be many times as great as they are today. The train is the heaven-sent response, in the field of transportation technology, to the challenge of the population-explosion in the field of demography. This point is demonstrated visually in the spectacle, seen from an hotel window in Tokyo, that has been described in an earlier passage. This advantage of the railway-train over the mechanized road-vehicle is a permanent advantage, and it is going to become a progressively more valuable one as the World's population increases, as the World-City comes into being, and as a larger and larger percentage of the World's population becomes urban. By contrast, the mechanized road-vehicle's advantage over the railway-train is an ephemeral one. It is a wasting asset because it is inherently self-stultifying; and it is already within sight of defeating its own purposes.

The train running on rails is the logical instrument for harvesting, to the full, technology's feat of harnessing the mighty physical forces of inanimate nature for use in traction. On the other hand the mechanized road-vehicle, which is the railway-train's belated supplement and which is, today, temporarily in the ascendant, is an illogical regression to the form of vehicle which was the most effective form possible in the age of muscle-traction but which has been an anachronism ever since the achievement of the mechanization of overland transport. By comparison with the railway-train, the mechanized road-vehicle is a wasteful instrument both in its consumption of power and in its occupation of road-space. The engine of almost any mechanized vehicle on the road could haul a much greater load than it does haul if it were to be fitted to a railway-locomotive; and, since there is only a limited quantity on this planet of the gasoline or other natural fuel with which a mechanized road-vehicle is powered, this unnecessarily extravagant use of fuel is an offence, on the part of the present prodigal generation, against its still unborn successors. However, the fault in the mechanized road-vehicle which is going to tell against it in the nearer future is its wastefulness of traffic-lane space.

The most capacious passenger-carrying omnibus or freight-carrying lorry is wasteful of traffic-lane space by comparison with the railway-train; the automobile, designed for private use, is still more wasteful of space, and in 1969 automobiles of this kind are far more popular and far more numerous than either of the other two kinds of mechanized road-vehicle. An automobile of normal size will carry, at the most, five or six persons including the driver. In other words it has no greater carrying capacity than its predecessor, the horse-drawn carriage. The automobiles that are to be seen on the World's roads today are, however, seldom filled to the full complement of their carrying capacity—a capacity that is not in scale with their engines' power. A privately-owned car may carry a whole family party at week-ends, but on working days it will, as often as not, be carrying one person only—a passenger who is also the driver; and it will be parked—again occupying space—for the greater part of the day. If the family can afford to own a second car, this too is likely to have a single passenger-driver, namely the wife and mother doing her shopping. When traffic-lane space is being used as extravagantly as this, it is no wonder that the World's road-traffic is becoming more and more frustratingly congested, in spite of the highway authorities' frantic attempts to keep pace with its increase by widening the existing roads and constructing additional ones.

In 1969 it is already manifest that the automobile's floruit is going to be brief, and that it has already passed its zenith. This zenith was attained a few years before the outbreak of the Second World War and, after the interdict on private motoring for the duration of that war, the zenith was passed within a few years of the war's end.

The automobile could not enter upon its heyday until the roads had been made fit to carry it; it could not prolong its heyday when the widening and multiplying of the roads failed to keep pace with the increase in the volume of the automobile traffic travelling on them. Even in the United States, automobiles did not begin to make their appearance on the roads in appreciable quantities until after the end of the First World War, and by that time the roads, which, in Western countries, had been reconditioned, almost up to Roman standards, at the heyday of the stage-coach, had been allowed to deteriorate for nearly a hundred years—ever since, that is to say, the stage-coach had been abruptly put out of business by the invention of the mechanically-hauled railway-train. I myself learned to bicycle at the turn of the nineteenth and twentieth centuries on the section of the Dover-to-London road between Dover and Canterbury. I learnt by trial and error, falling off my bicycle and remounting again and again. The thickness of the road's cushion of dust made my falls painless, and I was not in danger of being knocked down and run over by the occasional farm-waggons and dog-carts that were the only other wheeled traffic on that trunk road besides my bicycle. In Britain the roads were a paradise for the private motorist only during those two brief spells, just before and just after the Second World War, when the roads had already been sufficiently well reconditioned to make motoring agreeable, while the output of cars had not yet reached the volume at which the automobile-traffic began to frustrate itself by the congestion which is still increasing in 1969.

The respective prospects, in the coming World-City, of automobiles and of railway-trains have been made clear, beyond question, in a piece of evidence that was given by the American Transit Association in hearings held by the Joint Committee on Washington Metropolitan Problems in May–June 1958.[1] This evidence is presented in the form of estimates of the carrying capacity of a single lane for different forms of transportation—

[1] Quoted by Professor Gottmann in op. cit., p. 652, from which I have taken the following extract. The same story is told by the figures given on p. 331, footnote 29, in Professor Charles Abrams' *The City is the Frontier* (Harper Colophon Books: New York, Evanston, and London 1967, Harper and Row).

the capacity being reckoned in terms of the number of passengers per hour that could be conveyed. The figures are:

Passengers in autos on surface streets	1,575
Passengers in autos on elevated highways	2,625
Passengers in buses on surface streets	9,000
Passengers in streetcars [i.e. trams on rails] on surface streets	13,500
Passengers in streetcars in subways	20,000
Passengers in local subway trains	40,000
Passengers in express subway trains	60,000

These figures speak for themselves, and their verdict is conclusive. They tell us that, in the closing decades of the twentieth century, when the World's population will have at least doubled or trebled and when the World-City will have become an accomplished fact, railway-trains will have recaptured the primacy, as conveyances, that they possessed during the century ending in the nineteen-twenties, when automobiles began to win from them an ascendancy that has been sensational while it has lasted but that is now proving to be ephemeral.

In 1969 the day cannot be far off at which every section of the World-City will have to adopt Venice's practice of making it compulsory for mechanized road-vehicles, arriving at the city's outer edge, to halt and garage there. In keeping mechanized vehicles out of the interior of a city, Venice has actually been the pioneer in the Western part of the World, because the interior of Venice has never been traversable even for muscle-drawn wheeled traffic. In Venice, the principal arteries for traffic are canals, and the narrow alleyways, with their frequent steeply-arched bridges, are usable only by pedestrians. When the Venetian rule has been extended to all parts of the World-City, it will become practicable, in the interior of this world-conurbation, to provide public transport, in the shape of buses and taxis, that will be frequent, regular, rapid, cheap, and at the same time remunerative.

The only other automobiles that will be allowed to circulate within the World-City at all hours will be fire-engines, ambulances, doctors' cars, and police cars. Commercial vehicles will be allowed to deliver and collect at certain hours only—outside the rush hours, and preferably outside the whole of what, except for the drivers of such vehicles, will be the working day. During the hours allotted to them, commercial vehicles will necessarily be permitted to wait while they are being loaded and unloaded; but, except when they are on their rounds, they will be required, like privately-owned passenger-vehicles, to garage on the World-City's edges. In Rome in the Imperial Age, no wheeled traffic of any kind was allowed to circulate in daylight hours, except in a few special circumstances. The price of this boon was that the din of wagon-wheels, rumbling over the cobbles, and the clatter of hooves, kept residents awake at night. This was a hardship, but it was the lesser evil.

The surviving evidence bearing on the traffic-problem in the City of Rome in the Age of the Principate happens to be clear, authoritative, and also pertinent to the world-wide urban traffic-problem of the present day. We have the text of a law on municipal administration that was promulgated by Julius Caesar in the year 45 B.C., and, though the main subject of this law is, as its title *Lex Iulia Municipalis* implies, the administration of local self-governing communities of Roman citizens outside the City of Rome, this law does incidentally include a regulation for restricting traffic in the City of Rome itself.

The following regulation applies to streets, whether present or future, within the continuous built-up area of the City of Rome. From next 1 January onwards, no waggon is to be led or driven within this area during the daytime, that is to say, after sunrise or before the tenth hour of the day—with the exception that this provision does not apply to haulage or carriage of materials (i) into this area for use in the building of temples or in other public works or (ii) out of the City, including the sites aforesaid, on any demolition work that is being carried out under contract with the public authorities. Exceptions will also be made to provide for particular cases.

The present law is not to be construed as prohibiting the circulation of vehicular traffic during the daytime on the dates of events in the three following categories: (i) religious processions, involving the use of waggons, in which the Vestal Virgins, the Rex Sacrorum, and the Flamines are participants; (ii) [military] triumphal processions; (iii) festivals administered by the public authorities, within a radius of less than one mile from the City, and circus performances involving the processional use of waggons.

Furthermore, this law is not to be construed as prohibiting the presence in the City, or within a radius of one mile from it, during the ten hours after sunrise, of ox-drawn or horse-drawn waggons that have been brought into the City during the preceding night, if these waggons are returning empty or are carrying loads of night-soil.[1]

It will be seen that this Roman regulation of 45 B.C. for the City of Rome could be applied, with advantage, to the London of A.D. 1969. It could be enacted for London as it stands. The only verbal changes that would be needed would be the substitution of the annual Lord Mayor's Show and of an occasional Coronation Procession for the three classes of events set out in the second paragraph.

These restrictions on the circulation of vehicular traffic in Rome were imperative after the City had become the political capital of the whole Mediterranean World. The consequent increase in the size of the City's population had made the pressure of pedestrian traffic alone almost intolerably severe, as is testified in the following passage of a work written by a resident, L. Annaeus Seneca, who lived *circa* 5 B.C.–A.D. 65.

In this City, even in its broadest streets, the flow of pedestrian traffic is continuous, and consequently, when any obstruction occurs which checks the current of this rushing human torrent, there is a formidable crush. The City's population is of a magnitude that requires the simultaneous use of the auditoria of three theatres and the importation of food-supplies from all over the World.[2]

The hardship of being kept awake at night in Rome by the

---

[1] *Corpus Inscriptionum Latinarum*, I, 2, 593, lines 56–67: C. G. Bruns, *Fontes Iuris Romani Antiqui*, 7th edition (Tübingen 1909, Mohr), p. 105. A previous English translation of this passage will be found in E. G. Hardy, *Roman Laws and Charters* (Oxford 1912, Clarendon Press), p. 153.

[2] Seneca, *De Clementiâ*, I, 6, 1 (written *circa* A.D. 54).

din of the traffic is described in vivid words by Juvenal, who lived *circa* A.D. 60–130.

Here in Rome, many invalids die from being kept awake. . . . Where can you find lodgings that give you a chance of sleeping? In the City, sleep is a luxury that costs a fortune. This is the prime cause of illness there. The roar of the wheeled traffic in the City's narrow winding streets and the shouts of abuse when a flock of sheep gets into a jam— the din is enough to rob Drusus of his sleep, or to rob seals of theirs, for that matter.[1]

My sister, Professor J. M. C. Toynbee, who directed me to these three passages, comments:

I imagine that, when the fora of Julius Caesar, Augustus, Domitian, and Trajan were added to the Forum Romanum, there would have been no wheeled traffic, whether by day or by night, in the heart of Rome. But that was not a residential quarter, where people slept. It must have been rather like 'the City' [of London]—it must have been an area for business and for big places of worship.

In the present-day World it will be necessary to regulate the circulation of privately-owned passenger-carrying automobiles on surface throughways outside the bounds of the World-City or on underground throughways beneath the urbanized area that the World-City will cover. This long-distance traffic will not need to be banned, but it will have to be restricted. Every projected expedition of the kind will have to pass the test of the question, asked during the Second World War: 'Is your journey really necessary?' This preliminary question will be put, in the first place, by the possible traveller to himself, and it would seem likely that, more often than not, he will voluntarily answer it in the negative. This would seem likely because, as the number of people simul- taneously alive in the World, and the percentage of this number represented by the owner-drivers of automobiles, both continue to increase, driving will become less and less of a relaxation and a pleasure and more and more of a torment and a penance. It is to be hoped that, in these propitious circumstances, the necessary limitation of the traffic on the World's throughways will be

[1] Juvenal, *Satire III*, lines 232–8.

obtained mainly by voluntary abstinence. However, this may prove to be not enough in itself to keep the volume of the traffic within manageable limits. It may be found necessary to legislate that any would-be private user of a throughway must show reason why he should be granted a special permit before being given permission *ad hoc*.

Though these suggested limitations on the private use of the World-City's streets and roads by owner-drivers of mechanized passenger-vehicles may sound drastic and, to motorists, even harsh, the effect of them will not be to abolish the use of the private automobile as a means of conveyance. The effect will be merely to hold the use of it just within the limits within which it will be practicable to keep this traffic moving on those traffic-lanes on which it will still be allowed in limited numbers. The private automobile will not be put out of action, and of course it ought not to be; for, however massively our railway-traffic may be re-developed, the maximum practicable volume of road-traffic will be needed as well, considering the immensity of the coming increase in the numbers of the World's population. Just as, for the foreseeable future, we shall need to preserve our existing slums while exerting ourselves to the utmost to build sufficient new housing for the poor majority of mankind, so we shall need to preserve the mechanized road-vehicle—regressive though the invention of it has been—while exerting ourselves to the utmost to re-develop our railways, which, in the realm of overland transportation, are manifestly 'the wave of the future'.

The fate that is going to overtake the automobile is, no doubt, also going to overtake the aeroplane—the other fashionable new form of conveyance that, today, is temporarily diverting passenger-traffic from the railways.

The chief advantage of aviation is its speed, which is incomparably greater than that of any form of surface-transport on either land or water. If the traveller in even a slow-flying plane looks down, out of the window, on a moving automobile, train, or ship below, the surface-bound vehicle looks as if it were crawling as slowly as a centipede on tar. A second notable advantage of aviation is that a plane can 'post o'er land and ocean without rest' in its own three-dimensional element, whereas a traveller in surface-bound conveyances has to change from wheels to keel, or vice versa, when he crosses any of the dividing lines between land and water. An inhabitant of a small island—e.g. Ireland or Britain—who began his travels before the arrival of the Air Age is particularly well aware of the subsequent and consequent simplification and alleviation of a journey from Dublin or London to New York or Paris or New Delhi.

One of the countervailing disadvantages of aviation is that it is more dangerous. A vehicle that travels in a three-dimensional element cannot stand still there. A train or car can be stationary on terra firma, and a boat on water, without coming to grief; but a plane whose engines fail is likely to crash to the ground with probably fatal consequences for the crew and the passengers. A second disadvantage of travelling by air makes itself felt when the journey is latitudinal. By the time a passenger has been catapulted across a series of successive time-zones, he will have suffered a dislocation of his physiological and psychological rhythm from which it will cost him time and effort to recuperate. A third disadvantage of aviation is its inability to guarantee that it will fly to schedule. Aviation is more helplessly at the mercy of the weather's caprice than navigation is, and, on this point, rail is far superior, not only to air and to water, but to road as well.

However, in an age in which the whole population of the globe is being knit together into a single society, the possibility, provided by aviation, of swift travel from any point in the World-City to any other point would far outweigh all the drawbacks of air-travel if this, like road-travel, were not now being threatened with being stifled and stultified through congestion. By the year 1969 the increase in the volume of the World's air-traffic is already outpacing the increase in the number and the size of the World's airports; and the increase in the average speed of planes is being offset by increasing loss of time in waiting in the queue for the plane's turn to take off from a runway or in circling round and round above an airport until the plane's turn comes for being allotted a runway for landing. This incipient congestion of traffic at and above the World's airports suggests that the volume of air-traffic, like the volume of road-traffic, is going to have to be restricted drastically. If so, the tortoise-like train is, paradoxically, going to come out as the winner in its race with the hawk-like plane, as well as in its race with the hare-like automobile.

A ban on the circulation of privately-owned passenger-carrying automobiles in the interior of the World-City would work together with eventual slum clearance to revive the decaying centres of the former local cities that have been the World-City's original growing-points. Since cities became mechanized and consequently began to expand, they have been suffering from the configuration that had been the standard pattern during the static first five thousand years of their history. A city of the traditional size and shape was focused on a marketplace that was its main social centre, though not in all cases its exact topographical one. This central meeting-place was originally used for all purposes—political assemblies, judicial business, and religious ceremonies, as well as trade—though trade was the marketplace's original and indispensable function, since even the smallest and most primitive city has to buy its food by selling manufactures and services.

The focusing of a city's activities on a single business centre inevitably puts this centre-point under some pressure, both physical and psychological; but, in a city in which the marketplace was not more than ten minutes' walk from any of the gates in the city-wall, the difference in degree of pressure in the marketplace and at the wall never made itself felt severely—not even in business hours on ordinary days and not even on market-days, when the pressure on the centre was at its maximum. The smallness of the traditional city's area and population ensured that the pressure on the centre should not increase beyond the degree that human nature can bear with equanimity.

The traditional layout of a city, which had been natural and convenient during this first chapter of urban history, became a trap when the mechanized and therefore expanding city got on the move. The expanding mechanized cities which merged into each other to form megalopolises that are now coalescing into the World-City all started with a layout on the traditional plan. Even in those cases in which they were new cities planted on what had been virgin soil, they were still laid out to converge on a business centre because, in the past, this had always been a city's configuration and because the makers of the mechanized city did not foresee that their revolutionary transformation of the city's nature demanded a radical change in its physical structure. Consequently the mechanized cities' expansion, which was one of their novel features, took the form of successive additions of concentric rings —the form, in fact, that, in the realm of nature, is taken by the thickening of the trunk of a growing tree. In the realm of mankind's man-made artificial urban environment, this concentric physical expansion of the mechanized cities brought with it a proportionate progressive increase in the pressure on the centre.

A classical example of acute increase of pressure on the business centre of an old city that has been overtaken by industrialization is the experience of the university city of Oxford within the last half-century. When I was an undergraduate at Oxford in the years 1907–11, the sole factory there was a marmalade factory, and the increase of the pressure on Cornmarket Street (the principal shopping street in Oxford) that had been caused by the introduction of this industry was imperceptible. Since then, Morris's automobile manufacturing works and a pressed steel works have been set up in Cowley, which had originally been a village, separate from the city of Oxford, a short way farther down the Thames. The installation of these two major industrial plants at Cowley has attracted others; new residential suburbs have sprung up to match, and the much increased population of greater Oxford now congregates, for doing its shopping, in a shopping-centre that was laid out to serve the area within the medieval walls or, at the widest, the area enclosed within the Royalists' earthworks when Oxford was King Charles I's capital during the English Civil War.

The pressure on the centres of expanding cities has, in fact, rapidly become intolerable, and this is why the beginning of the mechanized cities' expansion was soon followed by an exodus first of the wealthier residents and then of industrial plants. Business offices have been the slowest to move out, because the various kinds of workers in these need to be in constant personal contact with each other for doing their work, whether they are merchants, bankers, brokers, lawyers, or members of any of the other professions that, between them, constitute the business community. They too, however, have felt the increasing price of continuing to work at the centre: the loss of time and the expenditure of physical energy imposed by the practice of commuting, and the lack of physical room for expanding their offices, even if they are able and willing to pay a fantastic purchase-price or rent per additional cubic foot. Moreover, the advance of technology—above all, the invention of the telephone, the continual improvement in its efficiency, and the world-wide extension of the telephone-network—has begun to make it practicable to decentralize business, as manufacturing industry and housing for the well-to-do have been decentralized already.

Thus, today, the original areas of the cities that are the World-City's historical nuclei are decaying. The former middle-class urban residential quarters are degenerating into slums; many, perhaps most, of the middle-class workers have moved their homes into new suburbs and have become commuters; industry has been dispersing; and even office business is now poised for dispersing in its turn. Before mechanization generated expansion, the configuration of a typical city—a city, that is, with a central marketplace and a surrounding wall—was like that of the solid wooden wheel of a primitive ox-cart which centres on an axle and is held together compactly by an iron rim. The typical configuration is now coming to be, not a solid disc, but a hollow ring—the shape of an automobile tyre when it has been stripped off its wheel.

If the decay of the centres of the historic nuclei of the World-City is to be arrested and reversed, it will not be enough to close these areas to private automobile traffic and to replace their slums by handsome public monuments and smiling parks. We shall also have to limit, and as far as possible reduce, the quantum of urban area and urban population that presses upon any one business centre; and this can be done only by creating new business centres that will be more convenient for the inhabitants of the new sections of the growing World-City.

This may not prove easy, as the example of Oxford indicates.

In terms of economic, as contrasted with academic, importance, Cowley may overshadow Oxford today, but, for inhabitants of Cowley, including its recently arrived additional population of industrial workers, the famous ancient city still has the prestige—not as a university city but as a shopping centre—that it acquired long ago, when Cowley was still only a neighbouring village. The people of the present-day industrial Cowley have shown themselves reluctant to give up their habit of coming into Oxford to shop, though Cowley could, if it chose, set up a shopping-centre of its own that would eclipse Oxford's Cornmarket Street. The establishment of new shopping-centres which, in effect, are the centres of new urban components of a megalopolis, has made better progress in the United States. Perhaps this is because no city there is yet old enough to have acquired the prestige of the more venerable of the cities of Western Europe.

What needs to be done to relieve the pressure by distributing it has been put by Dr. Constantine Doxiadis in geometrical terms that are illuminating because they are simple and clear. The closed city converging on a centre-point is no longer a workable configuration even for a single city now that it has been mechanized and is consequently expanding. *A fortiori* it cannot survive in an age in which cities have already coalesced into megalopolises and in which these, in their turn, are coalescing into the World-City. It is impossible to imagine the World-City's having a single centre-point. At a centre-point of a conurbation containing all but a fraction of mankind, and this at twice or three times mankind's present numbers, the pressure of human activity on the unimaginable Ecumenopolitan centre-point would be as enormous as the water-pressure of the Ocean on the Ocean's bottom at the points at which the Ocean is at its deepest.

As Dr. Doxiadis puts it, the closed city has now to be replaced by one that is open-ended. Long before the pressure on a particular city-centre has increased to a degree at which it would be intolerable, the increase must be halted by diverting the further quanta of the mounting pressure to another centre—and then to another and another, in a continually lengthening echelon, as population and construction and production and traffic continue to increase.

Since Dr. Doxiadis is both a thinker and a doer, he has already put this precept of his into practice in the planning of human settlements in a number of different parts of the World.

This revolution in the configuration of urban settlements is going to limit the pressure under which the World's work is done; but the human worker, unlike the robot worker-bee or worker-ant, is a person first and foremost and a worker only incidentally. 'Man shall not live by bread alone.'[1] Man is not a cipher, not a reference-number, not a computer-card; he is a living soul. To make his working conditions tolerable for him is necessary, and to achieve this is much, but it is still not enough. Man cannot live in a state of spiritual rootlessness; deracination threatens to drive him mad or to goad him into taking to criminal courses, and this threat hangs over all the hundreds of millions of human beings who are now streaming into the slums and shanty-towns of the rising World-City out of the villages in which they and their ancestors have been living since the invention of agriculture about eight thousand or possibly ten thousand years ago.

The ex-rural urban worker must be enabled, in his unfamiliar and formidable new urban environment, to continue to live the life of a human being. This means that he must continue to have neighbourly personal relations with a small enough group of fellow human beings to allow the relations between him and them to be close and intimate. This, in turn, means that the immediate social setting of the inhabitant of Ecumenopolis must be on no larger a scale than that of the rural village—a settlement whose inhabitants are neighbours in the positive sense of being in personal relations with each other. In an urban community on the village scale the waif, marooned in the World-City's 'lonely crowd', will have a chance of becoming once more a member of a community; and this is a human waif's birthright, since Man is by nature a social being. In virtue of its performance of this social function the village-size component of the World-City will be the most important one of all; but it will be only the minimum-scale component in a hierarchy of social and administrative units rising, in an ascending order of magnitude, to the ecumenical

[1] Luke iv, 4.

scale of the World-City itself. In this hierarchy the neighbourhood unit will be a ward of one of the civic centres that will be the 'open-ended' World-City's direct constituents; and, if the humanization of life at the ward level is not to be lost at the civic centre level, each civic centre must be kept within the dimensions of the standard-size city of the past—say, third-millennium-B.C. Ur or late-eighteenth-century-A.D. Weimar. In other words, the constituent cells of the coming World-City must be settlements on the scale of the traditional local city. In the World-City there will be hundreds of thousands of these units, and they will be juxtaposed in a continuous mosaic, instead of being scattered thinly over a predominantly rural *Oikoumenê*. But, in this new setting, each unit must aim at being a Weimar or an Ur *rediviva*.

This need to humanize life in Ecumenopolis is one of Constantine Dioxiadis' fundamental postulates, and, whether or not he considers the siting of Brasilia to have been well-chosen, this audacious experiment of erecting a new capital city in the wilderness has given an opportunity, which has been taken, of trying to put this precept of Dr. Doxiadis' into practice on the all-important basic minimum scale. The residential parts of Brasilia have been laid out in the form of *quadros* (i.e. square units of settlement), and each *quadro* has been designed to be, as far as possible, self-contained, and to be on a small enough scale for its inhabitants to be acquainted with each other personally. Inside the four sides of a *quadro* there are no streets open for mechanized traffic. There are only apartment houses, schools, shops, community centres, lawns, gardens, and paths for pedestrians connecting the *quadro*'s various components. The wives and mothers can do their shopping and their washing within their own *quadro*'s four corners, and the children can walk between home and school without being exposed to the risk of being run over. This pattern of residential settlement in Brasilia is a reproduction, on a rather more lavish standard, of the pattern that Dr. Doxiadis had originated in his layout of the new settlements, in the environs of Karachi, for the Muslim refugees who had flocked to Karachi after the partition of the former British Indian Empire between Pakistan and the Indian Union.

The general subject of the present chapter, which is the concluding chapter of this book, has been the exploration of ways and means of easing the current transformation of the rapidly increasing mass of mankind from peasants living in villages and subsisting by agriculture and animal husbandry into urban industrial and office workers living in a World-City—a new form of human settlement that has no precedents in mankind's past history. Will human nature be able to stand so radical and so rapid a revolution in mankind's way of life? This is the question towards which this book has been leading. We do not know the answer. This will be revealed only in the event, and, meanwhile, we can do no more than make guesses.

The quality in human nature on which we must pin our hopes is its proven adaptability. This has been demonstrated impressively under the test of the apocalyptic events that mankind has brought on itself within the lifetime of people, now still alive, who, like myself, have turned eighty. Human adaptability has also been revealed in an earlier technological, economic, social, cultural, and spiritual revolution which our ancestors did succeed in surviving, though it was an even more radical revolution than the one by which we, their descendants, have been overtaken in our time. About eight thousand or perhaps ten thousand years ago, our ancestors transformed themselves from vagrant food-gatherers, hunters, and fishermen into sedentary tillers of the soil and breeders and shepherds of livestock. Their survival of this previous testing transformation is a precedent that offers us grounds for hope that we, in our turn, may be going to survive our own ordeal. Our experience feels severe, but our knowledge of our ancestors' ordeal tells us that it was still more severe than ours is. Since our ancestors rose to the occasion, we, their descendants, are presumably capable of emulating them if we display the courage, vision, and inventiveness that were our ancestors' salvation.

Index

Index to Maps

References are to Map number and page. Where the map occupies two pages, the page on which the particular name appears is given: thus Anshan is on p. 118, in Map 4.